Striptease Culture

From advertising to health education campaigns, sex and sexual imagery now permeate every aspect of advanced capitalist culture. *Striptease Culture* explores this 'sexualisation' of contemporary life, relating it to wider changes in post-war society. Divided into three sections, *Striptease Culture* first traces the development of pornography from the mid-nineteenth century, following its movement from elite to mass culture and the contemporary fascination with 'porno-chic'. In Part 2 McNair considers popular cultural forms of sexual representation in the media. Moving from backlash elements in straight male culture and changing images of women to the representation of gays in film and television shows such as *Ellen* and *Queer as Folk*, McNair argues that the high profile of sexuality in contemporary culture, rather than evidence of moral decline, is a positive expression of post-war liberalism and the advance of feminism and gay rights, as well as a key contributor to public health education in the era of HIV and AIDS.

In Part 3, *Striptease Culture* turns to the uses of sexuality in contemporary art, examining the artistic 'striptease' of Jeff Koons and others, who have used their own naked bodies in their work. McNair also considers how feminist and gay artists have employed sexuality in the critique and transformation of patriarchy. In a concluding chapter, McNair considers the implications of the rise of striptease culture for the future of sexual politics.

Brian McNair is Reader in Film and Media Studies at the University of Stirling, and a member of the Stirling Media Research Institute. His books include *Mediated Sex* (1996), *The Sociology of Journalism* (1998) and *Journalism and Democracy* (Routledge, 2000).

Striptease Culture

Sex, media and the democratization of desire

Brian McNair

London and New York

For Katherine Granger

First published 2002
by Routledge
11 New Fetter Lane, London EC4P 4EE

Simultaneously published in the USA and Canada
by Routledge
29 West 35th Street, New York, NY 10001

Routledge is an imprint of the Taylor & Francis Group

© 2002 Brian McNair

Typeset in Galliard by
Keystroke, Jacaranda Lodge, Wolverhampton
Printed and bound in Great Britain by
Biddles Ltd, Guildford and King's Lynn

British Library Cataloguing in Publication Data
A catalogue record for this book is available from the British Library

*Library of Congress Cataloging in Publication Data
has been requested*

ISBN 0–415–23733–5 (hbk)
ISBN 0–415–23734–3 (pbk)

CONTENTS

List of figures   vii
Preface and acknowledgements   ix

1 Sex matters   1

2 From Wilde to Wild: the end of patriarchy, or is it all just history repeating?   15

PART 1
Cultural sexualization: from pornosphere to public sphere   **35**

3 The amazing expanding pornosphere   37

4 Porno-chic, or the pornographication of the mainstream   61

5 Striptease culture: the sexualization of the public sphere   88

PART 2
Sexual representation   **109**

6 'Women, know your limits!'   113

7 The mainstreaming of gayness   129

8 Men behaving sadly: the crisis of masculinity?   149

PART 3
The aesthetics of sexual transgression   **163**

9 Men, sex and transgression   167

Contents

10 Queer culture   179

11 Bad girls: sexual transgression as feminist strategy   191

12 Conclusions   205

    Notes   208
    Bibliography   228
    Index   235

FIGURES

1.1	Defining terms: sex, sexuality, gender	2
1.2	Sex matters	4
2.1	History repeating?	16
3.1	'Porn Spirit of '76'	45
3.2	Porn for women	46
4.1	*i-D*: the 'Skin and soul' issue	77
4.2	*The Face*: L'Édition Sexe	79
4.3	Dunlop tyre film advertisement	80
5.1	Bill and Monica 1	92
5.2	Bill and Monica 2	94
6.1	*Basic Instinct*	123
6.2	*Starship Troopers*	125
7.1	Kronenbourg film advertisement	130
8.1	*Viz*: The Joy of Sexism	161

PREFACE AND
ACKNOWLEDGEMENTS

Striptease Culture is my label of convenience for the media of sexual revelation and exhibitionism which proliferated in the capitalist societies of the late twentieth century, and continue to be among their most visible and controversial features in the early years of the twenty-first. 'Striptease' in this context has both literal and metaphorical meanings, embracing a range of texts and images including pornography, the sexualized art of the body, documentaries about strippers and confessional talk shows. These media forms make up a culture in which public nakedness, voyeurism, and sexualized looking are permitted, indeed encouraged as never before. In describing that culture and examining its sociological meanings I roam freely across the media landscape in my mapping of the texts of high art and low porn; of those made by, for and of gay, straight and queer; the constructions of masculine and feminine in TV and cinema; the sexualized products of the music, fashion and advertising industries.

That is a lot to try and cover in one book, and I am aware that any of the following chapters could be expanded to fill a weighty tome in itself. There are indeed many such books already out there, more specialised and technical in their approach than this one. While I have sought to avoid writing an extended review of that literature, the footnotes and bibliography which accompany the text will serve as a guide to further reading, whether for learning or research purposes. But the starting point of *Striptease Culture*, as Chapter 1 argues, is that sex matters to us all. I have tried, therefore, to write a book which will be of interest to more than just a specialist readership.

Despite the broad scope of the work it is not exhaustive, and there are inevitably omissions. For reasons of economics and linguistic competence, my empirical focus is on the United States and the United Kingdom, with examples drawn from Japan, France, Korea, Russia and other countries as appropriate. The products of art and culture selected for discussion below are of course not necessarily 'the best' in aesthetic terms, nor have they always been the most commercially successful. Some reflect the subjective intervention of my own personal preferences. But all, I would submit, have made significant contributions to the culture of emotional and physical striptease which characterizes our time, and to the *democratization of desire* which, I will argue, has accompanied its proliferation.

Preface and acknowledgements

The writing of *Striptease Culture* has benefited from conversations with, and feedback from, many of the two hundred or so students who have taken my *Sex, Society, Media* class at the University of Stirling in recent years. Doctoral students Mark Brownrigg, Lynne Roper and Maggie Magor kindly read the manuscript before submission, as did Stirling Media Research Fellow Matthew Hibberd. The editorial team at Routledge, and the readers who viewed proposals and drafts on their behalf, provided constructive criticism and advice throughout. Their comments and suggestions were of great value, and I thank them here. Thanks are due also to *The Face* and *i-D* magazines, and to John Brown Publishing for permission to reproduce copyright material. Stills photography and video captures were provided by Media Services at Stirling University. And thanks to Richard Purden for 'Porn Spirit of 76'.

Brian McNair
June 2001

1

SEX MATTERS

People say to me – or imply in the frowns and jokey asides which still tend to accompany discussion of the sexual even in the grown-up world of academia – what's a nice media sociologist like you doing in a dirty sub-sector of the field like this? To which I reply: sex is the most important thing in the world. Or if that seems excessive: sex is one of the three or four most important things in the world. We eat, we excrete, we fuck, we sleep, if not necessarily in that order. In the human journey from birth to death, only those activities are truly essential to the production and reproduction of life. All else – the way we dress, the shapes of the houses in which we live, the work we do, our art and culture – are, to a greater or lesser degree, epiphenomenal decoration and artifice; the socially and culturally mediated product of our precocious species' ability to advance technology at an ever-accelerating rate, to command and exploit its environment, to reflect on its achievements and failings, to learn (and sometimes not to learn) from its mistakes.

If eating and excreting are essential because they are the means by which we process food, dispose of the waste products, and thus replenish our bodies then sex, the means of *genetic* reproduction, is the prerequisite of it all. The fundamental human sex act – that which takes place between a male and a female, requiring vaginal penetration by the penis and the ejaculation of male sperm leading to fertilization of the female's egg – is the only natural biological mechanism for the transmission of genetic information from one person to another, and from one generation to the next. From this clumsy exchange of bodily fluids a new human being can be made, and genes passed on. All other means of reproduction, welcome though they may be to those who are unable to produce children naturally, and with access to the technology which makes assisted conception possible, are the artificially enhanced fruits of scientific progress.

Defining terms: sex and sexuality

Sex in our time is not reducible to reproduction, of course. Its possibilities and permutations are constrained neither by the mechanics of male–female intercourse, nor the immediate survival needs of the gene or species. The *biological* imperative to transmit genes through sexual intercourse has over hundreds of millennia evolved

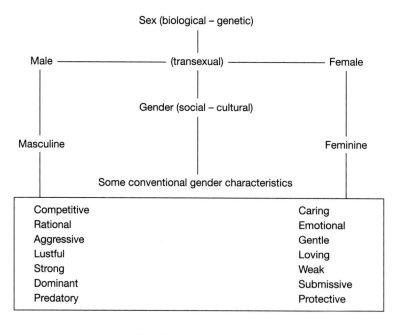

Sex (biological – genetic)

Male ——————— (transexual) ——————— Female

Gender (social – cultural)

Masculine   Feminine

Some conventional gender characteristics

Competitive	Caring
Rational	Emotional
Aggressive	Gentle
Lustful	Loving
Strong	Weak
Dominant	Submissive
Predatory	Protective

Sexuality (psychological?)

Heterosexuality

Homosexuality

Bisexuality

Perversions, paraphilias and fetishises

Figure 1.1 Defining terms: sex, sexuality, gender

into the *psychological* capacity to feel sexual desire and experience orgasm as an especially intense form of physical and emotional pleasure (Figure 1.1).[1] Sex has become sexuality; or rather, sexualit*ies*.

The structures around which human sexuality is organized – the persons, behaviours and objects on which it is focused – have diverged from one society to another throughout human history, and from one person to another within any given society at any given time, but the specific shape of our individual desires defines for each one of us, here and now, our own sexuality. In addition to what we might think of as the default mode of male–female attraction, men can feel desire for men, women for women, men and women for inanimate objects, textures, sounds, smells. The biological predisposition to male–female sex has evolved into a social universe of multiple sexualities which, as Michel Foucault observed in his influential history of the subject (1990), have since the advent of sexology in the mid-nineteenth century been named and categorised in evermore precise medical, moral and pathological terms – heterosexual, homosexual, bisexual; fetishistic, paraphiliac, nymphomaniac; normal, deviant, perverted.

We human beings, it is generally believed, are unique among terrestrial species in being in command of our sexuality. Within the constraints imposed by economics, politics and conventional morality we can experiment with it, refine and manipulate it, enhance it, and (where contraceptive technologies are available) detach it from the reproductive function entirely. We can make art from it, celebrating its pleasures and pains (as Prefab Sprout once put it, 'when love breaks down, when love breaks down'[2]) in literature, painting, and every other medium of cultural expression used by human beings through the ages.

Gender

Alongside this proliferation of socially constructed sexualities the biological category of sex has become enmeshed with another, predominantly *cultural* category – that of gender. The anatomy of maleness corresponds to something most of us will recognize as 'masculinity'; a set of behaviours and beliefs which distinguish the masculine from its bipolar opposite, femininity. Although maleness and femaleness can be described in terms of biological characteristics which, if they are not universal, fit the vast majority of individuals well enough (particular configurations of sex organs, certain genetic and hormonal profiles leading to the physiological features associated with male and female), the gender characteristics associated with masculinity and femininity – and routinely displayed in what some theorists would call the 'performances' of men and women in society,[3] – are to a significant extent learned, ascribed qualities, signified by speech and behaviour patterns, modes of dress, and other markers which are conventional rather than biological, changing over time and across cultures. Although most men are masculine, in other words (as most women are feminine), not all are, and none need be.[4]

The content of gender roles in any given society will change over time, as they will differ from those prevailing in other societies. If our biological sex is fixed at birth (and, with the possible exception of those transsexuals who embark on sex-change surgery, it probably is) the way that sex is expressed culturally, through gender, is in large part a product of socialization, overlaid and personalized with elements of individual creativity and lifestyle choice.

It is fair to say that no one has conclusively explained how, and for what reason, the biological necessity of human sex became the complex emotional and psychological minefield that is sexuality as we live it today, nor how the act of procreation became the vehicle for such a diversity of pleasures and pains as are now associated with it. And for the purposes of this book it doesn't really matter whether the explanations for that transformation lie in evolutionary biology, Freudian psychoanalysis, structural anthropology or divine intervention.[5] I prefer to start from the simple observation, made without any statement of personal preference or moral judgement, that we inhabit a world of plural sexualities and polymorphous perversities, and that this diversity of sexual identities exists alongside many other elements of modern life which are far removed from the 'natural' human state as it may have been in some distant prehistorical past, but which we value and preserve nonetheless as taken for granted elements of contemporary life. Whether or not any of our sexualities can be defined as 'natural', in other words, is less important to my argument than the fact that they exist at all, and that there is no reason why freedom of sexual expression should not, in the advanced capitalist societies of the twenty-first century, be considered a human right[6] (I exclude from this generalization any form of sexuality – paedophilia, for example, or non-consensual sexual activity of any kind – which involves the violation or abuse of other's human rights).

Sex and power

Sex is about reproduction, then, and it is also about power (Figure 1.2). Because of the centrality of sex to social, as well as biological reproduction (through the role of bloodlines in the cross-generational transfer of property, for example; or the role of the patriarchal family in the reliable supply of well-disciplined and properly nourished labour power to industry) – roles which are always threatened by the

BIOLOGY
birth
sex
reproduction

PSYCHOLOGY
desire
sexuality
pleasure
art

ECONOMICS
business
money
sex sells

POLITICS
power
patriarchy
resistance and struggle

PATHOLOGY
epidemic
HIV/AIDS
death

Figure 1.2 Sex matters

4

anarchic, disruptive effects of the desires which sex inspires – sexuality and its representation have tended to be subject to state and church control, and thus politically charged. Throughout human history and in every form of society the state has, with varying degrees of severity, regulated sexuality and policed desire through legal controls on marriage, ages of sexual consent, and prohibitions on sexual practices of various kinds. These laws have functioned to maintain social discipline and order, almost always on behalf of what feminist theory and historiography have accurately characterized as a patriarchal ruling class. Sex and the control of it (who has it; what they can do with it; and to whom) has been the basis, for at least the seven millenia of recorded history, in virtually all civilizations across the world, of systems of social stratification dominated by men, in which women, homosexuals and those defined as sexual deviants have been oppressed and persecuted.[7]

Power is never exercised without challenge, however, and for some time now the power of, first the churches, then the state, to regulate sexuality and police desire has been echoed by the efforts of once-subordinate sexual communities – women in the first instance, followed closely by homosexuals and other groups whose sexual identities and lifestyles deviate in some way from the patriarchal heterosexist norm – to assert their socio-sexual rights. Anthony Giddens has correctly observed that 'sexuality is a terrain of fundamental political struggle and also a medium of emancipation' (1993, p. 181). Despite the private, intimate nature of sexuality, these struggles have taken place in the public domain, often through the channels of the mainstream, commercialized media, making the sexual social, the personal political, and both more than marginally profitable. The post-World War II period, characterized by the decline of class-based ideological polarity, has been one of especially intense campaigning around issues of sexual identity, and for what sociologist David Evans has called *sexual citizenship* (1993).

This has been one consequence of an environment where groups defined by their sexuality have become consumers wielding significant economic power. Between the 1950s and the 1970s the number of female wage labourers doubled, and their presence in the wage economy has increased steadily since then (see Chapter 2) with obvious implications for their spending power. As of 2000 it was estimated that the gay community in the United Kingdom earned collectively £95 billion, of which £10 billion was available for them to spend as disposable income. This earning power was reflected in an expanding culture of sexual consumerism focused on 'gay villages' and services, and facilitated through e-commerce websites like queer.com.

Where there's muck there's brass: sex sells

The phenomenon of the 'pink pound' is one manifestation of the fact that the pleasurable, recreational dimensions of sexuality have long made it the lucrative object of capitalist entrepreneurship, based on the transformation of desire and the promise of sexual pleasure into various types of commodity (pornographic books and films, sex aids, fashion and appearance enhancers of various kinds, and all the sex-saturated products of art and popular culture. Sex sells indirectly, too, routinely used in advertising and pop video as a powerful promotional tool to sell other commodities in the marketplace). In all these ways sex is about money, and never more so than in the capitalist societies of today, which have nurtured sex industries to rank in size and profitability, if not yet respectability, with the more established and institutionalized sectors of the culture economy such as Hollywood cinema and pop music. Precise figures for the size of the sex industries are hard to come by (see Chapter 3 for some estimates of the size of the porn business in the United States and Britain) and those which do surface from time to time should always be treated with caution, given the political motivations which so often underpin their use by journalists and lobbyists. But that commodified sex in all its forms, targeted at most sexual communities with the resources to indulge their preferences, is of major economic significance in the cultural capitalism of the twenty-first century, is indisputable.

Sex and death

The evolution of sexual culture and politics took a new turn in the 1980s with the emergence of a disease which confirmed what had always been known, but largely forgotten in the relatively liberal, often hedonistic atmosphere which followed on the sexual revolution. Sex is important, we were reminded then, because all too often it turns out to be about sickness and death, as well as pleasure and money. Sex is the transmitter of genes, and the source of life, but also of viruses and bacteria which can cause life to be damaged and extinguished. There have been many catastrophic sexual epidemics in human history, but none so panic-inducing for our present-day societies as that of HIV and the many life-threatening illnesses it causes (collectively known as Acquired Immune Deficiency Syndrome, or AIDS). Between the discovery of the hetero-immuno deficiency virus in the early 1980s and the turn of the century some 29 million people are estimated to have died from AIDS throughout the world, and a further 30 million were believed to be infected with the virus.

The discovery of HIV in the early 1980s required as a matter of public safety that the explicit representation and discussion of sexual behaviour become part of mainstream health education. In that process the traditional boundaries which had separated the private practice of sex from the public display and discussion of it were subjected to unprecedented stresses. Already breaking down in the wake of the sexual revolution HIV and AIDS exposed those censorial practices as positively harmful to the health of billions of people – a process which even the moral conservatives who dominated the US and British governments in the 1980s were unable to resist.[8] And when it finally came, anti-HIV education for both gay and straight audiences necessarily broke taboos in the public discussion of sexuality and sexual behaviour, provoking widespread awareness of and interest in the subjects.

For all of these reasons – the high stakes surrounding the politics and business of sex; its biological and emotional centrality to our individual lives and collective survival; the threats to public health which certain kinds of sexual activity had come to pose – the late twentieth century saw the development of a cultural environment pervaded by sexuality and its representation. Today, across the range of artistic, promotional and journalistic media we are likely to view, discuss and think about sex with greater frequency and attention to detail than at any previous stage in history. What was significant about the Monica Lewinsky scandal of 1998–9 was not, after all, the revelation that US presidents have messy and potentially scandalous sex lives (we have known that for a long time), but that we got to hear so much about this particular president's intimate moments, and were then encouraged to form a view as to whether oral sex is or is not 'sexual relations'; on the forensic significance of semen stains on blue dresses; on the erotic possibilities of unlit cigars.[9]

Taking offence: critical perspectives on cultural sexualisation

All of this has been recognized and commented on for some time now, generating a relentless talking about sex and the sexualisation of culture which shows no signs of exhaustion. Barely a day goes by without someone, somewhere in the public sphere adding further fuel to the debate about the perils of mediated sex. Usually, and regardless of whether the author is a religiously inspired moral conservative, a Marxist sociologist, an anti-porn feminist, or a freedom-loving liberal, these commentaries are couched in the critical tones of cultural pessimism. Melanie Phillips, for example, warns us with the apocalyptic certainty typical of the journalistic commentator that 'it's in the interests of everyone to confront the sexualisation of our culture which is leading us all, gay and straight, into a spiritual and emotional desert'.[10] The essayist Bryan Appleyard complains that 'the new sexual revolution is all about flattening sex until it becomes just one more product on the counter of consumer choice'.[11] A recent essay by Tom Wolfe is cynical about what he sees, speaking of the United States in particular, as 'the lurid carnival taking place in the mightiest country on earth'.[12] Wolfe's compatriot Roger Kimball has complained that 'anywhere and everywhere in American society the foulest possible language, the most graphic images of sexual congress and sexual perversion abound.'[13] (Kimball is not referring here to the content of the multi-million-selling 1986 Meese report on pornography commissioned by the Reagan administration,[14] nor even to the Starr committee report on the Clinton–Lewinsky affair, available to billions of fascinated surfers on the internet from late 1998, but to the proliferation of explicit sexual imagery, 'high' artistic and 'low' popular, observed across the range of media outlets in America and elsewhere in the West as the century closed[15].)

Some forms of cultural sexualization have been more vilified than others. Pornography continues, as it has since the emergence of anti-porn feminism in the 1970s, to be implicated in the incitement to sexual violence of men against women and children. The internet-driven spread of 'cyberporn' and the potential for abuse of sex-related online chat rooms have given that concern a new urgency, fuelling a moral panic to which legislators in the United States and the United Kingdom have felt obliged to respond with censorial measures of various kinds (though without much success – see Chapter 3).

The less explicit forms of sexual imagery deployed by the advertising and fashion industries are charged with disseminating distorted and damaging views of both femininity and masculinity, as well as breeding dissatisfaction and disappointment among sexually frustrated consumers everywhere. Advertising has been blamed for what the psychologist Oliver James refers to as the 'overheated [sexual] aspirations and unreal comparisons' alleged to preoccupy so many in modern capitalism.[16] The heady mix of babes and beer contained in the 'new lad' generation of style magazines are criticized for championing a reactionary masculinity, while the 'new' women's magazines allegedly construct women as, to quote the authors of one study, 'sex-mad, silly and selfish'.[17]

Though differing in their motivations, assumptions and emphases, these arguments usually end up agreeing that in nearly all of its manifestations cultural sexualization is bad for us – bad for individuals, male and female; bad for the family, nuclear or otherwise; bad for society in general. There is, as I have pointed out elsewhere (McNair, 1996), no hard evidence for this conclusion, which is almost always premised on the application of particular moral or ideological assumptions (about the sanctity of sex, for example, or the evils of commercialization, or the inherent misogyny of sexual objectification, to name the three most common). Assertions of a link between the sexual content of media imagery and the allegedly anti-social values, beliefs and behaviours of the consumers of those images are founded on, at best, questionable models about how media products work in, and on, the societies within which they circulate. The communication process is by its nature chaotic and non-linear. That is to say, simply, that it is sensitive to the initial conditions within which the communicative act takes place. These conditions, rather than anything inherent in the content of the message, define its meaning and thus the effect it will come to have later in the communicative cycle. The content of any media image, and of any sexual representation in particular – fictional or factual, fantastic or journalistic – cannot be reliably predicted to have any effect in isolation from the context of its reception by real people in their physical and social environments. What any particular image means, and what it may predispose, provoke, or persuade someone to think or do are as much the product of that individual's personal circumstances (an infinitely complex amalgam of individual and familial history, education, cultural tradition, and all the other elements which shape and constrain a person's existence and conscious being) as they are of the image-content. The lines of cause and effect between media text, individual consciousness and social action are dependent on too many variables to be reliably known.

The fundamental uncertainty at the heart of the communication process renders all debates about the effects of media images on individuals circular and repetitive – not because there *are* no effects but because effects cannot be isolated, measured or predicted in any but the most speculative of ways. Some individuals may be sexually turned on by looking at pornography, for example, while others may be disgusted. Some may read an advertisement or a fashion shot depicting a well-known supermodel like Naomi Campbell as an attractive and pleasing image, to be emulated in one's own choice of clothing and 'look'; others will see it as 'body fascism', or as incitement to anorexia, or at the very least as an assault on the right of women not to be squeezed into a particular model of womanhood. Each of these responses is valid. None precludes the others. Each springs from and gives rise to different patterns of thought and behaviour.

The media and the sexual revolution

But if media effects are complex and virtually impossible to prove, there is no shortage of evidence to substantiate the view that the twentieth century was a period of significant change in the conditions of existence of women in capitalism, as it was for other suppressed sexual communities, and homosexuals in particular. Chapter 2 presents that evidence in more detail. Here, let us recall that in 1895 Oscar Wilde was given three years' hard labour for having sex with another man. In 1999 a senior figure in the British Conservative Party, Michael Portillo, could admit to having had gay sex in his youth and still be regarded as a potential prime minister. In the years just before World War I women were literally dying for the right to vote. In November 2000, as Hilary Clinton basked in the glory of a successful New York senate race, the idea of a female US president no longer seemed outlandish. Clearly, between the *fin de siécle* and the millennial turn attitudes to sexuality had altered radically. That they did so in parallel with the sexualization of culture is equally apparent.

Less obvious is the precise role played by the mass media and the culture industries in making possible (if not inevitable) a gay Tory prime minister, or a female US president. Tom Hickman's book on *The Sexual Century* argues that the media were 'the main engines of the sexual revolution' (1999, p. 245) and that the cinema in particular 'gave shape and form to sexual desire' in the twentieth century. That is a nice idea, evoking the silver screen's golden age of sultry screen goddesses and dashing leading men. Who can doubt that from Clara Bow to Uma Thurman, and Douglas Fairbanks to Tom Cruise, cinema has spoken to and of the changing sexualities of western societies?

But if the cinema, and the media in general, *have* played this role, it has been because of their broader function as the 'main engines' of *cultural* capitalism: that phase of capital's development in which the sources of profit are increasingly informational, data-based, imagistic – newspapers, magazines and books; music, films and computer games; the hardware to access all the different media on which cultural commodities are stored and distributed. Not all cultural products exist as commodities, of course. Very few television programmes are paid for directly at the point of consumption, but through advertising costs passed on to consumers when they buy their breakfast cereals or motor cars, or in state-levied licence fees such as those paid by British audiences for access to the public service BBC. But whether a cultural artifact comes with an upfront cover price or not, a large part of its success is measured by the numbers of people who watch, listen to or read it. In this sense, even publicly funded culture is subject to commercial pressures and market disciplines. The BBC, to the chagrin of many critics, is as much ratings-driven as its commercial competitors in the British media marketplace.

The software components of this new cultural economy – the image-content of books, films, CDs, DVDs and the rest – are unlike oil, cars and washing machines in that they embody ideas and values as opposed to merely *value*.[18] It is their 'statements' which make them sellable, rather than the shiny plastic discs or video-tape on which they are stored. And statements of rebellion and opposition are, in this economy, just as saleable as, if not more so than, those of submission to, or acceptance of, the state of things as they are. In their engagement with increasingly sophisticated and knowledgeable consumers aware of and possibly living out the ideologies of feminism and gay rights, and in so far as their aim is to realize profit in a crowded media marketplace increasingly responsive to considerations of style and taste, commodities must resonate with and express the ideas which constantly emerge from the complex, chaotic interaction of people with each other and their media. In doing so they become vehicles for the dissemination and transformation of those ideas; the memetic 'engines' of their ongoing evolution. Take the example of *Big Brother*, discussed in Chapter 5. Irrespective of what the ten individuals who participate in this programme say or do on air, their mix of ethnicities, sexual orientations, political affiliations and demographic profiles amounts to an ideological macro-message about the state of Britain in 2001 (and the same applies to the other countries which have produced versions of *Big Brother*). The programme says: this is Britain, and here is a microcosm of the people who live in it. Isn't this diversity, and the ease with which such a diverse group of individuals can live together, a good thing? And, judging by the audience response (more young people participated through the internet or telephone in the second series of *Big Brother* than voted in the general election of 2001), people generally agree that it *is* a good thing.

On the BBC's *Changing Rooms* (the most successful of many 'lifestyle' television programmes which have featured prominently in recent years) one sees a gay couple, participating alongside a straight couple in the show's 'you do my room, I'll do yours' format. Sexuality is not presented as an issue, but there is a message about sexuality contained in the programme nonetheless – there are gay people, and they are just like straight people in the things that matter, such as interior decoration.

And take, finally, a movie such as Spike Lee's *Summer of Sam* (1999). The film features one gay character, and one bisexual. The former is written as a camp queen, subject to routine homophobic abuse from his macho Italian-American peers. The bisexual central character Ritchie is also victimized, and indeed nearly killed by their prejudice and ignorance. In the end, however, the homophobic masculinity of the straight male characters is unambiguously constructed as destructive and dangerous. *Summer of Sam*, at face value an account of the real-life media and moral panic which developed around the activities of serial killer Sam Berkowitz in late 1970s New York, is also Lee's celebration of the humanity and dignity of alternative sexual lifestyles. As with his breakthrough film, *She's Gotta Have It*, *Summer of Sam* is a statement about sexual politics, as well as a commodity for sale in the cultural marketplace. The ideological effects of its success in that marketplace cannot be measured, but the mere existence of such a message in mainstream culture is significant in itself (Lee's earlier films, such as *Do the Right Thing* and *Malcolm X*, have engaged in similar fashion with issues of racism and ethnicity).

These examples illustrate how changes in the social relations of capitalism – such as the mass entry of women into the labour force after World War II; the gradually improving social status of homosexuals from the 1970s onwards; the slow but steady marginalization of racism – have economic and political effects which are reflected in culture, generating media images and discourses which inevitably feed back into the political, social and economic environments, generating a virtuous circle of media-driven change in attitudes to sexuality and gender.

Cultural commodities are ideological, then, in so far as they are the products of human authorship and thus tell us things about the world we live in and how to behave in it (and may even, through skilful packaging and promotion, have the power to make us believe them). But they are also *counter-ideological* – part of the process by which we are empowered to talk back; to resist reactionary or oppressive ideas; to make the marginal mainstream; to change the world, or at least some of the things in it. This can be one of the aims of cultural producers, or it can be the accidental by-product of the fact that cultural commodities can be interpreted in many different ways and lack, as Richard Dyer has observed, 'ideological uniformity both as texts and in how they are read and enjoyed' (1992, p. 8). My reading of *Summer of Sam* or *Big Brother* may not be yours, in other words, and nor is it necessarily more valid. That there is something disruptive of conventional attitudes to masculinity and heterosexuality in Lee's film cannot be denied, however.

New technologies and the democratization of desire

Another, more concrete contribution of the media to the sexual revolution relates to technology, and the fact that the late twentieth century saw the emergence of a global media system which national governments have found increasingly difficult to control and regulate. The long-term sociological consequences of this trend are profound, going way beyond issues of sex and morality to overarching questions about the maintenance of political authority and social stability. In the specific context of our present discussion, the introduction of successive waves of new communication technologies (from printed word to digital code) has led to accelerating flows of sexual information within and between national boundaries, and erosion of the patriarchal state's capacity to block out or censor that information. This revolution in the means of communication has fanned the growth of a less regulated, more commercialized, and more pluralistic sexual culture (in terms of the variety of sexualities which it can accommodate), and thus promoted what I will describe as a *democratization of desire*. By that I mean, on the one hand, expanded popular access to all the means of sexual expression, mediated and other-wise (the availability of hard core porn to anyone with access to the internet, for example), and on the other, the emergence of a more diverse and pluralistic sexual culture than has traditionally been accomodated within patriarchal capitalism (as illustrated by the proliferation of 'niche market' television targeted at diverse sexual communities). The following chapters describe and analyse these processes as they have been reflected in the various categories of sexual representation I am grouping together as 'striptease culture'.

The scope of the book

The categories to be looked at include that of pornography, which has evolved from its sixteenth-century aristocratic, libertinist origins into a highly visible, profit-able sector of the culture industries. *Striptease Culture* is not only, nor even mainly about pornography, but the pornographic is clearly central to anunderstanding of cultural striptease. As the first chapter of Part 1 on Cultural Sexualization argues, not only is pornography the form in which self-revelation, physical nakedness and voyeurism are most obviously and explicitly required; its evolution has been the catalyst for the broader sexualization of mainstream culture which has characterized recent years. Pornography is the totem around which contemporary attitudes to trends in sexual culture revolve: an index of sexual democratization to some; to others, a denunciatory label attached to those forms of cultural sexualization judged undesirable.

Striptease culture also includes the *meta-discourses* of pornography which populate the contemporary media: feature films like *Boogie Nights* and *8mm*; television and feature-length documentaries and series, book-length inquiries and analyses of the pornography business and its appeal. The proliferation of these forms of 'porno-chic', as Chapter 4 calls them, is among the most prominent sub-trends in the wider process of cultural sexualization, amounting to what I call the *pornographication of the mainstream*. If the channels of mainstream culture continue to be bracketed off from what Chapter 3 calls the *pornosphere*, they have engaged in an unprecedented flirtation with the codes and conventions of the pornographic, producing texts which constantly refer to, pastiche, parody and deconstruct the latter.

The near-ubiquity of porno-chic provides the bridge between the pornosphere and the public sphere, where sex (including its mediated form, pornography) becomes the subject, in non-explicit contexts, of public debate. These forms of sexual discourse – the focus of Chapter 5 – comprise striptease culture in its most literal sense. They include the examples of sexual self-revelation pursued through the media by celebrities and non-celebrities alike, from the pin-up calendar produced by the English Women's Institute in 1999 to the *Naked . . .* photo albums of American photographer Greg Friedler and the *Vanity Fair* front cover depicting a nude, pregnant Demi Moore. Chapter 5 is devoted to these forms of 'striptease culture', and also discusses the journalistic media of sexually confessional, revelatory subject matter and images (as in the Lewinsky scandal, or the 'fifty-seven varieties' of confessional programming which have been a feature of US and British television in recent years).

Part 2 contains three essays exploring the impact of a rapidly evolving system of sexual stratification, and the progressive sexual politics which have accompanied it, on sexual representation more broadly.[19] If, as I am arguing, there has been not just a sexualization of capitalist culture (hardly contentious any more), but a democratization of desire, Part Two asks if and how these trends have been reflected in the representations of masculinity, femininity, homo- and heterosexuality which occur elsewhere in the culture. Thus, Chapter 6 examines the changing content of images of women and femininity, against the backdrop of feminist-inspired political and socio-economic change. Chapter 7 takes a similar approach to representations of homosexuality in an era when it is generally acknowledged that the politics of gay liberation has made significant advances. Chapter 8 discusses how, against that backdrop, the 'crisis' of heterosexual masculinity has been refracted in key cultural forms such as popular cinema and advertising.

Striptease culture includes the art of sexual transgression, and in particular the sexualized art of the body (where the body stripped bare is often that of the artist him or herself). Part 3 comprises three essays linked by their consideration of the contributions made by this art to the articulation of sexual identity by male and female, gay and straight artists.

But before embarking on these explorations, Chapter 2 presents an assessment of what, precisely, *has* changed in the sexual sphere, and what has not, in the century and a bit since Oscar Wilde's prosecution and imprisonment for gross indecency. Since the ignored plea of Wilde's lover Bosie for a sympathetic understanding of 'the love that dare not speak its name' the system of sexual stratification, and the culture which surrounds it, has changed beyond what those late-nineteenth-century martyrs of a new sexual politics might have thought possible. Chapter 2 plots the scope of that change, and the limits which nature and nurture have placed upon it.

Some qualifications

The division of the material outlined above is not the only one which could have been adopted, and I am aware that it implies some ambivalent category distinctions. For example, my routine use of the terms 'art' and 'popular culture' should not obscure one of the most interesting characteristics of postmodernity: that the two are often the same, and that the boundaries are not always clear. Madonna is discussed as a 'bad girls' artist in Part 3, and as a key figure in the 'porno-graphication' of mainstream pop culture described in Chapter 4. She is, of course, both artist *and* pop star, in that her 'art' has achieved immense commercial success, as well as a more grudging critical appreciation. In the visual arts the same could be said of such as Robert Mapplethorpe and Keith Haring, whose images are today as likely to be found on greetings cards, kitchen calendars and T-shirts as on the walls of museums and galleries. In short, my use of 'art' and 'pop' should not be taken to imply acceptance of the high–low distinction still applied by many culture critics. On the contrary, I celebrate the emergence of a culture in which art can be popular, and popular culture can be considered art.

I also distinguish in the following chapters between straight- and gay (or queer)-authored representations, although lingering homophobia means that many gay men and women in the culture industries continue to feel obliged to masquerade as straight, and that many 'gays' resist the adoption of that label, preferring not to be pigeonholed into any sexual category. My division of cultural producers into straight, gay or queer corresponds to the public self-identifications of those concerned, where they are known. I acknowledge where appropriate the uncertainties and ambiguities involved in the too-rigid classification of sexualities.

One final qualifying remark. This is a book about the sexual cultures of advanced capitalist societies, at a particular historical moment characterized by relative economic affluence and moral liberalism (even if these attributes are not shared equally amongst all the members of a given society). Its arguments and conclusions are not necessarily applicable to societies where progress on such issues as women's rights and the decriminalization of homosexuality continue to be held back by the impositions of patriarchal dictatorships and religious fundamentalisms of various kinds. The ruling elites of such societies continue to be more concerned with containing what they perceive to be the 'threat' of sexual reform and revolution presented by the media than with advancing sexual equality in their own jurisdictions. They will find little comfort in these pages, in the unlikely event that they should ever have occasion to read them, since one of my conclusions must be that sooner or later, at a pace determined by local conditions but as certainly as the spread of the internet and its technological offshoots is rapid and unstoppable, the processes described below will impact upon them too.

2

FROM WILDE TO WILD

The end of patriarchy, or is it all just history repeating?

There is an argument that the last years of the twentieth century and the passage from one millennium into another have witnessed not a sexual revolution so much as a recurrence of events and processes which first took place over one hundred years ago. Adherents to this view point out that the late nineteenth century, or *fin de siècle*, was, like today, a period of radical and far-reaching social change, fuelled by the politics of women's liberation. Then as now advanced capitalist societies were afflicted by widespread sexually transmitted disease approaching epidemic levels, in the form of frequently fatal infections like syphilis and gonorrhea. In our own time, while these diseases still affect the sexually active population, it is of course the human immuno-deficiency virus (HIV) which is perceived to be the most dangerous sexual infection.

Other comparisons are drawn. Elaine Showalter (1992) notes the similarities between the late-twentieth-century anti-pornography campaigns of one wing of the feminist movement and the anti-prostitution and social puritanism campaigns of the *fin de siècle*. In both cases women warned other women away from what they perceived to be male-originated sexual danger, in campaigns fuelled by what Lucy Bland describes as an 'ideology of female moral superiority and altruistic maternity' (1995, p. 304). Like the anti-pornography feminists who pushed the Minneapolis Ordinance to the forefront of the US public agenda in the 1980s, argues Bland, 'repressive purity feminists [of the 1880s] acted in and through the state in an effort to transform the sexual morality of the time' (ibid., p. 123). Avedon Carol sees in late-twentieth-century anti-pornography feminism 'precisely the view of women and sexuality that was central to the traditional social purity campaigns [of the nineteenth century]: women as sexless, men as rapacious; women as victims, men as brutes; sexual pleasure as dangerous and anti-social, repression as necessary to social stability' (1994, p. 5). Wendy McElroy compares late-twentieth-century anti-porn legislative efforts with laws such as the Contagious Diseases Acts and the Criminal Law Amendment Act of the late nineteenth century – laws which sought to place control of sexuality in the hands of the patriarchal state (1995).

And history is repeating, from this perspective, not just for women and feminists. The late nineteenth century saw the emergence of homosexuality as a distinct sexual identity and lifestyle, similar in some respects to the last three decades of the twentieth century. The *fin-de-siècle* suppression of homosexuality signalled by the trial of Oscar Wilde has been compared by some authors to the 'gay plague' anxieties which accompanied the 1980s discovery of HIV and its subsequent association with the sexual lifestyles of gay men. Both produced what Showalter calls 'a moral panic that inaugurated a period of censorship affecting both advanced women and homosexuals' (1992, p. 171).

The parallels are compelling, and underpin a view of history as cyclical process following more or less predictable patterns of ebb and flow, progress and reaction (Figure 2.1). They make sense of confusing contemporary events in terms of the better known past, and frame evaluation of their significance in the comfortable (because familiar) context of what past experience has demonstrated to be the limits of the possible. They are then put to the service of a variety of more or less pessimistic perspectives on the role of culture and the evolution of sexual relations within capitalism which end up by downplaying the notion that there can be any positive change – lasting change of depth and significance, as opposed to superficial, commercially driven change – in these relations.

Susan Faludi's *Backlash*, for example – more than a decade old but still influential and oft-quoted in this context – is unambiguous in its assertion that feminism had provoked by the 1980s a 'post-feminist' conservative male reaction – the backlash of her title – expressed culturally in such works as Adrian Lyne's 1987 hit movie *Fatal Attraction*, or in the fashion trend which came to be known as 's&m chic'. As she put it then, 'in times of backlash, images of the restrained woman line the walls of the popular culture gallery' (1991, p. 93). In the same way, Elaine Showalter compares *Fatal Attraction* with Robert Louis Stevenson's tale of *Dr Jeckyll and Mr Hyde* (1886). In both narratives fallen women are punished and men who might be tempted to dabble in the pleasures of the flesh warned off with threats of annihilation. Both, suggests Showalter, enter the culture and become iconic at times of feminist advance.

	fin de siècle	*millennial turn*
sexual revolution	New Women; aesthetes	feminism; gay liberation
sexual epidemic	syphilis	HIV/AIDS
patriarchal backlash	The Bostonians	Disclosure
moral puritanism	anti-prostitution	anti-pornography

Figure 2.1 History repeating?

This view is appealing in its neatness, if misleading in so far as it tends to downplay the very real and quite unprecedented changes which have taken place in the century or so separating Wilde (Oscar) and Wild[1] (the artist). While there are obvious similarities in, for example, the anti-prostitution and anti-pornography campaigns of the nineteenth and twentieth centuries respectively, or between the syphilis and AIDS epidemics, or indeed between the responses to these events of some artists and critics then and now, the social contexts in which they occurred are so different, the economic and political environments surrounding them so radically altered, that to compare them in this way is of limited value in the understanding of the advances in sexual relations and culture which characterize our time. And also morale-sapping, if such comparisons can be allowed to suggest that heterosexist patriarchy and its relations of inequality, exploitation, and sexual discrimination are eternal.

The simple truth is that much has changed in the sexual sphere, and that most of that change has been for the better. Which is not to deny that there *has* been a backlash of sorts, evident in at least some of the cultural output to be examined later on in this book. But to recognize the fact of backlash is not the same thing as saying that we live in a 'backlash culture', if that term implies a cultural environment in which patriarchal resistance to feminism is ascendant or hegemonic. Writers in the 1990s who asserted this did not specify the precise extent of the backlash they had in mind, instead conjuring up images of an all-consuming wave of misogynistic reaction pushing back whatever limited advances second-wave feminism of the post-1960s era had achieved. 'Backlash' was and remains a particular kind of response by some men, but not all, to the picture of progressive socio-sexual change which emerges from a fair examination of the evidence.

This change, if indeed it can be shown to have occurred, has not come about by accident, nor through the beneficent instincts of men – the ruling class of patriarchy – enlightened by feminist-inspired good sense after millennia of unreflective domination of their womenfolk, but precisely – and only – because of the struggles of politicized women and homosexuals to further it, supported by those amongst the 'straight' male population who have supported their campaigns. Change has been the *product* of sex-political struggle, just as much as the reform of capitalist working conditions in the nineteenth and twentieth centuries could not have been achieved without the efforts of trade unions.

But change there has been, as a statistic or two, highlighted by Showalter, demonstrates. In 1897 there were only 844 women studying in English universities. Only eighty-seven doctors in the whole of England were women. These were times in which women were effectively segregated from their male masters – politically, culturally, economically – and all but excluded from the spheres of 'serious' work (most working women were employed as domestic staff), as they were prevented from reaching the highest levels of achievement in art and government. They were denied the fundamental human right to vote, as they were denied their sexuality by male establishments.

Now, as the media frequently remind us, women outnumber their male peers in most academic subjects within education, and perform on average qualitatively better. In 2000, for the first time, more women achieved first-class honours degrees from British universities than men.[2] By 2000 females were also performing better in school, leading to much public debate about the future of male children in a post-feminist world. That summer, as A level and GCSE exam grades were published in the United Kingdom, the British media were trying to come to terms with the fact that, for the first time in British educational history, but certainly not the last, girls achieved more A levels, and more A levels at 'A' grade, than their male peers, and performed better on average across the range of grades.

Once out of school, in professions where they were once, if not entirely excluded, routinely discriminated against, women are climbing the ladders of achievement, and reaping the financial rewards. A 1998 report found that, up to the age of 35, women in the British journalistic profession earn some 25% more than men of the same age.[3] Thereafter men are ahead on income, and the more familiar pattern of male domination is reasserted at the most senior levels of the profession. In journalism, as in many other occupations, the relative positions of younger men and women are much more 'equal' than those of their older colleagues, showing that the most radical change is occurring lower down the scale. New generations of women, formally and informally educated to expect equal treatment in their dealings with men, are now more likely to receive it. Older generations, both men and women, reared in pre-feminist values and ideas, are more likely to reflect these in their career development. The pressure for change is generational, comes from below, and takes time to work through the system.

To assert that the glass ceiling is being raised as it becomes thinner and more fragile does not preclude the recognition that it remains in place. A BBC *Panorama* documentary broadcast in January 2000 described the problems faced by women who aspire to participate as equals with men in the labour force, while at the same time having and rearing children. Achieving a balance between their traditional maternal role, and the pursuit of a career outside the home, is no less difficult and demoralizing for many women today than it was two or three decades ago. Research commissioned for the BBC showed that of 560 mothers who returned to full-time work after the birth of their first child, 36 per cent had given it up again within two years, removing themselves entirely from the paid labour force (19 per cent) or opting for part-time employment (17 per cent). The reason for this drop-out was, in most cases, the fact that while women now had equal access to jobs and careers from which they were once excluded, little or no allowance was being made in their places of employment for the parental demands made on them. Increasingly, the programme reported, and in the absence of greater workplace flexibility by male-dominated managements, women are required to choose *either* children *or* career,[4] rather than be enabled to have both.

In work as in society generally, my female readers will not need reminding, men are relinquishing their privileges only with reluctance, and often not before inflicting physical and emotional damage on wives, partners, employees, or others within their reach who might wish to take advantage of the achievements of the feminist movement in the conduct of their own lives. My argument here is not that such resistance no longer exists; it is that those who would most resolutely mount it are in serious long-term retreat. In the historical scheme of things women in contemporary capitalism occupy a social world fundamentally transformed from that in which their mothers, grandmothers and great-grandmothers grew up – a 'post-feminist' world, indeed, a world in which feminist ideas and presumptions have not been superseded so much as become part of the fabric of the culture; accepted, at least in public, by the great majority of powerful and influential males; taken for granted in a way that has been true of no previous type of society, anywhere in the world. Sexism is now recognized as a blot on the cultural landscape. This doesn't mean that sexism is dead, nor even that it is close to dying out; only that it is in measurable decline, increasingly marginalized as a 'bad thing'. In her introduction to Annie Liebowitz's 1999 collection of photographs of women Susan Sontag noted just how much had changed in their socio-economic and cultural position, and just how quickly.

> There is something new in the world, starting with the revoking of age-old legal shackles regarding suffrage, divorce, property rights. It seems almost inconceivable now that the enfranchisement of women happened as recently as it did: that, for instance, women in France and Italy had to wait until 1945 and 1946 to be able to vote. There have been tremendous changes in women's consciousness, transforming the inner life of everyone: the sallying forth of women from women's work into the world at large, the arrival of women's *ambitions.* (her emphasis)[5]

As for the patriarchal enemy, Sontag continued in the same piece, 'male behaviour, from the caddish to the outright violent, that until recently was accepted without demurral is seen today as outrageous by many women who not so long ago were putting up with it themselves and who would still protest indignantly if someone described them as feminists'.[6] As women have advanced on the socio-economic front men in patriarchy have had to give ground, contributing to what was by the late 1990s being called by academic and journalistic observers alike the 'crisis of masculinity'. Regarded by some as a long overdue recognition of and necessary adaptation to the achievements of feminism, and by others as signalling the collapse of civilized society, the 'crisis' signified a real shift in the status of men *vis-à-vis* women in advanced capitalism.

Gay men and women also greeted the millennium in a very different situation from that faced by Oscar Wilde and his peers. In Britain at the beginning of the twenty-first century, as the previous chapter noted, being openly gay was no longer a bar to mainstream commercial success in the worlds of art and entertainment, nor even to attainment of the highest political and public office. The gay journalist Andrew Sullivan conceded in 1995 that 'despite extraordinary resources marshalled against homosexuals – culturally, economically, politically – the twentieth century has seen fissures of liberty become chasms' (p. 75).

So how did it happen? How did societies like Britain and the United States advance from the states of female subordination – slavery in all but name – and the brutal suppression of homosexuality which existed a mere century ago, and which still exists in much of the world, to the position Sontag and Sullivan describe?

The feminist revolution

The emergence of 'first wave' feminism in the countries of the western world[7] – although the term was not then in common usage – was a product, on the one hand, of changes in the organization of work and family life associated with modern capitalism, and on the other, of advances in nineteenth-century science and political philosophy which delivered among other things Darwin's theory of natural selection, Marx's theory of capital, and John Stuart Mill's theory of democratic government. The rational, socially progressive thrust of these various thinkers, on the back of widening suffrage and educational provision, and in the radicalizing context of a viciously exploitative, untamed capitalism produced the conditions for a campaigning focus on women's rights (or the lack of them), and organized movements dedicated to the pursuit of those rights. In the United States the nineteenth-century campaign to abolish slavery was also a factor in this process, in so far as it encouraged some anti-slavery women to look more carefully at the causes and consequences of their own oppression as females, and to begin to fight against it. For feminist historian Sheila Rowbotham, 'feminism came, like socialism, out of the tangled, confused response of men and women to capitalism' (1977) as it matured in the nineteeth century. When male-dominated trade unions and nascent labour parties began to campaign for such reforms as a humane working day and the abolition of child labour, women were politicized too, but quickly discovered that, left to their own devices, men were unlikely to deliver significant improvements to women's status. Men could reform capitalism, but not patriarchy, within which even the humblest male proletarian stood in a privileged relationship of domination to the women around him.

Some of the early feminists, nonetheless (such as Eleanor Marx, Karl's daughter), defined themselves principally as socialists, subordinating 'the woman question' to a broader anti-capitalist struggle. This strand of 'Marxist' or socialist feminism shared historical materialism's thesis[8] that all forms of social exploitation were founded on class relations, and that class struggle was the driving force of history. These feminists found an ideological home in the Marxist-Leninist inspired communist parties of the twentieth century, which viewed any other approach to the liberation of women as a bourgeois deviation from the class struggle. In the Soviet Union and other 'socialist' countries, feminists were routinely persecuted as dissidents.

Other feminist campaigners were inspired to action by the extent of the prostitution industry, and the threat which they perceived it to pose to women's health, morality and well-being (principally in the form of the syphilis epidemic of the late nineteenth century). For this group, sex represented a threat; a danger from which women had to be protected. Marie Stopes's pioneering work on birth control, welcome as it may have been to women at the time (and attacked by the guardians of patriarchal morality when it was published in 1918 as *Married Love*), was inspired by a eugenicist agenda of improving the 'race' by reducing the numbers of the lower classes, whom she believed to be breeding rather too prolifically for the good of polite society.[9]

Others campaigned not for less sex but more, in the form of 'free love', challenging patriarchal norms of family life and female sexuality. These women, and the men like Edward Carpenter who inspired and supported them, anticipated the sex-radical feminism of the late twentieth century[10] believing, like their successors a century later, that the personal and the political were 'inseparable and that sexuality could be the basis of social change' (Showalter, 1992, p. 47).

These early feminists' understanding of their own, distinctively female sexuality was influenced by the development of the medical sub-discipline of sexology. Though pioneered and largely monopolized by men, sexology gave women a new and rational-sounding scientific vocabulary with which to articulate their sexual problems and needs. As was the case with the homosexual community (see below), the development in the late nineteenth century of what Michel Foucault called a *scientia sexualis* (1990) created a discursive framework for sex talk to proliferate, leading on to new possibilities for political action. This sexualization of Victorian culture led, as did the explosion of mediated sex a century later, to a certain amount of public anxiety. Tom Hickman's *Sexual Century* quotes the author of a 1913 edition of the journal *Current Opinion* to the effect that 'a wave of sex hysteria and sex discussion seems to have invaded the century. Our former reticence on matters of sex is giving way to a frankness that would startle even Paris' (1999, p. 53).[11] Pressure for political rights for women, and a growing awareness of female sexuality, coexisted with a widespread public fear of the 'new woman' and her impact on settled family and social life. Lynda Nead's study of the female nude in art describes the press outrage which accompanied the 1914 vandalism of Velazquez' *The Toilet of Venus* by the suffragette Mary Richardson, and the 'representation of the affair as the frenzied attack of a militant feminist on an image of perfect womanly beauty' (1992, p. 42). Fear of feminism also took the form of imprisonment of activists and other legal sanctions, and cultural backlash of the type seen in Henry James's *The Bostonians*, with its negative portrayals of feminism and feminists.[12]

At the same time as feminists were being satirized and denigrated by male politicians, journalists and artists, however, 'New Woman' writers like Sarah Grand and Emma Brooke were selling millions of copies of their novels, and the movement for women's suffrage made steady progress on both sides of the Atlantic Ocean until the upheavals of World War I finally forced major concessions from the patriarchal state. The trauma of global conflict, the consequent shortage of labour, and the enhanced socio-economic leverage which this bestowed upon women, built on the political pressure coming from various branches of the feminist movement to end at least some of the primitive sexisms of nineteenth-century patriarchy. In 1918 British women over the age of 30 at last won the right to vote (though full voting equality did not come until 1928), and in 1920 the voting rights of American women were enshrined in the Constitution for the first time.

Following these victories, however, and until the 'second wave' of feminism arrived in the aftermath of the 1960s sexual revolution, the international movement for women's rights went into forty years of decline, for reasons which still divide feminist historians. Some argue that the achievements of the suffragettes temporarily removed the edge from the struggle and encouraged a premature complacency amongst women. For others, the period between the first and second world wars, during which economic upheaval was accompanied by the rise of fascism and the threat of renewed international conflict, inevitably pushed feminist demands to the margins as the survival of global capitalism itself came into question. Whatever the cause, as Lucy Bland puts it, 'the sense of an enormous energising movement disappeared, and with it went the biting critique of male sexuality' (1995, p. 309) which had driven 'first wave' feminism.

The experience of World War II, however, and the movement of women *en masse* into 'men's work' such as shipbuilding and armaments production which it necessitated, laid many of the foundations for the eventual resurgence of feminism in the 1960s. As the classic documentary film *The Life and Times of Rosie the Riveter* (Connie Field, 1980) demonstrates, images of women doing 'men's work', and doing it well, would turn out to be powerful propaganda in the feminist battles to come later in the century, even if the immediate post-war period was one of moral and sexual conservatism, reinforced by the ideological rigidities of the Cold War and the need to get returning war veterans back into productive employment. The sexual mores of that time were satirized a half century later in Gary Ross's movie *Pleasantville* (1998) which in its (literally) rose-tinted depiction of a half-remembered United States also exposed the oppressive sexual conservatism of the 1950s. Presented at the time as an ideal for both men and women to live by, the kind of nuclear family depicted in *Pleasantville*, and the moral values which supported it, were not sustainable, the film suggests. The separations caused by war had put great strain on many relationships, increasing the incidence of divorce, adultery, pregnancy outwith marriage, and many other deviations from the marriage-with-two-point-four-kids ideal portrayed in much of post-war popular culture.

The ideal was a fiction, but the post-war drive to reinstate pre-war sexual ethics and morality might have fared better had it not been for the economic boom and the culture of triumphant hedonism which victory permitted, and which a rapidly expanding media system encouraged to become fashionable through such sexually charged movie and music icons as Marilyn Monroe, Marlon Brando, Elvis Presley and James Dean. As commercialized forms of youth culture emerged in the 1950s moral conservatism seemed increasingly anachronistic and out of date, giving way to *Playboy*, *The Wild One* and teen hysteria associated with the burgeoning pop music industry.

Feminism and the 1960s

The sexual revolution of the 1960s built on this gradual undermining of hitherto solid family values, as well as important changes in the economic and social status of women. These were fuelled in turn by technological advances in contraception which undermined the notion that all sex had to be procreative in function. In 1962 American author Helen Gurley Brown published *Sex and the Single Girl*, the core text in the construction of what became known as the 'Cosmo girl'. Betty Friedan's *Feminine Mystique* appeared a year later. These books announced the arrival of a new generation of economically empowered, sexually assertive women who were, by the standards of their time, 'liberated' from the stereotypes and norms previously applied to women in even the most advanced of capitalist societies. Many of them were readers of the new *Cosmopolitan* magazine, edited by Brown, and which pioneered the frank discussion of female sexuality and the role of women in work.

As the decade progressed and hedonistically rebellious youth culture (or sections of it) became highly politicized anti-Vietnam war counter-culture – the New Left – women were actively involved in radical organisations such as Students for a Democratic Society, campaigning alongside their male peers. Part of this politics was an assertion of the benefits of 'free love' and a rejection of the sexual conservatism favoured until then by the parent culture. What this turned out to mean in practice, however, was the subordination of women within a male-led cultural revolution; domination by a macho left which neither understood nor was interested in the specific issues women might have wished to put on the agenda. Beatrice Faust recalls that 'women became accessories to porno politics: idealistic women were needed to paint banners, do clerical work, and provide creature comforts – of which coffee and cunt were the most in demand' (1980, p. 110). From this experience of exclusion, subordination, and downright denigration at the hands of 'right-on' males sprang the separatist feminism of the late 1960s and after – a necessarily segregationist politics which recognized that, on their own, men were incapable of delivering a sexual revolution worthy of the name. Political women broke away from the male left and began to organize themselves.

These radical feminists embarked on a wide-ranging critique of patriarchal culture and its role in the oppression of women. Advertising, cinema, pornography – all were implicated in the construction of women as objects of male possession and domination, and denounced as vehicles for the imposition of what Laura Mulvey famously described as the 'male gaze',[13] now viewed as the defining characteristic of patriarchal culture. Pornography in particular became a symbol of patriarchy's oppressive essence, its sexual objectification of women viewed as the purest manifestation of predatory male voyeurism. Throughout the 1970s and into the 1980s this reading of the pornographic, and of male-authored sexual representation in general, was hegemonic in the feminist movement as it advanced its anti-sexist agenda in various arenas. By the late 1970s slogans like 'pornography is the theory, rape is the practice', had become articles of radical feminist faith.

The sex wars

As the arguments of feminism gained wider acceptance they were reinforced by the growing economic and social independence produced by the pill and the entry of women into the paid labour force in ever-greater numbers. Women were making slow but steady material progress, increasingly living feminist lives, even if they did not always call themselves feminists. Those who embraced the label divided themselves into radical feminists, liberal feminists, lesbian feminists, Marxist feminists, and socialist feminists, all digging away at the foundations of patriarchy with varying degrees of militancy and separationism. Through it all the possibilities for women to live as independent economic, political and sexual beings were expanded (if not to the point at which anything like 'equality' had been achieved). Between 1950 and 1975 the percentage of women in paid employment rose from 25 to 50 even if, as Anne Oakley observed, 'compared to men, women are concentrated in occupations which reflect the domesticity of the conventional female role' (1974, p. 79). For all its limitations, however, the movement of so many women into paid jobs and careers had a major impact on sexual culture. As the sociologist David Evans put it in the early 1990s:

> Women . . . as they have become free wage labour have become socially and morally freer to be sexual or, more accurately, to negotiate with competing sexualising discourses. Still severely prescribed by femininity, female sexuality has nevertheless become active, recreational, material, independent, consumerist and consumed, a key site of conflict, resistance and division.
>
> (Evans, 1993, p. 41)

Many of those women were reluctant to endorse the more extreme positions of radical feminism, and in particular the labelling of all sexual representation, including the pornographic, as oppressive. Thus began the intra-feminist 'porn wars', marked by such events as the 1981 publication of the *Coming to Power* manifesto by the sado-masochistic lesbian SAMOIS group; the publication of the *Heresies* journal's 'sex' issue in 1982; the 1984 Barnard conference; and the founding, also in 1984, of the lesbian feminist *On Our Backs* periodical. In a collection of essays published under the title *Women against Censorship* Anne Snitow argued that feminists 'need to be able to reject the sexism in porn without having to reject the realm of pornographic sexual fantasy as if that entire kingdom were without meaning and resonance for women' (Snitow, 1985, p. 117). Lynne Segal made a similar point when she wrote that 'while the voices recognised by mainstream culture as "feminist" remain those busy demonising male lust and pornography as a metaphor for evil, it will not be possible to find any confident – or even hopeful – popular affirmation of a feminist sexual politics' (1994, p. 69).

These developments signalled that feminism, by its successes in advancing women's socio-economic and political status within patriarchy, had created the conditions for a flowering of diverse and frequently 'unfeminine' female sexualities, not all of which could be comfortably accomodated by the then still-dominant anti-porn wing of the feminist movement. Deborah Bright records that 'the porn wars of the late 1970s and 1980s pitted those women who explored sexual subjects and eroticism as a necessary intervention in a territory historically reserved for male commerce and privilege against those who believed that any sexualised images of women's bodies, without exception, promoted misogyny and violence against women' (1998, ed., p. 7).[14] In her essay to accompany the 'Bad Girls' exhibition which toured Britain in 1994 Laura Cottingham noted that 'whereas in the late 70s and early 80s, a general critique of mainstream pornography was an assumed premise of those who considered themselves feminist, now the majority of academics, artists and activists who [do so] are openly hostile to the pornographic critique' (ICA, 1993, p. 56). In the 1990s, with the publication of Madonna's *Sex* book and other cultural manifestations of a female sexuality which often borrowed overtly from the codes of pornography, the porn wars became part of popular culture, its competing arguments disseminated to a wide audience in a new generation of raunchy women's magazines like *Marie Claire*, *Company* and *New Woman*.

Rosalind Coward observed at the end of the 1990s that 'feminism has been a dramatically successful social movement' (1999, p. 1). On the basis of this success women reopened, on their own terms, debates on the nature of femininity, and the extent to which men and women really *were* different. As the *Panorama* programme cited above showed (in addition to criticizing the lack of childcare facilities and other resources required to give women genuine equality in the workplace), women in the early twenty-first century were questioning their ability, and their need, to do everything – to bear and raise children; to compete with men in the office, factory or university. The debate about, and search for, 'authentic' femininity – as distinct from the femininities imposed on women by patriarchy – was moving on, but on the foundation of thirty years of femin*ism* and the achievements it had won. Though initially condemned by Susan Faludi and others as part of the patriarchal backlash,[15] this rethink made sense in terms of the new possibilities which feminism had made possible for women, particularly those younger generations brought up in a world where ideas which had once been the province of radical feminism were increasingly viewed as self-evident common sense. That recognition contributed further to intra-feminist debate around the question of what forms of sexual representation and discourse were appropriate to the new environment. The opposing positions taken in the specific context of the porn wars were extended to discussions of sexual representation in pop music, art and advertising, mainstream Hollywood and independent cinema. In all these arenas, images which would once have been defined (and denounced) as the expression of male sexism were being invested with new meanings and significance by feminist women.

Indicative of the changing political environment was the fact that when, at the turn of the millennium, Andrea Dworkin surfaced in the mainstream British media with calls for the establishment of a women-only country on the model of Zionist Israel, controversial allegations of 'date rape', and the advocacy of castration and capital punishment for sex offenders,[16] she was greeted with embarrassed silence by most feminists. Around the same time that Dworkin was calling for her women's republic Lynne Segal seemed to be more representative in advocating a feminism that was 'optimistic, imaginative and inclusive, that said no to sexism but yes to whatever sort of sexual pleasure a woman could find; that took issue with misogyny and male domination, but welcomed engagement with generous, thoughtful men'.[17]

The homosexual century

If the feminist struggle for women's rights made significant advances in the twentieth century, and thus changed the context in which much sexual discourse and imagery was received and understood, so did the struggle for gay liberation. During the writing of this book, a number of things happened in the United Kingdom which were indicative of the progress being made towards civic and social equality by homosexuals at the millennial turn. First, the Labour government of Tony Blair effectively ended the ban on homosexuality in the British military, until then an offence punishable by dishonourable discharge and even court martial. Then, the same government equalized the age of sexual consent as between heterosexuals and homosexuals. Gay teenagers of 16 (and their partners) were no longer committing a crime if they had sexual relations. And third, in 2000 the infamous Section 28 of the 1988 Local Government Act was repealed in Scotland (in England the House of Lords obstructed its final stages, against the wishes of the government, though most commentators expected that the second term of Tony Blair's administration would push it through). This law – the most contentious element of which banned teachers from 'promoting' homosexuality in schools – had been introduced by the Conservative government of Margaret Thatcher in response to the perceived advances of the gay community in British society. Although no one was ever actually prosecuted under the legislation its presence on the statute books was a symbolic reminder of the institutionalized homophobia of British society. Its removal, therefore, in combination with the other measures cited, was a moment of comparable symbolic resonance – the point at which deep-rooted trends in British popular culture indicating increased mainstream acceptance of homosexuality (see Chapter 7) were matched by legal changes in the status and civil rights of homosexuals.

Since 1997 there had been known to be three gay men in the British cabinet (Nick Brown, Peter Mandelson, Chris Smith) and many gay members of parliament, male and female (not all of them 'out', of course – Mandelson himself was 'outed' for the first time on national UK television by the gay journalist Matthew Parris, though the then-Northern Ireland minister's sexual orientation was an open secret). These were not just members of the Labour and Liberal Democrat parties (perceived, rightly or not, as historically less homophobic than the Conservatives). In one of the most significant developments in what one might describe as the normalization or 'mainstreaming' of gayness in Britain, the man widely predicted to be a future leader of the Conservative Party – Michael Portillo – admitted in a 1999 newspaper interview to having had homosexual experience as a student. He then went on to win a safe Tory seat in the House of Commons, proving that the taint of queerness was no longer a bar to a successful career anywhere on the political spectrum.

These developments in the United Kingdom were foreshadowed in the United States by Clinton administration pro-gay reforms earlier in the 1990s, although in America a strong Republican lobby in the Congress inhibited the pace and scope of change (parallelling the role of Conservative peers in the British House of Lords). As this book went to press overt homosexuality remained inadmissible in the US military, and George W. Bush was not expected to alter that situation, although at least one openly gay man was working in his first administration. In America as in Britain, it was possible to argue with some conviction that the millennial turn was a period of progress, rather than reversal, in the socio-economic, politico-cultural and legal fortunes of gay men and women; the fruition of a process which had begun with the Stonewall riots of 1969 in New York and which, to the surprise of many, had survived the tragic consequences of the HIV/AIDS crisis.

Before Stonewall: discrimination, persecution, invisibility

Archaeological records suggest that same-sex sex (and indeed love) have been present in all pre-existing human societies (Taylor, 1996). In ancient Greece it was practically compulsory among a certain class of wealthy, cultured male, for whom 'the love of a man for a boy who had passed the age of puberty' (Tannahill, 1992, p. 85) was perceived as an aesthetic refinement and a philanthropic duty. This form of what we would categorize as paedophilia was not homosexuality, in the sense that we use the term today. Foucault observes of boy-love in ancient Greece that 'our notion of homosexuality is plainly inadequate as a means of referring to an experience, forms of valuation, and a system of categorisation so different from ours' (1992, p. 187). *Homosexuality*, as opposed to the same-sex activities of the Greeks, or the sins of sodomy and buggery proclaimed by the Christian church, is a relatively new 'invention', by no means synonymous with same-sex sexual activity in general. A significant number of males and females in our societies who would resist categorization as homosexual have sex with other men and women – prisoners in jail, for example, perhaps because it is their only means of sexual contact with another human being (or because they are forced to by other prisoners, who may be no more homosexual than they); servicemen and women, again because there may be no other form of sexual activity available in their immediate environment; teenagers in single-sex schools, for whom same-sex experimentation is sometimes part of their initiation and progress to adulthood. All of these may have 'homo' sex but do not necessarily view themselves, nor wish to be viewed by others, as homosexual.

Homosexuality as we use the term today refers to a kind of *person*, a sexual orientation, rather than an *activity*. Prior to Karoly Benkert's coining of the term in 1869, and for most of the period of judaeo-christian ascendancy in Europe, same-sex love was perceived as sinful behaviour indulged in by the morally weak, rather than a fixed quality of an individual's essential being. Although the punishments of those times were brutal and inhumane, Reay Tannahill notes that between the sixth and sixteenth centuries those referred to as 'buggers' and 'sodomites' 'were in fact treated no more harshly than couples who practised contraception' (1992, p. 159). Sodomites, like adulterers, were punished because they departed from the theologically imposed notion that all sex had to be procreative in purpose, and conducted within the framework of marriage. Gradually, as the influence of Thomas Aquinas[18] and anti-sex moralism spread from the thirteenth century onwards, 'homosexuals as a group were to find neither refuge nor tolerance anywhere in the Western Church or state.' As late as 1828 the 'abominable crime of buggery' was still punishable by death in Great Britain, and Aquinas's views still structure the Catholic Church's public hostility to homosexuality.

Following the development of a scientific discourse of sexual pathology in the late nineteenth century homosexuality was recognized for the first time as a distinct sexual *identity* rather than a sinful choice. It continued to be punished, nonetheless, and was formally outlawed in the Criminal Law Amendment Act of 1885 used to prosecute Oscar Wilde. The Wilde trials, argues Lucy Bland, 'were important in creating a public image of and for the homosexual; as decadent, artistic, white, upper class – and male' (1995, p. 289). There were also female homosexuals, of course, although the law (and, famously, Queen Victoria) did not care to acknowledge their existence. The Wilde trials ushered in, as already noted, an era of censorship and repression of homosexuals. Henceforth they practised 'the love that dare not speak its name'. While homosexual women artists like Radclyffe Hall were censored and banished from visibility, gay men were euphemistically referred to as 'aesthetes' or 'decadents', and required to suppress the public display of their sexual identities – a legally and culturally imposed invisibility which lasted, in Britain as elsewhere in the western world, for more than sixty years. Homosexuality was still socially marginalized, persecuted in the courts, and mocked in the media at the height of the 1960s sexual revolution.

Stonewall and after

Whatever its limitations, however, that revolution (and the partial decriminalization of homosexuality which accompanied it) laid the foundations for the gay liberation movement of the 1970s. Drawing on the sexual hedonism of the 1960s counterculture, and taking inspiration from the feminist critique of patriarchy described above, the homosexual community began to come out of the closet, tentatively at first, but with growing confidence. The first gay scenes – 'gay' becoming a common term of homosexual self-identification in the 1970s – formed in liberal American cities like San Francisco, Los Angeles and New York, but the trend was evident throughout the United States, western Europe and Australasia, as gay spending power connected with the liberal sexual culture of the times and began to translate into cultural visibility.

Reacting to these trends, on 28 June 1969 members of the New York police department carried out their famous raid on the Stonewall Inn, a gay bar. Rather than skulk away into the night, however, as might hitherto have been expected of those harassed in this manner by New York's finest, the patrons of the Stonewall Inn fought back and in doing so launched the era of organized, politicized resistance to heterosexist oppression. The militant mood created by Stonewall led to the formation of the Gay Liberation Front in 1970, and the subsequent development of a gay rights movement throughout the western world. This was a movement characterized by the politicization of sexual hedonism. Post-Stonewall, and in reaction to the long period of persecution and enforced invisibility which preceded it, the construction of a gay sense of community and identity initially revolved around the 'fast-lane', sexually promiscuous lifestyle of discos, bath-houses and leather bars which Robert Mapplethorpe would later document in his photography, and which Armistead Maupin would make the subject of popular literature with his *Tales of the City* books. For homosexuals in the 1970s the political campaign for gay rights and the public celebration of homo-*sexuality* were intimately connected.

HIV and AIDS

This politicized sexual hedonism could not survive the HIV epidemic, which first trickled into public consciousness in the early 1980s as the 'gay plague'. People, it later emerged, had been dying from HIV infection and AIDS since the 1950s, but the disease was first recognized and named in the 1980s when it began to strike down gay men in New York, San Francisco, and other population centres. The onset of the HIV/AIDS crisis at first encouraged a moral conservative backlash to the progress which the gay rights movement had been making since Stonewall, with AIDS identified as the wages of sin. For gays themselves, as Randy Shilts passionately described in his 1988 book *And the Band Played On*, it forced painful and divisive examination of post-Stonewall assumptions about the legitimacy and viability of the promiscuous, multiple-partner sexual lifestyle. For the first time 'safe sex' became an issue for gays and straights alike, and one which had to be addressed head-on and in public. Andrew Sullivan recalls that:

> HIV acted as an unprecedented catalyst for the collapse of the norms of public discussion of homosexuality. It made the subject not merely unavoidable; it made it necessary. And it made hypocrisy unsustainable. The public-private compact between heterosexuals and homosexuals had to be renegotiated.
>
> (1995, p. 124)

HIV/AIDS forced a broad cultural coming to terms with homosexuality in all its manifestations. As a consequence, and notwithstanding the personal tragedies which the virus brought upon so many of its members, the gay community was better placed – socially, legally, economically – at the end of the 1980s than it had been at the beginning. This can be attributed in part to the fact that during the 1980s and 1990s, in response to official neglect of the HIV/AIDS problem throughout the western world, gay liberation activists developed a range of innovative and highly effective campaigning strategies designed to put their demands on the mainstream public and political agenda. First, they aggressively asserted their 'queerness' (as black Americans in the 1980s reclaimed the word 'nigger' from white racists), by which they meant to convey a rejection not just of straight stereotypes of gayness, but those which had been endorsed by the gay community itself.[19] Queer activists and artists like film director Todd Haynes wanted 'to question the conformity [of gay life], instead of just replicating the structures we've been trying to free ourselves from'.[20] This meant confrontation with conservatism of both the gay and straight varieties. Members of ACT UP, Outrage and other groups pursued strategies of gender and identity subversion such as 'outing' in which closet gays had their 'real' sexualities revealed against their will. The English activist Peter Tatchell established a reputation for doing so in hitherto sacrosanct spaces like church pulpits. On one widely reported occasion he provoked a minor diplomatic incident by confronting the homophobic leader of Zimbabwe, Robert Mugabe, during a state visit to the United Kingdom.

Another wing of the gay movement focused on the socially transformative possibilities of the mainstreaming and commercialization of gayness through the development of 'gay villages' in big cities, and the recognition by business that there was a substantial 'pink pound' or dollar to be earned from the servicing of gay consumerism. The economic power of homosexuals in the 1980s and 1990s, like that of women in the 1960s, encouraged capitalist economies to make space for a gay public in the cultural marketplace. Homosexuals in general have not been anti-bourgeois so much as anti-heterosexist, and the cultural capitalism of the late twentieth century had matured to the point of being able to recognize the difference, and to profit from it.

The tension between militant strategies of 'outing' and the integrationist tendencies of commercialisation and mainstreaming echoed debates within the feminist movement about pornography, and led to analogous splits and divisions around cultural politics and aesthetics. Some queers greeted growing acceptance of homosexuality by the straight world as a form of betrayal or collaboration, preferring to maintain a stance of rejectionism and anger. Like the feminists who defined all male sexuality as predatory and aggressive, some in the gay movement actively pursued strategies of alienation and separation from the straight world, and even from those in the gay world who viewed accomodation with the straight as a legitimate political approach. Through it all, though, real, tangible process was being made in the extension of civil rights to homosexuals. In the US state of Hawaii in the late 1990s, same-sex marriage was given legal recognition. In Britain, the right of gays to become adoptive parents was accepted by the courts. In Israel, in May 2000, lesbians were given the legal right to adopt for the first time anywhere in the world. In Britain that September leading New Labour supporters (and prominent gay couple) Lord Ali and Charlie Parker declared their support for some form of legal recognition of the status of long-term gay relationships.

But then, just as the new century dawned, it seemed that in the United Kingdom at least there might be an anti-gay backlash underway. In both the Westminster and Scottish parliaments, Labour government manifesto commitments to repeal Section 28 of the Local Government Act were greeted with carefully orchestrated hostility by religious and other conservatives, most notoriously the Catholic Cardinal Thomas Winning in Scotland, who spoke of homosexuality as a 'perversion', and compared gay rights campaigners to the Nazis. The anti-repeal 'Keep the Clause' campaign in Scotland was given further profile by the revelation that Brian Soutar, multi-millionaire boss of the Stagecoach company, was funding it to the tune of £500,000. For a few months, in both the Scottish and UK media, the debate around Section 28 kept hard-pressed news editors in stories, and saw the resurgence of a particularly nasty homophobia in some tabloid newspapers. Despite these reversions to type, however, it was possible to argue that the struggle for gay rights had by the year 2000 reached an historic watershed. Certainly, as the Section 28 controversy showed, homophobia had not gone away, but it had become increasingly marginalized as a preserve of the elderly, the conservative and the ignorant. Opinion polls showed conflicting levels of pro and anti opinion on the Section 28 issue, but all agreed that opposition to repeal grew with age. A Channel 4/National Opinion Poll survey published in December 1999, for example, showed that while two-thirds of the British population in the 15–24 age group supported the government's policy of repeal, only one-third of over-65s did so. To this extent the outrage stirred up around Section 28 in early 2000 was something of a storm in a teacup – a last stand of the homophobes before calm once again descended on a society increasingly unshocked by public homosexuality. As Jonathan Freedland put it in the *Guardian* that year, 'wherever you look, Britain has become a nation at ease with sexual difference'.[21]

Straight masculinity in crisis

What about straight men, then – the ruling class of patriarchy, and hate figures of some thirty years of feminist and gay rights discourse? How did they cope with all this change, and the threats to their privileged positions which it presented?

Some, perceiving that their right to be 'real' men was under attack, sought refuge in the cultivation of a quasi-mythical, primitive masculinity. The phenomenon of Iron John exemplified this movement, as did the character of Frank 'T.J.' Mackie played by Tom Cruise in P.T. Anderson's *Magnolia* (1999).[22] Other responses included the 'New Man' of the 1980s, 1990s 'new lad', and a succession of more laboured attempts to reconfigure the elements of an authentic masculinity in the post-feminist era. Some of these identities embraced the lessons of the feminist and gay critiques of straight masculinity, and encouraged men to 'get in touch with their feminine sides'. Others were defiantly reactionary, reaffirming precisely those features of patriarchal masculinity which feminists had most criticised – the unreflective consumption of pornography, alcohol and football in misogynistic, female-free environments, for example. Others ('soft lad') combined elements of both responses, in uneasy amalgams of 'feminine' emotionality and sensitivity with traditionally masculine confidence and decisiveness. But if the responses of straight masculinity (or, to be more precise, the gurus and arbiters of male taste) to sex-political change were often clumsy and contrived, it was undeniable that, as Helen Haste noted in 1993, 'men are changing, challenging in different ways the entrenched assumptions of masculinity, tying to find ways to escape the anxiety' (1993, p. 246).[23]

The cultural expressions of this 'changing and challenging' are explored in Chapters 8 and 9 below. Here I restrict myself to the observation that at the beginning of the twenty-first century, thoughout the advanced capitalist world, it was no longer accurate (if indeed it ever was) to speak of a single, hegemonic masculinity to which all men aspired. In response to the economic, social and ideological transformations brought about by advances in the distinct but connected spheres of women's and gay rights, there were many straight masculinities available for a young male to clothe himself in. For those men who wanted to try them on for size (and not all did, of course; nor were all able or willing to overcome the constraints of upbringing and peer group pressure so that they could) the range of identities compatible with being a 'real man' had greatly expanded.

So is it all just history repeating?

Our twenty-first century societies are not merely repeating processes gone through one hundred years ago. There are thought-provoking parallels to be drawn, certainly, between the millennial turn and the *fin de siècle*, but the cultural and political environments within which feminism and gay rights are pursued today, and in which the notions of masculinity and femininity are understood and lived out, are very different from those of a century ago, reflecting transformed political, technological and economic conditions. *Fin de siècle* feminism was an ideological movement ahead of its time, conducted in the absence of women's access to political and economic power. Contemporary feminism, by contrast, is backed up with rights won from a capitalist system which, if still patriarchal in the character of its socio-sexual stratification, is one in which the assumptions of patriarchy are under unprecedented challenge. Women (and men) have access to reproductive tech-nologies which give women control over their own bodies, an advance which undermines once and for all any religious code or value system premised on the biological necessity or moral desirability of procreative sex. The impact of technological change on capitalist social relations has meant that the ideological force of contemporary feminism, and also of gay liberation, go with rather than against the grain of *material* circumstances, as manifest in the growth of sexual consumerism, the increased range of viable lifestyle choices, and reformed laws which confirm the sexual citizenship status of previously disenfranchised groups.

There has, in all these ways, been an unprecedented sexual revolution in recent years, if by that we mean what Anthony Giddens calls 'the flourishing of homosexuality, male and female', and of 'female sexual autonomy' (1993, p. 28) within capitalism. That revolution, as we shall see, has been cultural, as well as economic and political.

Part 1

Cultural sexualisation: from pornosphere to public sphere

3

THE AMAZING EXPANDING
PORNOSPHERE

As recently as 1972, according to a US federal study, the market for pornography in the United States was worth only $10 million. By 1996 the *US News and World Report* put the figure at $8 *billion*.[1] That same year, according to this source, 8,000 pornographic titles were released on video, distributed across a network of 25,000 video stores. In 1998, according to the trade periodical *Adult Video News*, 686 million pornographic videos were rented in the US,[2] a ninefold increase over ten years. By 2001, at the heart of the US porn business in San Fernando Valley, California 10,000 X-rated movies were being produced each year, employing 20,000 people in 200 companies and generating $4 billion in revenue for the region. One observer argued that, on this evidence, 'pornography is fast becoming America's defining cultural form and is already its quintessential business'.[3]

In Britain, where the regulatory and cultural environment is very different from that of the United States (until 2000 there was no legal hard core porn[4] for sale in the United Kingdom, for example), comparable figures are unavailable. Surveys conducted in the late 1990s claimed that 75 per cent of men had used pornography, and one-third of couples. UK porn magazines claimed monthly sales of 2 million copies in 1998, part of a larger sex industry estimated to be worth £2 billion per annum.[5]

None of these figures is entirely reliable, since questions about individual porn use are unlikely to be met with complete honesty, and the pornography industry has tended to shun openness and transparency. The aforementioned *Adult Video News* estimate of 686 million hard core rentals in 1998, for example, was reported to have generated $23 billion in revenue for video stores, a figure which seems unlikely, implying as it does a rental fee of at least $33 per tape. The circulation figures of legally available, 'soft core' pornographic magazines are not available through the usual channels (the Audit Bureau of Circulation in Britain, for example, does not list even the most respectable and biggest-selling of the top shelf magazines like *Penthouse*). The pornography industry is still, despite the liberalization of the media environment described later in this chapter, largely hidden from public view. The pornographers' reticence to reveal information about their industry makes any discussion of its size and structure somewhat speculative, therefore, as does the fact that anti-pornography campaigners (journalistic or otherwise) have an interest in giving the public at large the impression that the industry is both bigger and nastier than it really is. For all that, there is little doubt that in the United States and many other countries the legal market for sexual products (including, in addition to the mediated form of pornography, telephone sex, striptease clubs, sexual aids and so forth) now exceeds those of both the mainstream movie and popular music markets.

The process by which pornography became an economically significant sub-sector of the culture industries has been both demand and *technology* led. To deal with the latter first, each new innovation in the means of mechanical, electronic and most recently digital reproduction of images has enabled easier manufacture and consumption of sexually explicit material, lowering at both points barriers to entry to what I will call from now on the *pornosphere*. The most recent of these technologies to find application by the pornographers – video, DVD and the internet – have been especially effective in allowing individuals to evade many of the negative psychological consequences hitherto associated with the acquisition and use of porn, bringing it further into the private domain of the home and away from the furtive, socially sanctioned world of peep shows and adult book stores. The consumption of pornography traditionally involved a prior public declaration of one's interest, even if that was only across the counter to a storekeeper. New information technologies have made possible the *de facto* routinization of the pornographic experience, and removed some of the moral inhibitions traditionally imposed on its use for many otherwise 'decent' people.

The invention of photography in the early nineteenth century was a key moment in this process, revolutionizing as it did the reach and accessibility of all representation, and beginning the commodification of sexual culture which in turn led to the category of 'pornography'. Before that, the invention of printing in the late fifteenth century had allowed the restricted circulation amongst aristocratic libertines of texts such as Aretino's *Sonnets* (1527), judged by some historians to be the first 'pornographic' work, since in it sexually explicit words and images were united within the body of a book. *L'École des filles* (1624) was an important literary text in seventeenth-century France. A century and a half later the works of the Marquis de Sade were in circulation, and John Cleland's *Fanny Hill* had been published in England. But the development of a truly *mass* pornosphere (as opposed to one accessible only to the educated and the wealthy) had to wait for the introduction of cheap photographic printing. With the invention of photographic daguerrotypes and the positive/negative process in the 1840s, sexually explicit representations became for the first time an affordable item of mass consumption.[6]

'Stag reels' – short, silent films, shot on celluloid – became available in the 1890s and dominated the market for moving image pornography for most of the twentieth century. Cheap colour magazines devoted to pornography appeared in the 1950s, proliferating in the 1960s and converging with the sexual revolution to make hard core pornography widely available for the first time in Europe and America. Video cassette players were introduced in the 1980s, making moving image porn accessible to domestic consumers, and in the same decade satellite communications made the pornography of one country available through the TV screens of another. In the mid-1990s the internet delivered another qualitative leap in the ease with which people could consume sexually explicit materials in their own homes and private spaces.

Developments in communication technology have also changed the way in which, and by whom, pornography is produced. In the late 1970s a feature-length pornographic movie shot on celluloid might cost $350,000. By the 1990s, with video cameras in routine use, companies like Evil Angel Video could produce tapes for a reported $8,000. The same technology which vastly increased the profitability and potential output of the commercial industry allowed pornography to be made by non-professionals. The Polaroid camera and home development kits had long made sexually explicit amateur photography a possibility but now, with hand-held video technology, members of the public with an inclination to do so could produce their own moving image porn, and did, for their own use and that of others. In the United States the Homegrown Video company found a niche distributing the best of these amateur productions around the country, thereby 'serving as a clearing house for the consumers of porn, supplying hard-core videos by the people, for the people'.[7] In Britain too a commercial market for 'amateur' pornography developed in the late 1990s, deploying inexperienced models in unrehearsed, unscripted scenarios, directed by producers of varying degrees of professionalism.

The impact of successive technological innovations on the form of, and audience for pornography has been well documented. The experience of the VCR and the internet in particular have confirmed the fact that 'new technologies are always used for sexual purposes' (Califia, 1994, p. 169) and that, conversely, sex has played 'a huge role in the advance of new communication technologies'.[8] The rapid spread of VCRs in the 1980s was fuelled not least by the unprecedented access which they provided to 'adult' films like *Deep Throat* and *Behind the Green Door*. The expansion of the internet in the late 1990s was facilitated by the availability and profitability of sex sites. By 2001, according to one estimate, online pornography was worth $366 million[9] in profits. As the internet boom turned to bust at the start of the new millennium sex sites were one of the few areas to be making money. US sites alone were generating an estimated $1 billion in revenues in 2001, with an expected rise in that figure to $5 billion by 2005. Some successful sites were reporting 50 million hits per month,[10] and estimates suggested that as of 2001 around 50 per cent of all internet traffic was related to sex sites like the Amsterdam-based Interclimax.[11]

Porn's pulling power

None of this technology-driven expansion would have been possible, of course, unless people wanted mediated sex, and if there was not quite widespread *demand* for what Michelle Aaron calls 'the consumption of dangerous pleasures' (1999, p. 3). The demand for porn in particular has been a driving force in the process by which successive generations of information technologies have become part of mainstream consumer culture. So what is its appeal?

To answer that question first requires some agreement as to what pornography is, and we might as well start with the standard dictionary definition of *explicit content with no purpose other than to induce sexual arousal*.[12] Pornography is defined in the first instance by its function – which is to turn the user on, leading to sexual activity such as intercourse or masturbation. This is not to say that images which are not pornographic cannot be erotic (sexually arousing), or that all pornography arouses. But in so far as there is any intentionality in the text pornography's aim is to make you horny by providing 'a graphic prompt to the sexual fantasies that initiate or accompany masturbation' (Abramson and Pinkerton, 1995, p. 74).[13]

The pornographic text achieves this (or its author does) by acknowledging and then reflecting back to the reader or viewer his or her erotic fantasies and sexual desires, in the form of scenarios reproduced in one or more representational modes – the written word; the photograph; the moving image. By 'fantasy' here I mean that the scenarios depicted are unlikely to be straightforwardly reproducible in real life – men in pornography are always erect, women always eager for sex. In the pornographic depiction of rape and other sex acts involving coercion and domination (sado-masochism, for example) desire is always seen to be present ('no' usually means 'yes'). In pornography the constraints, commitments and responsibilities which structure real-life sexual relationships – the demands of marriage and child bearing, for example – are nearly always absent. The pornographic world is an ideal one in which – while the user is immersed in it, at least – life is reduced to the mechanics of the sex act. A distinguishing feature of porn is thus the foregrounding of sexual activity within the narrative, with or without credible justificatory context. Where a non-pornographic novel or feature film may contain scenes of sexual explicitness (Oshima's *Ai No Corrida* [1972] and Catherine Breillat's 1998 film *Romance*, for example, both showed vaginal penetration, but were not – at least in the opinion of their directors – pornography[14]) these will be presented as subordinate elements in a broader narrative, which may or may not be about sexuality (Oshima's film purports to be about the self-destructive nature of sexual obsession; Breillat's is about a young woman's search for sexual identity and expression). In pornography, by contrast, sex is the story, with other plot elements functioning as incidental narrative devices. The pornographic film, novel or magazine photo-set proceeds from one sexual transaction to another, punctuated by scenes of sexual climax (in movies and photographs, the 'money shot', in which the male's ejaculation is visible and external to his sexual object). This structure is echoed in the user's own progress from arousal to orgasm through masturbation.

Locations and characterization in pornography function chiefly to propel the sexual action from foreplay to climax, then, and are rarely invested with the creative resources required to make 'art' of them. This doesn't mean that pornography cannot be artfully made, and that there is no difference between 'good' and 'bad' pornography. As P.T. Anderson's *Boogie Nights* (1997) showed with the affectionate homage to the genre characteristic of porno-chic (see Chapter 4), some makers of porn aspire to be artists, applying to their work the same production values and technical skills used in the production of non-pornographic texts. In the end, however, any authorial intervention which gets in the way of the sex is, in the terms by which pornography seeks acceptance as a genre (and, more importantly, success as a commodity), likely to produce formal failure, and to succeed only in frustrating (literally) the user. If porn has an aesthetic dimension it lies in the extent to which a text succeeds in its erotic ambitions – a quality largely independent of such elements as plot, script, character development, or production design.

The pragmatics of pornography

The functional purity of the pornographic text helps explain the form's appeal in our HIV/AIDS-infected times. Pornography acknowledges, stimulates and promises the satisfaction of sexual desire without the need for, or the complications of, real human interaction. Andrea Dworkin has called pornography 'mediated prostitution', which is a good way of putting it. She intends the phrase to imply pornography's role in the male exploitation of women, but it is also an accurate description of a function which in the era of HIV has acquired an enhanced social value. Prostitution is a form of displaced sexual activity (in the sense of displacement from the domestic environment) indulged in by men throughout history, from which women have largely been excluded (except in their capacity as prostitutes, of course). Men have used prostitutes in order to satisfy desires which could not be met in marriage, or with their permanent partners, perhaps because their relationships or religions did not allow such intimacy to occur, or because (religion again) they were ashamed of their desires. Some users of prostitutes are unable to have 'normal' sexual relationships due to physical or emotional disabilities, and find payment a convenient means of gaining access to sexual satisfaction.

Whatever needs have been met by the purchase of sex with a stranger, prostitution has always carried with it risks of infection and disease for both parties to the transaction, as well as violence and abuse for the women who have had to sell themselves. Pornography offers, as Dworkin's phrase recognises, a *mediated* version of the sexual transaction, increasingly satisfying as technologies of image reproduction have enhanced its realism, but without the risky personal contact associated with real prostitution. Pornography sells sex, certainly; commodifies it in a manner directly analogous to prostitution, but sanitizes and makes it safe at the same time. Always a factor in its appeal, HIV and AIDS have made this an important motivation in the recent spread of pornography. In conditions of sexual epidemic, pornography and the masturbation it encourages is the safest sex there is. As a consequence many governments have endorsed the use in anti-HIV public health education of what would in other contexts be defined as hard core pornography. Even in relatively censorious Britain, explicit (and erotic) videos and books with a strong safe sex educational content circulated legally amongst the gay community long before 'hard core' became legally available.

The personal underground

Pornography is not only convenient, safe and to the point. It is the most transgressive form of erotica, telling its fantastic tales without moral constraints.[15] This quality distinguishes it from other forms of sexually explicit representation and underpins its appeal, given that the nature of the transgressive and the taboo is a cultural variable, as a glance at Japanese porn quickly shows.[16] This raises the interesting question of what will happen to the concept of pornography if and when the censorial and legal boundaries of the transgressive are pushed back so far that they no longer exist in any meaningful sense and when, whether through the internet or some other means of uncensored and uncensorable communication, anyone can see anything, and everyone everything. We are not far from that position in the advanced capitalist world, even although self-imposed ethical constraints derived from religious and political beliefs are still important factors preventing many people from diving, or even delving into the pornosphere. Fenton Bailey, the producer of Channel 4's *Pornography: A Secret History of Civilisation* argues that 'there will ultimately come a point where pornography is so commonplace that it is rendered completely unsecret and without taboo'.[17]

That is unlikely, if only for the reason that sexual taboos appear to be a universal feature of human societies. To the extent that pornography relies on the violation of taboos it will always exist even if its transgressive content varies between societies and over time. Each generation discovers and transcends its own taboos, as well as inventing some new ones. In our culture, in our time, transgressing taboos has become, as we will see in the next chapter, 'chic', but images of the sexually explicit and forbidden would inevitably offend many people if they were to become part of mainstream culture, and would lose much of their erotic power in becoming accepted and familiar. Pornography is seductive because it represents the secrets of private sexual desire in all their taboo-breaking, transgressive exoticism. It is, by definition, a violation of public morality and taste – an affront to community standards in the sphere of sexual representation, whatever they may be.

For the time being, however, porn's outsider status – the product of the pornographer's determination to break societal taboos by revealing practices which familial, school and religious educations tell us should be forbidden, or at least remain hidden – is at the heart of its eroticism. The American sex guru Susie Bright defines the pornographic experience as being about 'secrecy, excess, the fear of violent reaction, the quease of perversion' (1997, p. 26). Pornography occupies the terrain of the forbidden, a normally repressed zone which in the interests of mental health and well-being requires recognition. 'What turns you on', she concedes, 'may not match your artistic values, your romantic choices in real life, your political views, but it is just as much a part of you, just as real and substantial, as any other aspect' (ibid., p. 153). To suppress it, by extension, is to suppress a part of oneself.

Camille Paglia argues from a similar perspective that 'pornography is pure pagan imagism . . . [the] ritually limited expression of the daemonism of sex and nature.

. . . Pornography shows us those eternal forces at work beneath and beyond social convention' (1990, p. 24). This is its value, she argues, in societies which elsewhere (and with good reason) suppress our instinctive, animal sexualities in the name of civilization and order. One doesn't have to go the whole way with this meta-physical, even mystical vision to recognize that pornography indeed occupies a kind of personal underground, the erotic equivalent of those Trotskyist news-papers sold at tube stations and in city centres on a Saturday morning – always on the margins, always placing itself beyond the realm of the respectable, the site of a small but significant rebellion against polite society. In this respect, argues Avedon Carol, 'pornography is subversive – it privileges individual pleasure, it ignores social convention, it allows us to step out of our roles and to play games' (1986, p. 5).

The potential subversiveness of porn is even more apparent in the case of the quiet rebellions necessarily engaged in by subordinate sexual communities such as gay men and women. For the former, 'fuck photos [and this source cites images dating back to 1893] have always had to serve not only as our stroke materials, but also, to a large extent, as our family snapshots and wedding albums, as our cultural history and political validation' (Waugh, 1996, p. 5). Porn, in this sense, has been a means of giving expression to otherwise silenced sexualities. For many women, emerging into feminist-inspired sexual freedom and experimentation, access to and use of porn is a marker of political progress.

Diversifying structures of pornographic desire

The content of pornography (pornography which is successful, that is) must reflect what I will call the *structure of the user's desire*. Pornography can only function erotically (i.e., act as a means of sexual arousal) to the extent that it achieves this mirroring. The user's desire, in turn, is structured by the pyschology of his or her individual sexuality (heterosexual or homosexual, for example), and defined by choice of sexual object (man or woman, usually) as well as a preference for particular behaviours (from 'normal' sexual intercourse to the myriad of more exotic practices documented in the *scientia sexualis*). The nature of sexual desire varies from one individual to another, and so therefore does taste in pornography, so that one person's offence and disgust may be another's erotic stimulation.

Pornography becomes a medium for the reflection and articulation of these desires when they are articulated by sexual communities with the financial and cultural resources to constitute a market, whether legal or underground, and occupy a sub-sector of the pornosphere. Thus, in the conditions of hegemonic patriarchy which have prevailed since pornography was 'invented' the form has tended to reflect the structures of male heterosexual desire, including of course those which take misogynistic forms. The sexualities of homosexuals, by contrast, and the pornographies which might reflect them, were suppressed throughout most of the last century and a half, taking the form of privately made, illicit snapshots and cine reels, or books which circulated clandestinely among small, closely guarded communities. Legal 'erotica' for gay men and lesbians was limited to the heavily coded, non-explicit images of the type found in physical culture magazines. Porn for straight women was practically non-existent until the 1980s.

Figure 3.1 lists the titles of the porn films which would be shown in a typical 'adult' cinema in 1970s Britain. Their casual references to the rape, violation and abuse of women propelled the feminist critique of porn which emerged in those years. Occupying small but no doubt lucrative niches of the contemporary pornosphere are those such as Max Hardcore and Rod Black, US producers who specialize in images of women being humiliated and abused, verbally and physically.[18] Pornography continues to play a role in the articulation of such desires and fantasies. But the sometimes ugly reality of what the pornosphere *has* been (and still is, in places) need not be taken as evidence of all that it *can* be. As Richard Dyer correctly observed in a 1985 essay 'a defence of porn as a genre is not at all the same thing as defending most of what porn currently consists of' (1992, p. 123). True in the early 1990s, it is even more so in an era when gay porn and porn for women form a substantial and growing segment of the sexual marketplace.

A stroll down San Francisco's Castro Street illustrates the point. The Castro district was the world's first fully constituted 'out' gay community, leading the way for the subsequent development of gay 'villages' in other north American, European and Australasian cities. Today the large Castro population of gay men (and a smaller number of lesbians) is supported by bars, restaurants, fitness suites, hairdressers, health food stores and, of course, sex shops, all dedicated to meeting the needs of the local community. In the sex shop window displays of magazines and videos men are dressed up as sailors, soldiers and policemen, posed, photographed and generally objectified for the sexual delight of other men. Some of the stores advertise themselves frankly as suppliers of 'porno'; others prefer the more respectable 'erotica'. All exist to supply the demands of an affluent, empowered sexual community, without a woman (not a straight woman, at least) in view.

Lesbians also have their distinctive forms of porn (or erotica, as some producers prefer to call it), today contained in legal outlets like the Canadian magazine *Lezzie Smut*, the San Francisco-based *On Our Backs*, and the proliferating network of websites targeted at lesbians (Figure 3.2). Where heterosexual women have emerged as a sexual community (as they have in Europe, the United States and elsewhere) there is a zone of the pornosphere dedicated to them too. 'Women have begun to engage with porn', notes one observer, 'with its power, rather than simply trying to say "no" to it or allowing *it* to extend over *them*' (Simpson, 1994, p. 143). The editor of the *Erotic Review* identifies 'a growing market for erotica aimed specifically at young women'[19] supplied by producers such as Candida Royalle, former porn star and now a key figure in the leading US porn-for-women company Femme Productions. Annie Sprinkle's 1982 film *Deep Inside Annie Sprinkle* is described by her as 'pornography made by women . . . something where the viewers are more directly involved, something more interactive'.[20]

The sexual revolution described in Chapter 2 has changed the content of pornography, then. For writer Mark Simpson the 'emerging homo- and hetero-

Porn Spirit of '76

Dr Feelgood Teenage Jailbait Model Hunters Girls Serve Their Apprenticeships Penelope Pulls It Off Sweet Sugar
Backseat Cabbie O Wow It's Cindy Kiss the Girls Where You Like Angelica the Young Vixen Black Emanuelle
Little Miss Innocence Yellow Bird Expose Adventures of a Taxi Driver Blondy Sex Rally Road Side Service
Diary of a Nymphomaniac Everybody's At It Erotic Dreams How to Succeed With Sex Sidewalk Cowboy
Stroke of Nine Three on a Waterbed Big Bust Out Notorious Cleopatra In Love With Sex Hot and Naked
Emanuelle Secrets of a Door to Door Salesman A Promise of Bed Dead Sexy Keyhole Report
Please Don't Eat My Mother Teenage Bride Sex Summer of 69 Sex After Six Versatile Lovers More Than a Ride
Forced to Love The Gun Runner Hard Ride Indian Raid Indian Maid The Pig Keeper's Daughter Finishing School
The Sex Thief ABC of Sex Strange Mistress Doctors of Oh Copenhagen Jekyll and Hyde - Adult Version
Sex Takers Sex Rituals of the Occult Girls in the Street Thar She Blows The Swinging Stewardesses
Sexy Swingers Gabrielle Trucker Girl The Rape Fraulein in Uniform Eyeball Joys of Jezebel Danish Modern
Lust For Money Hamburg City of Sin The Wicked Die Slow Knickers Ahoy Sex Crazy Secret Places
Street of a Thousand Pleasures Randy Widow Sappho Darling Confessions of a Male Escort I Do It My Way
Class Reunion The Erotic Housewife Come One Come All Orgy of Revenge Language of Love
Do You Believe in Swedish Sin I Million AC/DC Hotter Than Sex Wild Gypsies Very Private Party Give 'Em An Inch
Love Makers Tempt Me Take Me Copenhagen Sex Report Clamdigger's Daughter Cries of Lust Ramrodder
Bed Champion Golden Saloon of Sex Naughty Nun Excite Me All American Girl Teenage Milkmaid Sex Circus
While the Cat's Away French Kiss Bed Bunnies Linda Lovelace for President The Office Party Hot Dreams
Man Hungry Lust Girls Sex For an Adultress Fear of Love Jenny Gets on Top French Blue Black Leather Pants
Acquaintances First Time With Feeling Dropout Wives Take Me In Clockwork Nympho Sextet
I Love You, I Love You Not Fringe Benefits

Showing at the Tatler Club, Coliseum, Classic Grand and Classic Club, Glasgow

Figure 3.1 'Porn Spirit of '76'

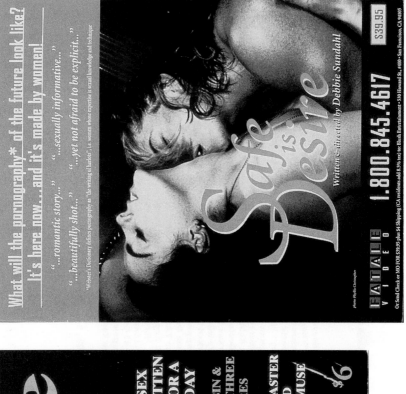

Figure 3.2 Porn for women

sexual female porn' portrays a world of 'commodified cocks, dethroned from their phallic positions, women behind the camera not just in front of it, and lesbians celebrating sex for the benefit of other lesbians rather than in some "Swedish Lesbian Lust" fantasy entertainment for straight men' (ibid., p. 148). If the majority of pornography hitherto in circulation has been male and heterosexist in orientation, not all of it has, and in the future none of it *need* be. There is, in other words, nothing essentially *male*, nor *heterosexual* about pornography. Contrary to one influential definition of it as 'male violence against women'[21] pornography is, like other modes of representation historically dominated by men (prose, poetry, narrative cinema, visual art, advertising), a form whose content and meaning are defined by and shaped in the interaction between the values and aims of its producers on the one hand, and the desires of its consumers on the other. In this respect the content of pornography, like that of mainstream Hollywood cinema or lifestyle magazines, is market driven, and where there is present in any given society a gay or a feminist community with the socio-economic status to constitute itself as a consumer group (as there has been in most western societies since the 1970s) a pornography targeted at them has emerged. As a result the expansion of the pornosphere has been accompanied by the diversification of its structures of desire, replacing the heterosexist near-monopoly of the past with a contemporary plurality of representations – linked in their form and function as pornography, but heterogenous in the sexual desires and object choices they assume in and reflect back to their users. The feminist-authored *Caught Looking* collection observes that contemporary porn is 'geared to every sexual minority population not included in the traditional nuclear family structure, as well as to those male consumers whose fantasies take them outside of that structure' (Ellis *et al.*, 1986, p. 4). A 1997 commentary observed that 'the manufacture and distribution of sexually-explicit materials, magazines and videotapes has never been so intensely competitive, catering to dozens of niche markets and continually searching for new target groups. Porn offers a textbook example of how free markets can stimulate and respond to consumer demand'.[22]

'Not your Dad's wank mag' – the new porno generation

What, then, of porn for straight men – the 'theory' behind what Robin Morgan famously called the 'practice' of rape? What is happening to old-fashioned, male, heterosexist sexual objectification in the amazing, expanding and diversifying pornosphere I have described? While still by far the dominant sector of the industry traditional 'top-shelf' porn was faced with two challenges in the 1990s.

First, in response to the uncensored wonders of the world wide web the audience was going online. In the week in 1997 when British newsagent chain W.H. Smith announced that its stores would no longer stock top-shelf magazines the commentator Mark Lawson pointed out that this was not evidence of a collapse in the market for pornography. On the contrary, he suggested, it was simply moving elsewhere. 'The real action', he speculated, 'is on the Internet'.[23]

At the same time as the liberalizing technology of the internet was threatening to make printed porn redundant a new generation of style magazines which, though not classified by the industry as pornographic, exhibited some of the characteristics of the 'soft core' top shelf titles, were taking over the men's market. In both Britain and the United States in the 1990s these magazines (and their televisual equivalents) rediscovered, if in a postmodern context, the pre-feminist pleasures of the pornographic. In Britain magazines like *Loaded*, *FHM* and *GQ* began to adopt the conventions of soft core top-shelf titles, with semi-nude models on their covers, explicit photosets inside, and correspondingly sexualized editorial content. In 1999 the newly appointed editor of *GQ* observed that 'women have become the lingua franca of the men's press, the defining language of publishing in the 90s'.[24] An industry analyst observed in 1997 that 'as top shelf pornography magazines became outdated and associated with men in dirty raincoats, these men's magazines have taken soft porn into the mainstream and made it more acceptable'.[25] These magazines, and their counterparts in the US market, were close in spirit and in substance to the *Playboy* model, remaking that publication's celebration of bachelor hedonism for a younger audience aware of feminism and the anti-porn movement,[26] but sufficiently post-feminist to be able to adopt an ironic distance from both (see Chapter 8).

In Britain, faced with the explicitness of the internet on the one hand, and the quasi-pornographic style of the new men's magazines on the other, established top-shelf titles began to reposition themselves in the sexual marketplace, shedding their 'wanker' associations and appropriating some of the trendiness of porno-chic (see next chapter). The relaunch of UK *Penthouse* in September 1997 – as 'a trendy style magazine about sex and the zeitgeist'[27] – explained the nature of this process in an editorial stressing what its publishers wished us to believe was the new respectability of porn, and its validity as a form.

> Five years ago the idea of persuading the country's best writers, photographers and designers to work for a top shelf magazine was inconceivable. Today it seems natural. . . . Sex is not the shameful or embarrassing subject it was for our parents. It drives our culture. It's on the net, the telly, cable and the catwalk. It's the advertising copyline for modern life. A new generation of Britons are growing up who do not want to repress sex. They want to discuss it, explore it and celebrate it. As we come to the end of our century there is a growing feeling – shared by men and women – that life is short and it ought to be fun. Erotica is coming out from under the mattress.[28]

In that context, the editorial continued:

> New Penthouse UK is not your dad's wank mag.

According to then-editor Tom Hilditch, with the onset of the internet 'print is redundant for masturbation, but not for discussing sex'.[29] In pursuit of this line the photographic and design style of the relaunched *Penthouse* bore a notable resemblance to photosets of the type contained in fashion magazines like the *Face*, *Dazed & Confused* and *i-D* – deliberately grainy, out-of-focus, sometimes monochrome images, not studio-bound and often featuring the waif-like, heroin-chic models popular at this time. The new *Penthouse* pin-up would not only be beautiful, but 'strong and confident', as only a post-feminist pin-up could be. Consistent with the vogue for women who were more than passive sex toys for the voyeuristic male reader (but still wanted to be looked at, if on their own terms), one feature depicted eight professional women (said to be from the worlds of public relations, television production, and graphic design, to name but three notably trendy occupations) 'shooting themselves', and explicitly challenging what the magazine confessed to be the tradition in male-oriented pornography – 'pretty girls in dodgy underwear shot by ugly blokes in over-bright studios'. Articles addressing such themes as 'the new porno generation' and 'top shelf terminology' further signalled the magazine's ambition to remake the meaning of pornography, and to convince its readers that

> Porno is a word already well on the way to Coolsville in the rest of the world – it's time to help it on its way in the UK.

At the same time, and with a view, presumably, to heading off some of the threat posed by the internet, the magazine emphasized the explicitness of its pornographic content.

> We are going to show you images of women who are really fucking: women, mid-orgasm, with a head full of endorphins.

They couldn't show you that, of course, given British censorship laws *circa* 1997, and they didn't. But the desire to project an aura of pornographic authenticity reflected an environment where the hardest of hard core material was available to anyone with a computer and internet access. And, like the non-pornographic print media faced with the challenge of the internet, top-shelf magazines like *Penthouse* and *Mayfair* could not restrict their response to a design make-over, but had to go on-line themselves, becoming part of the internet revolution before it left them behind.

The perils of the pornosphere: the high-culture critique

The evolution of the pornosphere I have described – technology and demand-led as it has been – hasn't proceeded without resistance. On the contrary, it has been accompanied at every stage by renewed bouts of public debate around what is and is not legal, obscene, dangerous, or immoral in the field of sexual representation. In a pattern consistent with societal responses to all previous leaps in the tech-nological means of delivering pornography to users, the 1990s saw a succession of moral panics in the United States, Britain and elsewhere around the threat of 'cyberporn' and its potential impact on Net surfers.[30] Reflecting on the porn-technology relationship in 1995 *Time* magazine observed that 'the history of pornography and efforts to suppress it are inextricably bound up with the rise of new media'.[31]

Three broad perspectives underpinned the critical response to 'cyberporn' (and the many panics which preceded it) and I will address each of them here. The first can be characterized as the elite-paternalistic or high culture school of criticism, which views the expansion of pornography as one symptom of a broader malaise produced by consumer capitalism. For adherents to this view porn is 'dumbed down' sexual culture, commercialized and degraded by profit-led submission to the base instincts of mankind.

The counter-argument to this view starts from the observation that, like sex itself, the desire of human beings to produce, display and disseminate explicit images of sexual behaviour appears to be, as far as the archaeological records can tell, universal. Sexually explicit cave paintings have been discovered amid the remains of prehistoric cultures all over the world, while the erotic artefacts unearthed in Pompeii leave little to the contemporary sexual imagination. Not only did the ancient Greeks and Romans have rather exotic sex lives, by the evidence of their own written accounts; they also liked to draw and paint their sexual practices on their living room walls, on their porcelain, in their places of religious worship. In Britain, the great figure carved into chalk on the North Dorset Downs of England is endowed with an unmistakeably erect penis, so in your face that the moral guardians of the Victorian era felt compelled to airbrush it out of their souvenir postcards and likenesses of the figure. These representations were not viewed by their makers as 'pornography', with all of that word's pejorative and shame-inducing connotations, but valued in societies where displays of sexuality and eroticism were regarded as normal elements of public life and culture (as of course were the exhibitions of ritual slaughter and sadistic, gruesome execution for the purpose of mass instruction and entertainment depicted in Ridley Scott's *Gladiator* – a film which reminds us that just because the ancient civilizations did something doesn't mean it was civilized).

The social meanings of explicit sexual imagery change over time and across cultures, then, and their precise functions are in many cases obscure to us, but it is believed that they have been employed at various times as accompaniments to religious ritual, as interior decoration, and as educational tools on sexual technique. Medieval religious architecture incorporated them into cathedrals and churches as a means of social control, often depicting alarming scenarios of sexual crime.[32] They were also used as erotica, and as vehicles for political satire. This latter function emerged in early modern Europe, in the context of the bourgeois struggle against decadent aristocracy. Lynn Hunt's ground-breaking collection of historical essays documents the 'philosophical subversiveness' of the work of Sade and others in the eighteenth century (1993). In these revolutionary times sexually explicit writings and their accompanying illustrations became a medium for the articulation of iconoclastic anti-feudal radicalism, complementing the more conventionally political writings of Thomas Paine and other reformers.

In the beginning, like all books, these sexually *and* politically transgressive texts were the property and currency of a wealthy male elite – progressive in their anti-feudalism and zeal for the meritocratic logic of capital, certainly, but a social universe away from the toiling masses, over whom they had just as much desire to rule as had the old aristocracy, and whose potential for social revolution they viewed with just as much suspicion and fear. With the invention of photography, and the expansion both of print media and of reading which characterized the Victorian era the lower classes (especially the urban proletariat) had access for the first time to sexually explicit images. Although the commercialized pornography of the nineteenth century had few of the subversive political overtones of eighteenth-century texts, becoming 'mass-produced texts or images devoted to the explicit description of sexual organs or activities with the sole aim of producing sexual arousal in the reader or viewer' (Hunt, 1993, p. 305),[33] elite unease about their disruptive social implications was widespread.[34] The category of 'pornography' emerged as a means of policing access to these texts.[35]

Growing state censorship of pornography accompanied the spread of a view of all lower class, lesser-educated individuals as akin to children, unable to regulate and control their own morality and behaviour, and thus in need of guidance from their socio-economically superior, better-educated, almost always male overlords. Women and children were seen as especially at risk from pornography – a view of the innate victimhood of these groups which continues to underpin most pro-censorship opinion to this day, wherever on the ideological spectrum it sits. The Obscene Publications Act of 1857 embodied this victimology, proscribing any texts which might 'deprave and corrupt' those perceived to be vulnerable and in need of protection by the moral watchdogs of the time. Depravity and corruption in this context meant, in effect, anything which might encourage deviation from the Judaeo-Christian norm of reproductive sex within marriage – sex before marriage, obviously, but non-reproductive practices like masturbation, fellatio and 'buggery' too. The 1960 prosecution of D.H. Lawrence's *Lady's Chatterley's Lover* under the OPA illustrated its paternalistic, patriarchal nature when the jury was asked if:

> you would approve of your young sons, young daughters – because girls can read as well as boys – reading this book? Is it a book you would wish your wife or servants to read?

That the category of pornography, and the legal means adopted to police it, then and now, were less the product of sincerely held moral beliefs than the assertion of patriarchal social control over an emerging mass sexuality (and a threatening female sexuality in particular) seems obvious in retrospect, not least because Victorian era moral censorship coexisted so easily with routine sexual promiscuity, adultery within marriage, and abuse of women and children by the male elites of the time. In the capitalist societies of the late nineteenth century, state regulation of sexual representation worked alongside religious ideas about the sanctity of marriage to reinforce a particular model of family life. Censorship continued to play this social role in the subsequent century, if with diminishing effectiveness.

This, it should be noted, was a function of patriarchal rather than merely bourgeois values. In the Soviet Union and other non-capitalist societies inspired by its example sexual censorship was equally severe, if justified not by reference to God's will and Christian morality but a secular, Marxist-Leninist ethic of work and sacrifice within which the public celebration of sexuality was seen not as sinful but as a bourgeois deviation. The Bolsheviks, of course (as well as the Maoists, the Castroites, the Kim Il Sung-ists and the rest), turned out to be just as paternalistic and hypocritical in their attitudes to sexuality as their bourgeois enemies, and used sexual censorship for precisely the same reasons – as a means of exerting control over a potentially unruly mass, for whom sexuality was one of the few pleasures in life which might distract them from the pursuit of socialist emulation and self-sacrifice to the party. Paul Goldschmidt observes that under Stalin and his successors 'pornography became associated with an ideology of free love that the state found more and more antithetical to its own desire for public control' (1999, p. 331).[36] In Gorbachev's Soviet Union, conversely, as in post-Franco Spain and other transitional countries (i.e., in the process of transition from authoritarian regimes of left or right to democracies) the decline of political censorship led to a long-overdue liberalization of sexual culture.

If the introduction of obscenity legislation throughout the industrialized world was a patriarchal imposition on the temptations perceived to be acting on lower class men and women it was also, as the Chatterley trial revealed, one element of a broader elite response to the growth of mass culture which accompanied the industrial revolution and its aftermath (made inevitable by the introduction of universal education and the spread of mass media). Just as late-nineteenth-century intellectuals developed a critique of popular journalism and literature which remains influential to this day (in the form of the 'dumbing down' critique)[37] so pornography became the category of illegitimate, because *popular* sexual representation. If painterly or carved nudes could be defended as legitimate cultural expression and hung on the walls of museums patronized by rich bourgeois connoiseurs, pornography circulating on cheap newsprint or on postcards was erotic trash – the sexual culture of the masses, unrefined and dirty.

Ever since, images which a particular critic or commentator finds offensive or distasteful are relegated to the realm of the pornographic in an attempt to have the text in question tainted with the latter's pariah status. The technique can be seen at work in Bryan Appleyard's denunciation of a 1997 novel about child abuse, *The End of Alice*, by A.M. Holmes. In an article headed 'Pornography all dolled up as literature' Appleyard frankly revealed his distaste for 'low' culture with the remark that 'Alice is a symptom of the infection of high art by the flattening demands of mass culture. . . . It is barren titillation'.[38] As opposed, presumably, to the high literary value of Nabokov's *Lolita*, in which paedophilia achieves the status of literary art[39] and is celebrated as the legitimate fantasy of a great genius. Susie 'sexpert'

Bright puts it with admirable simplicity when she writes that 'the critical issue here isn't sex, the issue is elitism. Some people think they are morally and intellectually qualified to view everything and then decide what's appropriate for the peasants' (Bright, 1997, p. 14).[40]

A century and a half after the Victorians introduced the term pornography remained the 'pariah of representational practices' (Ellis, 1992) for a certain kind of culture critic who could admit to having no interest in the form beyond the academic or the critical. Book reviews or articles on the subject were typically prefaced with a remark such as:

> I have never bought pornography, used pornography, even seen much pornography and never really wanted to.[41]

This rarely stopped the said commentator from presuming the intellectual authority to write about it, of course, nor from assuming the role of protector of those to whom porn might represent a danger. In the *Sunday Times* Peter Hitchens suggested that the proliferation (and popularity, he conceded) of pornography (or what he defined as pornography) put into question the wisdom of extending democratic rights to the masses, who were clearly incapable of using it properly. 'The torrent of coarseness and pornography', as he described it, 'which now overwhelms television, the cinema and stage suggests to me that we may not have the proper moral equipment needed to handle liberty'.[42]

Of God and porn

This brings us to a second broad source of opposition to pornography – that of religiously inspired moral lobbies, whose arguments are based principally on the belief that porn is blasphemous. The Victorians who invented pornography correctly understood, perhaps from the tinglings they experienced in their own groins as they beavered away in their secret museums, that the culture of the sexually explicit is a seductive, emotionally disruptive one; that it can encourage the private violation – and thus challenge the hegemonic status – of a society's public rules of morality; that it is implicated in the act of masturbation and other 'lewd and licentious' acts, because non-reproductive behaviours, and that for this reason if for no other it is profoundly subversive of moral values which have lain at the foundations of judeao-christian societies for centuries.

And in this, to be fair, they have a point. Pornography subverts the demand for sex and sexuality to be subordinated to the biological functions of reproduction, and to be pursued exclusively within the sacred framework of divinely consecrated marriage. That, indeed, is its appeal, and one can easily understand why its wanton, uninhibited character disturbs religious believers. The calls for the banning and outlawing of porn which routinely come from these groups, however, are usually justified with reference to the somewhat different claim that exposure to its images will undermine family life and values by leading to imitative behaviour of a morally disruptive kind. The man (or woman) who views pornography will 'do' pornography, so to speak.

The evidence for this latter view is circumstantial. The post-World War II spread of pornography parallels the rise in divorce and other trends associated with the 'permissive society', but can not be shown to have caused them. Much more likely causes of these phenomena were the mass movement of women into wage labour and the invention of the contraceptive pill. Both, as the previous chapter pointed out, created new opportunities for women in capitalism and removed many of the constraints which kept women (and men, for that matter) locked into unhappy marriages. In that context, the focus on the corrupting power of pornography (and of sexual permissiveness in general) has been a convenient means for religious leaders to explain away the fact that millions of people have chosen to live in ways deemed sinful by their churches.

Anti-pornography feminism

In pursuing this line the religious and moral conservative lobbies made strategic alliance with those sections of the feminist movement which, for reasons set out in Chapter 2, identified porn as the mediated essence of patriarchy. Anti-pornography feminists have accused both producers and consumers of porn of contributing to the reinforcement and reproduction of patriarchy, through its subjection of women to the oppressive male gaze. In a recent statement of the position columnist Charlotte Raven supports 'the feminist contention that uncontrolled exposure to imagery which treats people as commodities will result in desensitisation'[43] to the abuse of real women.

My earlier book on *Mediated Sex* (McNair, 1996) reviews in detail the evidence for and against the thesis that porn has harmful effects.[44] Here I will quote US Supreme Court Justice Brennan's conclusion (which echoes the findings of several expensive and high-powered commissions into the subject fundeded by both the British and American governments) that there is 'little empirical basis for the assertion that exposure to obscene materials may lead to deviant sexual behaviour or crimes of sexual violence'.[45] Despite that measured assessment – and it is one which has not required revision even after decades of research on the subject – anti-porn feminism continues to present shocking 'facts' in defence of assertions of direct causality. Catherine MacKinnon for example, in an essay I have selected at random but which is not unrepresentative of her style, claims that:

> Over a third of all women are victims of child sexual abuse; about the same proportion are victims of domestic battery; just under half are victims of rape or attempted rape.
>
> (1992, p. 474)

The ease with which such bleak (and widely contested) statistics are bandied about should lead us to be deeply suspicious of the claim which often follows – that pornography is responsible for, is a causal agent of, sexual violence and child sexual abuse. Stevi Jackson and Sue Scott put it well when they suggest that:

> A man does not rape as a direct reaction to a pornographic stimulus; rather pornography contributes to the cultural construction of a particular form of masculinity and sexual desire which make rape possible and which script the possibilities for its enactment.
>
> (1996, p. 23)

'Contributes to', as biblical texts, literary novels and many other cultural forms have contributed throughout the ages to the construction of misogynistic, sociopathic masculinities. In the United Kingdom, Glasgow's Bible John and Bradford's Yorkshire Ripper both also cited religious texts as justifications for their murders of women, but there are many disturbing associations between pornography and sexual psychopathy. The serial killer and child abuser Fred West used pornography. He also used the cheap video technology which has been widely available on the mass market since the 1980s to record his and his wife's crimes. But there is no evidence that West's misanthropy, dating back to his early adulthood in 1960s Glasgow, was *caused* by pornography or that, had pornography not existed, he and his wife would not have murdered. Indeed, the sexual abuse of young women and children (including members of their own family) which made him and his wife infamous is, if rarely with such horrific excess, regrettably commonplace in all societies across the globe, and long pre-dates the emergence of modern, mediated forms of sexual representation.

Rape, too – another oft-cited effect of pornography – is a depressingly universal crime, probably practised by all humanity in all ages, and certainly long before such a thing as pornography existed. Would that such social diseases were so easily diagnosed, because then they might begin to be cured. Valerie Steele, in her study of fetish fashion, makes a serious point in a witty way. 'Many people believe that pornography causes perversion and sexual violence. But this is like saying that country-and-western music causes adultery and alcoholism' (1996, p. 187). The consumption of country-and-western music may be *associated* with adultery and alcoholism, but who seriously suggests that it causes, rather than reflects and comments on the destructive behaviours which form the lyrical core of the music?

Perhaps the most compelling argument against the assertion that pornography causes male violence against women, or indeed sexist attitudes more broadly, is the stark fact that in so far as direct correlations between pornography and misogyny or sexual violence can be drawn they are more likely to be relations of *inverse* proportionality. To put it simply – the more pornography which exists in a given society, and the more open and diverse is its sexual culture in general, the more established – hegemonic, if you will – feminism and all that it stands for in the field of women's rights are likely to be. Compare the position of women in the sex-liberal Netherlands and Scandinavian countries, for example, with those in strictly censored Muslim countries. At the risk of stating the obvious, it seems relevant to note that the Taliban did not allow pornography,[46] and women in Afghanistan were prisoners in their own homes; that in parts of the Indian sub-continent pornography is prohibited, and women are burned alive because their fathers can't meet dowry payments, or because they dare to challenge arranged marriages. The feudal rulers of Saudi Arabia do not permit pornography, and compel their women to wear the *chador* at all times in public. These are extreme cases, it may be argued, but nonetheless illustrative of what appears to be a general rule – women through-out the world (homosexuals too) are subject to oppression in direct proportion to the severity of the sexual censorship prevailing in their society. Whether in Ireland or India, Cuba or Zimbabwe, Afghanistan or Saudi Arabia, wherever sexual representations are rigorously policed by patriarchal, heterosexist states, women and homosexuals are found to be worse, not better off than their peers in more liberal societies. When one adopts a historical, cross-cultural perspective on the question it becomes clear that there is no correlation between the availability of pornography in a society – and the level of explicitness displayed in sexual representation generally – and the sexual abuse or oppression inflicted on women or children by men. On the contrary, those societies in which pornography is most intensely policed are also those where women remain in the most extreme states of subordination (often little advanced from that of medieval feudalism) to men. Conversely, societies which are liberal with regards to pornography are also those where feminism and women's equality are taken the most seriously.

A paradox? Not if one accepts that cultural liberalism, indeed libertarianism, while good for pornography, is also good for the ethical values and sexual politics (such as feminism and gay rights) which dilute pornography's patriarchal, sexist power and open it up to alternative 'structures of desire'. If our contemporary sexual culture allows misogynistic pornographers like Max Hardcore and Rod Black to run successful businesses out of the San Fernando valley, it also tends to marginalize them in the context of the pornosphere as a whole (just as sweatshops in the textile industry are viewed as bad practice by manufacturers with sound ethical principles). Janice Winship writes that 'feminism *has* revealed pornography's abuse of women to women. . . . And feminism has given women a knowledge and a strength to act in the world which also allows them to laugh at and enjoy those images in a way many of us [feminists of the generation schooled in the politics of *Spare Rib*] cannot' (1987, p. 141). The success of feminist politics, in short – *including* its anti-pornography wing – has expanded not just the range of pornographic representation, but also the range of meanings to be drawn even from the images contained in straight male porn. In the process porn emerges as a cultural form like any other, its meanings (and its moral worth) defined both by what goes into it (the producers' intentions) and what audiences take out of it.

The crisis of censorship

These debates are, in any case, increasingly academic (in the popular sense of that term). In an article penned in 2000 to complain about the British government's censorial attitude to sexual representation the author Fay Weldon, in her capacity as a member of the UK Video Appeals Committee,[47] observed that 'the threshold of acceptance rises over the decades: a bared ankle shocked in Queen Victoria's day, as did a bared bosom in the *Sun* two decades ago. No longer. The 'Talking Dicks' of *Eurotrash*[48] would have been unthinkable on television ten years ago. To some, 'penetration' begins to seem more decent than a coy cutaway shot'.[49] That change in attitudes has not proceeded without opposition, as we have seen, but it has accelerated as a consequence of the internet. To a much greater extent than in previous technological leaps, which expanded the pornosphere within the confines of the nation state, the internet has globalized the porn industry, and eroded the capacity of individual nation states to police the consumption of sexually explicit material by their citizens (satellite broadcasting also had this effect, but on a much restricted scale[50]).

As access to the internet increases the most liberal of global standards are extended to the least liberal of countries. The peculiarities of British censorship (no erect penises) or Japanese (no pubic hair) make less and less sense in an environment where thousands of examples of the banned image are just a mouse click away. Short of outlawing computers (which the desperate rulers of some countries attempt to do, of course) the internet permits anyone, anywhere in the world with a computer and access to a net browser, to find and view anything he or she wishes. Existing obscenity laws which might make this activity illegal buckle under the strain of policing millions of net surfers, and cannot long survive as credible legal instruments. The internet delivers the final death blow to the traditional concept of community standards on which obscenity legislation is based. It removes the geographical basis of community, making it global and virtual. With the disappearance of 'community standards' defined geographically the legislation of obscenity becomes pointless. What then should replace it?

An inability to provide easy answers to this question has led to governments on both sides of the Atlantic Ocean struggling with the anarchic, anti-authoritarian qualities of the internet. Early in 1996, for example, the United States Congress passed the Communications Decency Act in an attempt to control cyberporn. In June that year, however, a Philadelphia court ruled the CDA unconstitutional on the grounds that it violated the First Amendment. The ruling judged that the CDA's criminalization of the 'patently offensive' and 'indecent' use of the net opened the door to arbitrary censorship, and would be ineffective as an anti-porn measure in any case, since much of the offending material originated outside US territory. More importantly, controls of the type proposed by the CDA were undemocratic. According to the judge on the case, 'as the most *participatory* form of mass speech yet developed, the internet deserves the highest protection from government intrusion' (my emphasis).[51]

More pragmatically, 'the digital mediascape is just too mind-bogglingly big to police effectively'.[52] Not only is it big; as is well known, it was designed to Cold War-era military specifications,[53] with the capacity to resist and evade all attempts at damage (including censorship), from whatever direction it might come (including national governments). Self-censoring software packages are available to parents concerned about their children's unsupervised use of the Net,[54] but for consenting adults nothing short of shooting down the satellites which distribute the traffic can destroy the system, or reverse the impact which it has had on the communicative environment. Commenting on the formation of the Internet Watch Foundation (a UK industry watchdog) in 1998 the chairman of the British Board of Film Classification Andreas Whittam Smith advised that 'in due course the means will exist for ordinary people to contrive that material they deem to be objectionable will be rejected. Each individual, each family will decide what to accept, and what to reject. Computer technology is not frightening but enabling. Properly used, it will allow us to become our own policemen'.[55]

The gradual acceptance of this more relaxed view impacted in turn on the regulation of non-pornographic media such as cinema and television, notwith-standing the efforts of New Labour's home secretary, Jack Straw, to hold the line in the United Kingdom.[56] The then-director of the British Board of Film Classification conceded in 1999, just prior to his retirement, that he was 'probably the last of the regulators'.[57] By 2000 BBFC chairman Andreas Whittam Smith had effectively 'overturned, by design or default, the more wilful sacred cows associated with the board during James Ferman's time as director – allowing hardcore pornography uncut at R18'.[58] Liberalization was a response both to the increasing impracticality of attempting to censor in the digital media environment, and to BBFC research showing that 'a majority of adults want information rather than censorship and see themselves as consumers entitled to choice'.[59] One observer remarked in 1999 that 'there's an obvious hunger for full-on sex on the British screen and, even more importantly, an evolution in the way that it is being presented, that is increasingly confounding the [regulators'] rigid rules'.[60] By the year 2000 films as explicit as Oshima's *Ai No Corrida* and Catherine Breillat's *Romance* were being shown more or less uncut on the subscription television channel FilmFour.

When images which some viewed as pornographic began to appear on mainstream television channels in the late 1990s (this material, though 'soft core' in its content, was nonetheless more explicit than anything ever broadcast on UK terrestrial television before) some critics objected to what they saw as the corruption of hitherto protected public space. When Channel 5 television began to broadcast series such as *Erotic Diaries*, and *Compromising Positions* it attracted criticism from the industry regulator, the Broadcasting Standards Commission, on the grounds that:

> The inclusion, for its own sake, of erotic material in a free to air television service is a step change in the use of sex on British television and begins to erode the difference between what is available on open access channels and that which is available through pay services.[61]

The columnist Melanie Phillips agreed that 'distinctions must be maintained: between open access channels and pay services; between sex within a dramatic context [acceptable] and sex for its own sake [not acceptable]'.[62] Sex 'for its own sake' was dangerous, in other words, to a mass public unable to make responsible viewing choices for itself. In fact, the distinctions so cherished by Phillips *have* been maintained within free-to-air British broadcasting – not by the impositions of paternalistic moral guardians so much as the use of careful scheduling and sign-posting of sexually explicit material. This approach appears to satisfy the majority of television viewers who, despite the anxieties of the BSC, Phillips and others of like mind, express no desire to return to the days of 'no sex please, we're British'. The broadcasting white paper of December 2000 acknowledged changing attitudes when it proposed a significant deregulation of British television. This was welcomed by one industry figure with the comment: 'When pornography on the internet is only a couple of clicks away, asking the ITC[63] to police a 9 p.m. watershed begins to look pointless'.[64]

And after all that, a more liberal approach to the censorship of more traditional media could not long be delayed. In 2000 long-standing UK prohibitions on photographic images of the male erection, sexual penetration, and ejaculation finally dissolved under the pressure of regulatory confusion and changing social attitudes.[65] Titles like *Playbirds Continental* and the deceptively-named *Whitehouse* (a cheeky homage to the leading anti-pornography campaigner, Mary Whitehouse) were able for the first time to honestly advertise themselves as 'hard core' magazines containing uncensored images of erections and vaginal penetration. In print, as elsewhere in the pornosphere, the end of a century and a half-long tradition of censorship had arrived.

A poll conducted by a Scottish newspaper in June 2000 found that the largest proportion of those questioned (44 per cent) – in what, for the benefit of non-Scottish readers, can reasonably be described as a relatively puritanical country – approved of pornography, compared to 31 per cent who disapproved. The balance in favour was even higher among the 25–34-year-old age group (50 per cent in favour), and among men (65 per cent of men surveyed approved of porn, as compared to only 23 per cent of women).[66] The lower approval ratings displayed for pornography by women may be presumed to reflect the historical dominance of the form by straight men, and the consequent near ubiquity of the objectifying 'male gaze'. Even among women, however, the stigma traditionally associated with the pornographic was giving way to an acceptance of its place in the culture. At the beginning of 2001 the British sex shop chain Ann Summers had forty-four high street stores throughout the United Kingdom, patronized by customers of whom 70 per cent were women. 7,000 female party hosts took Ann Summers' products into homes across the United Kingdom.

Even if censorship *were* a viable approach to the policing of porn in the age of digitalization and the internet, then, by 2001 it was not what people appeared to want from their media regulators. As this book went to press existing legislation already outlawed, in Britain and in most other countries, those kinds of porno-graphy in which real criminal acts are depicted (in particular, acts of child abuse and violence). Regulatory regimes did already, and looked likely to continue to, bracket off the pornographic from the non-pornographic in ways which protect those who would be offended from accidental and unwanted exposure. Beyond that, there was little public demand for stricter control of explicit sexual representation. The possession and use of pornography had lost not only their long-standing criminal status, but were well on the way to losing their stigma. Pornography had become 'chic'.

4

PORNO-CHIC, OR THE PORNOGRAPHICATION OF THE MAINSTREAM

In a 1996 article titled 'the sexual sickness at the heart of our society' the journalist Jeanette Kupfermann noted 'the degree to which pornography has infiltrated mainstream culture. There is', she continued, 'scarcely an image, entertainment, fashion or advertisement untouched by it'.[1] Elsewhere I have called this 'infiltration' the *pornographication of the mainstream* (McNair, 1996), and if the trend was clearly evident by the mid-1990s it has continued and intensified in the intervening period, as 'porno-chic' has spread across the range of popular and avant-garde cultural forms. A 1999 article in the *New York Times* noted 'the continuing push towards more explicit sexuality in advertisements, movies and on network television', and in particular 'the appropriation of the conventions of pornography – its stock heroes, its story lines, its low-budget lighting and motel room sets – by the mainstream entertainment industry, the fashion and fine arts worlds'.[2]

Porno-chic is not porn, then, but the *representation* of porn in non-pornographic art and culture; the pastiche and parody of, the homage to and investigation of porn; the postmodern transformation of porn into mainstream cultural artefact for a variety of purposes including, as we shall see, advertising, art, comedy and education. But as the title of the article quoted above suggests, porno-chic has provoked nearly as much criticism as the expansion of the pornosphere itself. For Bryan Appleyard porno-chic, and what he calls 'consumer sex' in general, 'is not about subversion, it is about reducing the act to one more aspect of the acquisitive society'.[3] Jonathan Freedland, writing for the *Guardian* in early 2000, complained strongly about what he saw as the deleterious effects of the 'mainstreaming of pornography'. Under this heading, and with the category confusion typical of the way the debate is often conducted in the press, he included everything from risqué advertising to comedians who say 'fuck'. In a line of argument directly descended from D.H Lawrence's 1936 anti-porn polemic[4] Freedland asserted that 'the greatest crime of the new pornographers is theft. They are stealing what should be a private, even spiritual part of the human experience and turning it into a commodity'.[5]

Perhaps. I want to argue in this chapter, however, that the rise of porno-chic

61

reflects a legitimate *public* (as opposed to merely commercial) interest in the pornographic and its transgressive, taboo-breaking qualities.

Porno-chic – a definition

Let's begin by recalling that, as a label, porno-chic is not new, first being used in the early 1970s to describe the remarkable box office success of *Deep Throat, Behind the Green Door*, and other feature-length, hard-core pornographic movies released around that time in the United States. Those were the days when Hugh Hefner's *Playboy* magazine sold nearly 7 million copies each month, and it was considered 'chic' to be seen queueing for entry to a cinema showing *Deep Throat* or *The Devil in Miss Jones*. For a brief time between the flowering of the sexual revolution and the emergence of the anti-pornography lobbies later in the 1970s the consumption of pornography was not viewed as the shameful obsession of emotionally stunted perverts, nor the sadistic pastime of patriarchal predators, but the valid entertainment choice of a mature, sexually liberated, 'swinging' society. In Britain, where hard-core material was illegal, a soft-core version of 'porno-chic' accompanied the mainstream cinema release of *Emmanuelle* (Jaeckin, 1974)[6] and the popular British sex comedies of the 1970s such as *Confessions of a Window Cleaner* (Guest, 1974). These films borrowed, if in heavily sanitized form, the narrative structures and tropes of the porno stag reel.[7]

These films *were* pornography, as defined by the censorial taste regimes within which they circulated, which at a particular moment had been given space in mainstream culture. The attempt to make them respectable was doomed to failure on both sides of the Atlantic, however, for two reasons. First, as suggested in the last chapter, pornography has to be *outside* and *beyond* the mainstream (if not actually outlawed) to perform its function and retain its value as a commodity. It must present a visible violation of moral values and sexual taboos, or it loses its transgressive erotic power. The attempt to make actual pornography into respectable cultural fare was founded on the false premise that what is taboo could at the same time have a presence in mainstream media channels.

The notion that porn could be fashionable was subject to a more direct political challenge by the anti-pornography arguments of the women's movement, the increased influence of which in the 1970s and 1980s was measured in the establishment of a broad public consensus around the idea of porn as a social evil. Labelled as patriarchal culture *par excellence*, outwith the publish-and-be-damned circles of Larry Flynt, Bob Guccione, Al Goldstein and the other porn kings it became distinctly uncool to concede an interest in pornography. Observing this transformation in porn's status moral conservatives added their voices to the early feminist anti-porn campaigns, uniting progressives and reactionaries around the idea that pornography was nothing to laugh about.

Consequently, when popular culture addressed the subject in the late 1970s, and for a long time after, pornography and the industry which produces it were typically cast not just as misogynistic and exploitative (reflecting the feminist perspective), but as dangerous, demonic influences on sexual morals and standards of behaviour (the moral conservative viewpoint). This 'porno-fear' is reflected in Paul Schrader's 1979 movie *Hardcore*, in which the search for a missing child leads a good Christian man, played by George C. Scott, into a dark pornographic underworld of exploitation and violence. Porno-fear is also present in the LA-based novels of James Ellroy who, when not engaged in long, gory descriptions of sexual violence and mutilation, overlaid with an unsettling authorial ambivalence towards black and homosexual characters, frequently incorporates pornography and pornographers into his plots, usually as the villains of the piece. Ellroy, like Schrader, constructs the pornographer as malevolent pied piper, leading the innocent towards decay and corruption. In Britain the leading literary novelist of the 1980s, Martin Amis, featured pornography in several of his key books, including *Dead Babies, Money* and *London Fields*. In these, as one critic put it, 'pornography became not an index of liberation but of an underlying cultural malaise'.[8] In fact, porn had not been an index of liberation in mainstream culture since the heady days of *Deep Throat*, and Amis's treatment of the subject – including his use of it as a metaphor for the exploitation and greed of the Thatcher years in Britain – was typical of even the most cutting-edge writers in the 1980s.[9]

Dark, violent representations of the pornographic remained dominant in popular culture until the late 1980s, when the transformation in porn's status began to 'infiltrate' the mainstream. This took the form of growing public interest in the nature of all aspects of the pornography industry, accompanied by a flirtation by cultural producers of all kinds with the iconography and conventions of porno-graphy as a genre. Unlike the first wave of porno-chic in the 1970s, the resulting texts were not porn as such, but *meta-pornographies* – works of all kinds, in every medium and genre, avant-garde and mainstream, fictional, scientific and journal-istic, which talked about, referred to, or assumed on the part of their audiences a quite sophisticated familiarity with and understanding of pornography, not to mention a popular fascination for the subject which could legitimately be satisfied within the parameters of mainstream cultural production. Porno-chic replaced the traditional demonization of porn with, if not always approval or celebration, a spirit of excited inquiry into its nature, appeal and meanings.

The academic community pioneered the trend (of which this book might itself be considered an example). Until the late 1980s, with very few exceptions,[10] only female academics could talk or write credibly about pornography, and then only in terms consistent with the hegemonic anti-pornography feminism of the time. Men who strayed into the territory were usually denounced as sexists, or as agents of patriarchal backlash. Some of them *were* those things, but not all. Bill Thompson (1994) and Hebditch and Anning (1988) are among those authors whose carefully researched book-length studies were subject to instant dismissal by feminists and feminist-inspired critics for no obvious reason other than that they diverged from the then-prevailing orthodoxy. This began to change when Linda Williams (1990), Camille Paglia (1990) and other leading female academics published weighty mono-graphs in which pornography and sexuality were treated as worthy topics of the kind of critical scholarly analysis long extended to other forms of culture. Gibson and Gibson's *Dirty Looks* (1993) exemplified the trend, contributing to an intellectual climate in which men too, if they showed appropriate sensitivity and care to what remained an emotive topic, could discuss pornography in print and not be denounced as vicious misogynists. Today the academic catalogues of Routledge, Arnold, Cassell and other major publishers prominently feature titles about pornography and sexuality. As one observer put it in 1997, with evident surprise, 'sexual activities that were once shunned as perversions are being debated in the media by academics'.[11]

Beyond the academy, in the spheres of art, journalism, entertainment and promotional media, porno-chic signalled the *postmodernization of the pornosphere* – the cultural transformation of pornographic, often disturbing sexual transgression into knowing, ironic, sexually charged play. This process occurred, moreover, in a variety of popular, commercialized cultural modes, similar to but distinct from what Leon Hunt calls the 'permissive populism' of the 1970s, when there was 'a popular appropriation of elitist 'liberationist' sexual discourses, the trickle down of permissiveness into commodity culture' (1998, p. 12). 1990s porno-chic emerged in a radically altered political context informed by feminist and gay liberation ideas.

Why this happened, at that particular time, must of course be a matter of speculation. Moral conservatives like Peter Hitchens blamed porno-chic on the nebulous effects of 1960s 'permissiveness'. Neo-Marxist successors to the Frankfurt school saw in porno-chic the pernicious influence of consumer capitalism and the degenerative effects of commercialization on all culture, not least the sexual. To these hypothetical causes can be added the sexual epidemic of the 1980s (HIV/AIDS), and the tendency which this produced towards more frank and direct sexual discussion in the public sphere. This development collided at the end of that decade with the accumulated impact of what had by then been twenty years of second-wave feminism and gay rights activism. These latter were not campaigns for pornography as such (indeed, they often opposed it) but they created publics – particularly among those generations reaching adulthood in the 1980s and 1990s – who were acclimatised to 'sex talk' and thus more likely to be receptive to porno-chic when it came. For these groups pornography was becoming the appropriate subject not just of serious debate and analysis by journalists and academics, but of pastiche, parody and aesthetic appropriation. By the early 1990s the conditions had been created for what Bryan Appleyard called 'a new revolution of sexual frankness . . . built around celebrity erotica and a clear insistence that sex was perhaps the biggest single consumer good'.[12]

The first signs of 'revolution' became apparent in the late 1980s (although it is misleading to suggest that one can identify a clear beginning to, or a single cause of something as abstract as a cultural trend. The German photographer Helmut Newton, for example, was engaging in what some considered 'porno-chic' as far back as the late 1960s[13]). An early example of artistic porno-chic, incorporating what we might recognize as a kind of 'celebrity erotica', was the American artist Jeff Koons's *Made in Heaven* series of photographs and sculptures. These depicted him and his then-wife Ilona Staller, better known as the Italian porn star Cicciolina, in the act of having sex. Although a subsequent messy divorce and child custody battle means that Koons today is rather defensive about these works, to the point of refusing permission to reproduce them in a book such as this, and has been anxious to distinguish them from pornography proper – in the *Jeff Koons Handbook* he wrote that 'pornography is alienation. My work has absolutely no vocabulary in isolation. It's about using sexuality as a tool of communication' (1994, p. 36) – they utilized much of the standard pornographic vocabulary (the money shot, for example, features in many of the images) and bore explicit titles like *Blow Job, Jeff Eating Llona* and *Dirty – Ejaculation. Made in Heaven* takes the pornographic figure of La Cicciolina, 'marries' it (in the literal sense) to the figure of the artist, and produces images which *look like* pornography (in the sense that they are sexually explicit, and are intended to arouse), but are culturally validated as art.

Though most of them were too explicit to be shown in mainstream cultural outlets (newspapers and television, for example), the images anticipated 1990s porno-chic in transforming the dirty, unrefined sexuality of porn into a much more sophisticated kind of text, considerably easier on the eye. The 'dirtiness' of their titles contrasted, as it was meant to, with the aesthetic gloss and technical proficiency of the images. The British censor, consequently, faced a dilemma in dealing with the work. While they were, by virtue of Koons's pre-existing reputation, art, and thus in theory not so vulnerable to the censor's attentions, the reproductions of *Made in Heaven* contained in the British edition of Taschen's *Jeff Koons* (1992) were published with Saudi-style black bars strategically placed over Koons's and Cicciolina's genitalia. In *Exaltation* Koons's penis is obscured, although his post-ejaculatory sperm can clearly be seen trickling down the side of Cicciolina's face (the censor apparently assuming that the viewer would not recognize this curious white stuff and thereby not be depraved and corrupted by the sight of it).

As the cultural trend which would be labelled porno-chic developed in the 1990s Koons's explicit images of himself and his wife were disseminated widely, and were frequently used to illustrate press and periodical articles about what it was. *Made in Heaven* pioneered what would become the ever more commonplace cultural flirtation with the form *and* content of pornography.

In the sphere of popular culture Madonna Ciccone is the figure who more than any other can plausibly be said to have made porno 'chic' with three key works produced during the years 1989–92. Having already achieved global superstardom with her highly sexualized late-1980s albums and accompanying video promos – in 1987's *Open Your Heart* she portrayed a striptease artist being watched by a young boy; *Like a Prayer* depicted a black Christ figure with whom she has sex; *Vogue* was a risqué camp celebration of gay sexuality – she released the single and video of *Justify My Love* in 1990. Steven Meisel's promo film placed Madonna in a bisexual *ménage à trois* scenario with sadomasochistic overtones, its performers dressed in sexy black underwear and fetish gear, eroticising her body with a directness rarely seen before in pop promos.

Justify My Love was not the first music video to challenge the existing boundaries of sexual representation, of course. Duran Duran and other pop bands had produced self-consciously 'adult' pop promos in the 1980s, and Frankie Goes To Hollywood's *Relax* video became notorious for its references to gay sexuality in 1985. *Relax* was sufficiently transgressive to be banned from the BBC's radio playlist (for its inclusion of the words 'come' and 'suck'), while performances of the Duran Duran videos were restricted to clubs, cable channels, and other adult-only spaces. These examples anticipated the trends of the 1990s, and are by no means insignificant in the history of late-twentieth-century sexual culture (the release of *Relax*, and its commercial success, for example, was an important staging post in the mainstreaming of gayness discussed later in this book).

Madonna, however, in the part-spoken, part-sung vocal for *Justify My Love*, as much as the sex scenes depicted in the video, makes repeated reference to the conventions of pornography, and goes much further in her sexualized self-display than either Frankie or Duran Duran had dared. *Justify My Love*, moreover, was only a taster for Madonna's full immersion in porno-chic with 1992's *Erotica* album (the CD's cover featured Madonna in the act of sucking a toe) and the *Sex* book of Steven Meisel's photographs.

Like Koons and his *Made in Heaven* there was a certain coyness evident in Madonna's packaging of this material as 'not-porn' – she called the album *Erotica* rather than 'Pornography', for example, and included a song called *Secret Garden*, after Nancy Friday's ground-breaking study of female erotica; in *Sex* she stated that 'I'm not interested in porno movies because everybody is ugly and faking it and it's just silly' – but the book was the closest thing to porn ever placed in the mainstream media marketplace. At the end of *Sex* is a pastiche magazine pull-out called 'Dita in the Chelsea Girl', depicting Madonna and her fictional friends – Bunny, Dex, Stella, Chiclet and the Stranger – working through a typical pornographic narrative of multiple sexual encounters.

By the nature of mainstream culture none of this material could stand classification as 'real' pornography. In seeking acceptance among a mass audience of Madonna fans (some of whom were children and young adults) it was necessarily 'soft' rather than 'hard', glossy rather than raw – a point missed in the criticisms which appeared in the gay press and elsewhere that it was not 'authentic'. But *Justify My Love*, *Erotica* and *Sex* were by any standards transgressive, explicit and sexy. Their *mises en scène* were quite intentionally those of the pornographer – masturbation, group sex, sadomasochism, lesbianism, and even simulated rape, all framed as the product of the star's sexual fantasies. Though marketed as erotica rather than porn – i.e. art rather than trash; beautiful rather than 'ugly'; true rather than 'faked' – this body of work stands as one of the first attempts by a popular artist, working in any medium, to appropriate the transgressive qualities of porn in a mass market context.

The *Erotica* album, companion piece to the *Sex* book, contained sexually explicit collaborations with black rap artists (*Did You Do It?*) and songs about cunnilingus (*Where Life Begins*). The video for *Erotica*, with its nudity and sadomasochistic references, replayed the taboo-breaking reputation of *Justify My Love*, receiving its British première on a post-watershed[14] Jonathan Ross television special, followed by an exclusive interview with Madonna herself, in which the conversational agenda included the pleasures of anal sex.

All of this output, like that of porno-chic in general, is distinct from pornography itself. Where porn stars are usually anonymous, porno-chic is celebrity-led. Where pornography is 'real' – i.e. the sex it shows is really happening – porno-chic is staged, and if not staged, then sanitized to remove its graphic rawness, as in Koons's work. Not porn, then, as it was defined in the previous chapter, but impossible to conceive without an understanding (and appreciation) of the perverse pleasures of the pornographic, *Sex* and the accompanying product brought the personal underground to the pop culture surface. Such a dramatic transformation in porn's cultural status reflected not just change in the broader sex-political environment, but was an important stage in the formation of a critical climate in which the meanings of well-established cultural pariahs (pornography, most obviously, and the objectification of the female body in the field of sexual representation more broadly) began to break down. Madonna's acts of explicit striptease encouraged writers and artists working in all modes, in every medium, to incorporate the pornographic as a source of inspiration, and to reject the negative associations traditionally associated with the form.

Madonna's contribution was important for other reasons. She was a successful, controlling woman in what had, until her own emergence in the 1980s, been very much the man's world of the pop business. To an unprecedented extent for a popular artist, she was the willing object of her own sexualization. If the anonymous near-naked girls who decorated Duran Duran videos like *Girls on Film* and *Rio* were clearly doing it for the boys, and it was the boys who were clearly in control, Madonna was just as clearly the one in charge of her own sexualized image. Madonna's early 1990s work was from the outset protected from the accusation of sexism (if not sluttishness) by the unavoidable facts of her sex and her power. Whatever she was doing, like Jeff Koons she was doing it to herself, and could not plausibly be positioned as a victim.

In the event, and despite their author's desire to be judged as the raunchy but ultimately respectable purveyor of erotic art, *Sex* and its soundtrack album were received by most critics as pornographic trash and condemned accordingly. Much of this criticism (particularly that of the tabloid newspapers) was predictable, driven by the familiarly patriarchal notion that nice girls didn't do such things, and that this particular woman was thereby a slut and a pop tart of the worst sort. Beyond the tabloids, and perhaps sensing a significant cultural moment in the making, most critics were reluctant to dismiss the work out of hand, but took the moral and/or high-cultural high ground to condemn the 'commodification' and cheapening of sex which Madonna appeared to be promoting. Some in the feminist movement condemned her objectification of herself as treason to the cause of women's liberation. One Mandy Metzstein complained that *Sex* was 'an insult which degrades Madonna, and humiliates women' (1993, p. 97). (It also, apparently, made her son cry.)

Whether the criticism of *Sex* and *Erotica* was based on aesthetic sensitivities, moral conservatism, straightforward sexism, or anti-porn feminism[15] mattered little, since it all contributed to making of the work and its author a global cultural phenomenon. The *Observer* newspaper dispatched Martin Amis – an author with a distinguished track record in writing about porn – to review the *Sex* book, and to pen a heavyweight intellectual essay on its cultural meaning. Even although the music was not well received (unfairly so, since the songs are as good as any she has ever recorded), and the *Erotica* CD sold less copies than her previous output (only 650,000 copies by 1994) Madonna's 1990–92 work established a popular cultural discourse which took for granted the existence of a personal underground, of something called pornography, and was not afraid to celebrate its place in a healthy, aspirational lifestyle of the type that someone like Madonna (or someone who wanted to be like Madonna) would enjoy.

Why did she do it? Clearly, she and her management were characteristically perceptive in recognizing that, after the decade of sexual anxiety caused by the spread of HIV and AIDS the moment was right for a reassertion of the pleasures of the flesh, and that she was the right artist to make the required leap. *Sex* celebrated the role of erotica and sexual fantasy in safe sex. It was also, in Madonna's own words, the product of twenty years of feminist struggle, of

> rage and rebellion against the way I was brought up. The repression, the sexual repression, the views on how girls are supposed to act. And once I realised, in the early part of my career, that my sexuality instantly branded me as an idiot – tainted everything I did with the idea that I wasn't very bright or I was just trying to seduce people – it made me want to go even further in that direction.[16]

Critics accused her of commercially driven sexploitation – albeit of her own body – but if that was a motivation it failed. This phase of her career was far from being her most successful in financial terms, and strictly commercial calculations might have suggested that she stick with the less explicit, less transgressive and sexually confrontational sounds and visuals of the 1980s. Far from representing the victory of trashy sexual consumerism, or 'celebrity erotica' over good taste, *Sex* and *Erotica* showed that sex does not always sell; or not, at least, in the quantities critical condemnation at the time might have led her to expect. *Sex* showed that playing with the iconography of pornography is not a surefire route to commercial success, even for a megastar. Approaching too closely to the sexual intensity of the authentically pornographic can provoke amongst audiences the anxieties and inhibitions associated with consuming porn proper. *Sex* certainly suffered from this reaction, frightening many people off with its fantasy rapes and its skin-headed, scissor-wielding dykes. In this sense, by dabbling in the pornosphere Madonna actually took a financial risk with her career, and it took some time (1998's *Ray Of Light*, six years later) for her record sales to recover to pre-*Erotica* levels.

What she lost in royalty payments, however, Madonna more than made up for in iconic status and cultural influence. This she achieved not only through the content of her work, but by sparking intense debate amongst journalists, academics, fans and non-fans alike about the ethics and meaning of her erotic displays. Newspapers, even while condemning her work, liberally reproduced images from the *Sex* book and quoted explicit lyrics from the *Erotica* CD. Academic books began to appear about the 'Madonna phenomenon',[17] while pro- and anti-porn feminists made of her a symbol of all that was good or bad (depending on their viewpoint) about contemporary sexual culture. Madonna's early 1990s work confirmed and intensified her status as a sexually assertive, in-control woman. The fact that she was a woman who identified herself as a feminist, and was already by then established as the world's foremost female pop star, meant that her use of explicit sexual imagery threw established paradigms for making sense of the pornographic into disarray. She disarmed, or at least confused, the key feminist arguments against porn. That Madonna could claim to be a feminist, and still appear naked in *Sex*, playing at being a porn star, announced the arrival of a new phase in western sexual culture, and the colonization of mainstream media by a new model of femininity, informed by feminism and publicly identifying with it, but cut from very different cloth than that worn by popular female artists before her.

Sex strongly influenced the sexual culture and politics of the 1990s because it broke a number of taboos (was transgressive) and was at the same time a popular commercial product. The cultural capital which she invested in the project ensured that it demanded attention even from those who hated it, pushing the debate on sexuality further into the heart of the mainstream. Madonna's *Sex* and *Erotica* contributed substantially to the creation of a cultural climate within which it became possible to treat porn as just another subject – not one which had to be ritually demonized as morally evil or politically reactionary, but could be treated as having some aesthetic interest and validity in itself.

The postmodern pleasures of porno-chic

After *Sex* two broad categories of porno-chic proliferated: texts, modelled on the example of *Sex*, which flirted with the aesthetic and narrative conventions of pornography; and texts which talked about pornography in various discursive modes (including the academic discourses of history, philosophy, art criticism, and sociology).

In the first category are all those works of art and popular culture which followed the lead of Koons and Madonna in seeking to look like porn, but not be labelled as porn. The adoption by artists of pornographic devices predates the late twentieth century, of course. The works of de Sade in the late eighteenth century and of later Sade-inspired artists such as Georges Bataille employed the structures of pornography (series of sexual encounters, unburdened by narrative context). These were not porno-chic, but intentionally provocative works intended to subvert the dominant moral values of the times in which they were made. Their present-day acceptance as art (the consequence of the post-1960s separation of art from porn in obscenity legislation) means that many of these works have ceased to be classified as pornography (if they ever were) and are freely available on the classics shelves of respectable bookshops everywhere. The original intentions of their makers is clear, nonetheless, and their efforts have inspired sexually transgressive art throughout the twentieth century (see Part III).

I want to distinguish here between that tradition of aesthetic transgression and the contemporary notion of porno-chic. The latter has no obvious aim to shock or scandalize (although it may, as Madonna intended with *Sex*, subvert sexual stereotypes). Porno-chic aims to transfer the taboo, transgressive qualities of pornography to mainstream cultural production, but in the knowledge that if media audiences are in general less easily shocked than in the past, mainstream culture remains a zone where real pornography is not acceptable. The resulting aesthetic tightrope can be a difficult path to tread, as several cinematic efforts show.

Paul Verhoeven, for example, flushed with the commercial and critical success of the sexually explicit *Basic Instinct* in 1992, went on to make *Showgirls* in 1994, combining images of striptease and lap dancing with the conventions of the Hollywood musical. Despite the visible on-screen luxury of its production, and Verhoeven's reputation as a popular auteur director, *Showgirls* was critically derided as too bland to be erotic, and too expressive of a traditionally male, voyeuristic gaze to be judged an aesthetic success. Lacking the self-reflexive postmodern distancing which is a feature of the best porno-chic, and in contrast to Bob Fosse's *All That Jazz* (1978), to which *Showgirls* bears some superficial resemblance, Verhoeven's film failed to win acceptance for its eroticization of a familiar Hollywood genre, and seriously damaged his career. The film critic Linda Williams typified the critical response when she argued that *Showgirls* failed because it was neither fish nor fowl in its straddling of the art/porn line:

> This is a film not bad enough to be good, nor wicked enough to be sexy. It is not even arousing enough to deliver what it promises: a feast for the male heterosexual eye, an explicit extravaganza of acts and body parts as yet unseen on mainstream screens. We have a quantity of images with which we are all too familiar (mostly focused on one or many topless women) rather than a qualitative leap in the possibilities of representation which challenge what can currently be seen and done on mainstream screens. Sex cinema directed with desire, the desire to stir viewers and change their viewing expectations as well as what they are allowed to see – this has yet to come.[18]

Showgirls showed that borrowing the conventions of pornography is fraught with pitfalls for a popular artist. If indeed authentic pornography can be defined as explicit sexual representation without narrative, devoid of all but the minimum of dramatic context, then to transform it into popular art or entertainment, as much as to make art which is self-consciously 'pornographic', creates an inherently unstable cultural category which in the end is likely to be pushed into being either art or pornography (never both) and judged accordingly – and nearly always negatively – as either too 'porny' to be art, or too arty to be porn.[19]

Some auteur-directors, such as Lars von Trier, have attempted to resolve this contradiction by embarking on the production of authentic porn films which willingly embrace all the trashy, sleazy connotations of the form, and make no effort to avoid labelling as pornography. In 1999 his production company Pussy Power released two hard-core porn films for women (*Constance* and *Pink Prison*). The Taiwanese artist Shu Lea Cheang's *IKU* (2000), described by one critic as a 'digital cyberporn film',[20] was premiered at the prestigious Sundance Film Festival (the first porn film to do so).

From *Hardcore* to *8mm*: how Hollywood learned to love pornography

Some cinematic auteurs have embraced a different approach to porno-chic, making films which are about pornography, but not necessarily *of* it. I referred above to *Hardcore* (Schrader, 1979) as an exemplar of what might be called porno-fear. Though Paul Schrader was at the time of *Hardcore*'s making immersed in a reportedly frenzied world of illegal drugs and promiscuous, sadomasochistic gay sex (Biskind, 1998) somewhat in opposition to the anti-porn moralism of his movie, his starkly negative view of the Los Angeles pornography industry was typical of a broad cultural queasiness towards the subject, in which the makers of porn were imagined as evil perverts, and the performers as pathetic victims. In *Hardcore* pornography directly threatened to destroy the family, and even the efforts of a doughty patriarch like George C. Scott were largely powerless to prevent it.

The People vs. Larry Flynt

For the next decade and a half *Hardcore*'s framework for making sense of pornography dominated the US movie industry, although there were no mainstream features which dealt so centrally with the subject. Then, in 1996, Columbia Pictures released Milos Forman's *The People vs. Larry Flynt*, starring Woody Harrelson and Courtney Love. The film was a biopic of the *Hustler* publisher and leading demon of the anti-pornography lobby Larry Flynt who, by the time of its release, was a millionaire paraplegic fighting a crusade against censorship. It was ground-breaking in its strong identification with the anti-censorship cause championed by Flynt, and its presentation of the pornography issue as one of press freedom and the preservation of the US constitution. In this sense it is old-fashionedly liberal, with the director playing devil's advocate. If freedom means anything, Forman is saying in the film, it means freedom for Larry Flynt. *The People vs. . . .* goes further, though, and normalizes Flynt by placing him firmly at the heart of entrepreneurial American capitalism. *Hustler* magazine is portrayed as the first sexually transgressive commodity to make it into the mainstream consumer market, and its publisher as a hard-working businessman concerned above all about the welfare of his employees and the quality of his product. 'We're breaking taboos', says Larry at one point, explaining his unique selling proposition, and neatly summing up the commercial appeal of the pornographic at the same time.

By the film's end, moreover, Flynt is positioned as the victim of a morally conservative and dangerously authoritarian US establishment – a major reversal of how he and other pornographers had been depicted hitherto. In so far as it deals with the ethics and victimology of pornography itself there are references to the famous 'meat grinder' issue of *Hustler* which became a symbol of patriarchal misogyny for the women's movement. In this respect the film acknowledges that there was at least a debate to be had around the image-content of porn, but the director's emphasis is very much on the satirical, anti-establishment (anti-male establishment, that is) essence of *Hustler* magazine. It isn't the female models who appear as victims in Forman's film, but Flynt's wife Althea (Courtney Love), whose descent into drug addiction and death is portrayed as a consequence of the boredom induced by celebrity and wealth rather than pornographic exploitation (at their first meeting Flynt is shown nobly refusing to have sex with her, because she is under age).

Although the film won several Oscars – a clear measure of its success in bringing pornography into the mainstream of American and thus global culture – initial critical reaction was ambivalent. *Sight and Sound* declared that it 'never resolves its fundamental dilemma: how to make a Hollywood film about a hard core pornographer. What ensues, therefore, is an often witty and dramatic sanitisation exercise during which any potentially disruptive or dangerous elements are spruced up and subsumed into the pervasive purity of the mainstream form'.[21] Similar criticisms were made of Madonna's *Sex*, and a similar response is appropriate in defence of this work. Mainstream culture, we have seen, has evolved to the point where artists can talk about and refer to pornography in quite explicit terms, as both *Sex* and *The People vs. Larry Flynt* do (although one scene in *The People vs . . .* had to be airbrushed for cinematic and video consumption). Their work cannot *be* pornography, however, or it would by definition no longer be porno-chic. Such texts *must* be sanitized, if they are to find a space in mainstream culture. *The People vs. Larry Flynt* is porno-chic not in its pornographic representation of sex (which it avoids) but in its efforts to overturn the long-standing 'fear and loathing' extended to Larry Flynt and the American porn industry in general, and to confront the hypocrisy which has surrounded the pornography debate. Flynt's greatest enemy on the moral frontline, Frank Keating, is revealed by the film's end as a financial swindler who cheated millions through his involvement in the savings and loans debacle; the religious right is linked, at least in spirit, with the attempt to murder Flynt which deprived him of his ability to walk, and we see him evolve from born-again Christian to iconoclastic atheist in response.

Due in large part, no doubt, to the artistic reputations of those involved in the film, but also some measure of the changed status of pornography in late 1990s western culture the film's producers were rewarded with box office success to go with their Oscar statues. Moral conservative critics naturally hated the film, as they had hated *Sex*, for mentioning what had previously been unmentionable in public. But with *The People vs. Larry Flynt* the genie of porno-chic was well and truly out of the bottle. Here as elsewhere in popular culture the meaning of the pornographic was being positively redefined.[22]

Boogie Nights

If *The People vs* . . . sought to reclaim a legitimate culture role for the pornographic by appealing to the sacred tenets of the American constitution, defining the issue as one of free speech, Paul Thomas Anderson's *Boogie Nights*, released a year later, contained a yet more positive endorsement of the form, and contributed at the same time to a parallel late 1990s trend: 'retro-chic', in which the 1970s – 'the decade that taste forgot' – and the porn industry in particular, were rediscovered as an era of innocent hedonism, good times and, as Anderson's film directly suggested, unending boogie nights down the disco.

Like *The People vs* . . ., *Boogie Nights* is not just a film about pornography, but one in which the porn industry supplies the stage, the characters and the dramatic twists required to illuminate broader themes. This time the thematic focus is not civil liberties and freedom of speech, but family, celebrity, and dealing with change. *Boogie Nights'* radical departure is in approaching these themes through a pornography industry which is portrayed as a benevolent rather than corrupting force. In *Hardcore* pornography was seen to be destroying the bourgeois family by corrupting its innocents. In *Boogie Nights* the pornography industry, and its personification in a small-scale, low-budget production company run by Jack Horner (Burt Reynolds, in a well-received comeback role) provides a surrogate family for a group of individuals who are victims of family breakdowns of various sorts. Eddie Adams (Mark Wahlberg) is oppressed by a neurotic mother and her ineffective husband, finding replacement parents in Jack Horner and his senior female 'star' Amber Waves (Julianne Moore). Amber herself has been deprived of her child in a custody battle because, we are told, of her involvement in the porn industry. Eddie and the others are her real children. Rollergirl, too (Heather Graham) seems to be orphaned, and to have adopted the Horner circle as her family. Little Bill's breakdown, in which he kills his wife and then himself, is the consequence of her violation of the husband–wife contract in sleeping promiscuously with anyone, anywhere, and flaunting the fact of her promiscuity before him and the rest of the 'family'. Far from being a gateway into hell the pornography industry is portrayed as a refuge. Though they fuck each other regularly in the course of their work the love they share is platonic rather than sexual. The sex is not sanitized beyond what is necessary for the film's marketing as a mainstream release, and it is clearly framed as business rather than pleasure; a job of work for those to whom it provides a decent, even dignified living.

As a meditation on the impact of celebrity, meanwhile, *Boogie Nights* follows the career of porn star Dirk Diggler from the late 1970s through to the early 1980s.

Although the fame on display here is far from mainstream, contained wholly within the narrow, specialized world of the Los Angeles porn industry, Diggler's progression from naïve newcomer to coke-crazed burn-out is no less compelling than any we might imagine to be experienced by an A-list celebrity. The temptations and corruptions of fame are the same at the bottom of the status hierarchy as they are at the top, the film suggests. Crucially, it is not the business of pornography which corrupts Eddie, but the affectations and indulgences which come with success in any walk of life, and the entertainment industry in particular. Porn is portrayed as a sub-set of Hollywood (albeit of relatively low status), and *Boogie Nights* is a film about Hollywood as much as its pornographic offshoot.

Dirk Diggler doesn't deal well with the changes which come upon him in *Boogie Nights*, and the impact of change on the pornography industry itself is a parallel theme running through Anderson's script. As the 1970s pass into the 1980s we see Jack Horner and his family grappling with the transition from celluloid to video, and from adult cinema to backroom booth. He resists what he sees as the loss of a golden age. We know, of course, from our contemporary vantage point, that he is doomed to failure, because the age of the VCR is coming soon and will render even the modest aesthetic pretensions of celluloid porn redundant. Working through this theme allows Anderson to raise questions about the nature of the pornographic, and to present Jack Horner as the bearer of a porno aesthetic which if not 'authentic' is at least worthy of celebration. Horner wants to make 'real' films – i.e. films which, though 'adult' and 'exotic' have good scripts, believable characters and decent production values. In this sense he is idealistic, but his artistic aspirations are doomed to failure because, as Anderson acknowledges, pornography needs no context; indeed, is better off without quality scripts and the accompanying paraphernalia of 'real' movies.

Boogie Nights is postmodern, like *Sex*, in so far as it unapologetically repackages and remakes the meanings of symbols and texts once viewed as beyond the ideological and semiological pale. The film contains some acutely observed reconstructions of Horner's productions, parodying the unreconstructed sexism of the 1970s. But anti-porn feminism is the other spectre (alongside video) haunting Jack Horner and his naughty children as the 1980s begin. In *Boogie Nights* pornography loses its demonic qualities, and those who make or appear in it are humanized. Anderson confirms that his intention was to 'romanticise the hey-day of porno',[23] which his film certainly does, if not without intimation of a darker surrounding context. One of the most disturbing sequences in the film is when Horner invites a man into his limo to be videoed having sex with Rollergirl. This is where video technology leads us, Anderson suggests – to the loss of dignity and any redeeming value which pornography could be argued to have in its heyday. Elsewhere, however, the film's tone is resolutely non-judgemental, and the characters are even more sympathetically drawn than Forman's picture of Larry Flynt and his court.

The success of *Boogie Nights* encouraged a broader cultural interest in the nuts and bolts of the pornography industry, as seen in the work of photographers like Ken Probst and Jeff Burton. Probst's work has documented what his publisher calls 'the absurdities, pathos and business of the pornographic film industry'[24] and, in the manner of *Boogie Nights*, comments on 'the banality of manufacturing desire'. For the US critic William Hamilton, Probst's work belongs to that school of contemporary art which 'draws from the politics, graphic subject matter and hit-and-run production values of adult entertainment'.[25] The photography of Jeff Burton shares Probst's interest in the iconography of porno-shoots. One critic suggests that 'Burton's images speak of the industry itself: the tacky makeshift sets, the actors' flaccidity between takes and, ultimately, the marketing of the sexual body'.[26] In these respects the debt of both Probst and Burton to *Boogie Nights* is obvious. From Koons's *Made in Heaven* to Madonna's *Sex* to Anderson's *Boogie Nights* and Probst's *Pornografic*, the connections are clear.

8mm

In what seems more than mere coincidence 1998 saw the release in the United States of *8mm*, directed by Joel Schumacher. Having given birth to two major productions in which pornography was cleansed of its demonic qualities *8mm* can be read as Hollywood's attempt to take a step back into the territory mapped out in Schrader's *Hardcore*. Indeed, *8mm*'s plot has much in common with the earlier film, down to the scenes in both where the naïve central character is introduced to stag reels for the first time, and the role of a photogenic, youthful insider in guiding the older man through the pornographic underworld. In both films, an honest, hard-working, all-American father figure (Nicholas Cage in *8mm*) reluctantly enters that world in search of a missing girl. In both, a daughter figure is lost to porn. Though *Hardcore* allows her to be reclaimed by her natural father the missing girl in *8mm* is revealed to have been murdered in a snuff movie, and Cage's character must return to the safety of his own family for redemption (having first noisily despatched the baddies, of course).

Porn threatens that family, this time through the unsettling pyschological impact all this porn-watching has on Cage's character. In vivid contrast to *Boogie Nights* Schumacher's pornosphere is populated by tatooed psychopaths and serial killers who delight in violent s&m. The milieu is that of sleazy porn stores, dark dungeons, and basements where innocents are readied for the slaughter. As in *Hardcore* porn is equated exclusively with violence, perversion and snuff. 'It's a thriller, it's a murder mystery,' director Joel Schumacher states in the film's production notes, 'but most important, it's a study of a human being who starts off feeling very much on top of his game and thinking he's quite normal and in control . . . and then losing all sense of himself in a whirlpool of terror, and discovering that the only way he can redeem himself is to go to a very dark place himself.'

If the similarities of plot and mood between the two films are obvious there was a significant divergence in the responses of critics to them – a difference which illustrates the cultural shift manifest in 1990s porno-chic. Where *Hardcore*'s stern rebuke to porn was received with some deference in the 1970s, twenty years later *8mm* was critically panned, and not merely by pro-porn libertarians. This 'vision of porno hell merely demonstrates', wrote British critic Mark Kermode in his *Sight and Sound* review of the film, 'that 70s sex-industry sensationalism has become laughable now that Larry Flynt is opening *Hustler* coffee-shops and porno-chic is de rigueur among artists as unthreatening as Lars von Trier. The porn industry just doesn't look scary anymore'.[27] Even with the state of the art techno-thrash of Aphex Twin's *Come to Daddy* playing at ear-splitting volume over the climactic scene *8mm* could not escape the criticism that it was tired caricature; a glossy realization of the most baroque visions of anti-porn campaigners, anachronistic in a culture increasingly at ease with pornographic iconography.

Fashionable fetishism and the pornographication of style

As porn became sexy in the 1990s its codes and conventions were increasingly adopted by the media arbiters of cultural style, taste and fashion. Just as top-shelf magazines like *Penthouse* borrowed from the design and typographic innovations of titles like *i-D* and the *Face* in their efforts to reposition pornography as 'cool' (see previous chapter), the style magazines repaid the compliment and openly flirted with the look of porn. In keeping with the postmodern mood of the decade, and following the example set by Madonna, pornographic iconography was just transgressive enough to be *outré*, while allowing for plentiful representations of pleasing erotic imagery to be packaged not as porn but as fashion. This became easier when fashion too embraced porno-chic and its variant, 's&m chic' – the label given to a wide variety of 'fetish' garments made of leather, rubber and PVC, and by the 1990s turning up on catwalks all over the world. What had been the defiantly sub-cultural interest of Vivien Westwood and others in the 1970s, and a still marginal feature of 1980s haute couture[28] (when Susan Faludi, Naomi Woolf and others condemned it as part of the patriarchal backlash) had become by the 1990s a feature of high street fashion.

These trends were already evident in the early 1990s, and peaked by the end of the decade, when it seemed that no style magazine could avoid devoting at least one issue to looking like, or talking in depth about, pornography. The *Dazed & Confused* issue of August 1995, for example, attracted attention with its images of eroticized violence and fetish gear. The magazine's third anniversary cover shot (August 1997) featured a 'scratch and see' photograph of model Helena Christensen, her breasts obscured by a grey panel which could be removed to reveal all. *i-D*'s 'skin and soul issue' (May 1999 – see Figure 4.1) pastiched what had by then become a style culture cliché. From a front cover depicting a bikini-clad model the magazine promised 'obscene amounts of sex', 'constant stiffies', 'kinky sex among animals' and 'tight little bums', all served up with a knowing wink. Here was embodied the 'have your cake and eat it too' tactic of employing porno-chic's playfully transgressive content while positioning *i-D* above the run-of-the-mill sex-obsessed publication. Inside, an alternative 'cover' – '*i-D* really' – featured singer Sharleen Spiteri in an unglamorous, decidedly non-pornographic pose. Under the risqué title headings inside the magazine contained thoughtful, well-researched

THE SKIN & SOUL ISSUE NO.186

cover star: **heidi klum** photographed by **max vadukul may 1999**

i-D

£2.80 US$7.25

9 770262 357044

LIRE 13,500 DM 18.00 PESETAS 890 D KR 76

bad sex

size does matter

what scares
men in bed

sex, scandal and
other wild things

obscene amounts
of sex

mountains or
molehills: the great
big tit debate

wildlife - kinky sex
among animals

teach the wife to
bellydance

constant stories

why men are
scared of you

any woman,
any time: pick up
tricks that never fail

sexy husband tricks

do you and him
want more sex?

make your own
sexy video

get weird in bed

lovers on the
rampage

tight little bums

twice as much sex:
who's having it,
how to get it

hot new reasons
to have sex

Figure 4.1 i-D: the 'Skin and soul' issue

articles about sexualized art and fashion, and meditations on the evolution of sexual representation. Stuart Shave's 'Constant stiffies', for example, invited the reader in with the statement that 'artists have always been concerned with the body but the current crop seem nothing short of obsessed, displaying nude models in museums and even spreading their legs for porn mags'.[29]

The Face's 'L'Édition Sexe' (November 2000) reprised this approach a year later, to the extent of coming in a lurid pink plastic bag adorned with three large 'X'es (Figure 4.2). Subjects covered inside included 'Nadia', the star of techno band *Add N To (X)*'s sexually explicit video promo for their song 'Plug me in'; a review of the delights to be found on internet porn sites; and a profile of *Richardson* magazine. *Richardson* combined all the elements of porno-chic discussed thus far in a provocative, expensive, self-consciously arty package: sexually explicit images, taken by artists (as opposed to pornographers) and featuring models (sometimes the artist him or herself) dressed in high fashion garments. As the *Face* article asked: 'when is a porn mag not a porn mag? When it's an £18, beautifully shot fashion event sold in the Tate Modern, containing self-fisting yanks, wanking and pissing Japanese teenagers'.[30]

Selling sex: porno-chic in promotional culture

Porno-chic was also embraced by the advertising industry. Recognizing the broad public interest in the sexual, including the more deviant and perverse variants of it, advertisers produced work which sought to exploit the appeal of the sexually transgressive in a promotional context. Tony Kaye's 1994 film for Dunlop tyres played on the rubberiness of the product by featuring models clothed in fetish gear and wielding whips (Figure 4.3). On the soundtrack the Velvet Underground (the band's name, of course, is taken from a classic sadomasochistic novel) performed *Venus in Furs*. Pop culture, fetishism, references to pornography and sadomasochism were all united around the selling of a commodity not hitherto perceived as especially sexy.

Sexual representation in advertising does not have to be erotic, of course, as long as it attracts the attention of the audience to the virtues of the product being sold. This may be done in an ironic or humourous way, as in the Guinness ad which appeared in the *Face* in August 1996. At the cost of criticism from the UK's Advertising Standards Authority the ad depicted a middle-aged man hanging from a ceiling, bound in chains and black fetish gear in familiar bondage style. Whether by coincidence or design, the ad appeared not long after the accidental death of the closet gay Tory MP Stephen Milligan in an episode of autoerotic asphyxiation gone disastrously wrong, and was interpreted as a rather tasteless reference to this tragedy. More straightforwardly comic, but speaking equally to the culture's fascination with the perverse which often lies at the heart of porno-chic, were the 'Sadist' and 'Masochist' television ads produced for the Tennent's lager company. Apart from depicting sadomasochism in the context of primetime television advertising, the clips also satirized and commented on the changing structure of

Figure 4.2 *The Face:* L'Édition Sexe

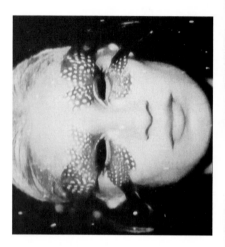

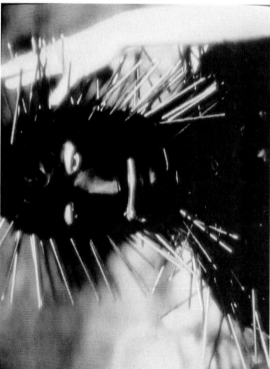

Figure 4.3 Dunlop tyre film advertisement

sexual relationships and stereotypes, presenting the man and woman who featured in the ad as engaged in a game of sexual one-upmanship. In 2000 television ads for Grolsch lager were set on a porno-shoot.

Using sex to sell commodities through advertising is a well-established promotional strategy, of course, dissected with anthropological precision by Erving Goffman as long ago as 1976,[31] and by Judith Williamson in her ground-breaking *Decoding Advertisements* (1978), both of which pay close attention to the construction of sexual identity and gender stereotypes in advertising. The advertisements described above are not selling sexism, however, nor can it be argued that they exploit and objectify the female body in the traditionally sexist manner. Indeed, they do not offer titillation so much as invite the viewer to share the 'adult' sophistication of the product, and to participate in the pornographication of the mainstream which their primetime presence signifies. They are more likely to subvert sexual stereotypes than to reinforce them, as in the Tennent's clips, and to bring to the public gaze practices and identities which less overtly sexualised advertising would be unable to use. In these respects porno-chic in advertising has reflected changing public attitudes to sexuality and gender roles.

Porno-chic in the public sphere

These images have in common the attempt to integrate the aesthetics of pornography into non-pornographic forms of art (popular and avant-garde) and promotional culture. They reflect the collision of the ideological shifts caused by decades of sex-political struggle with a postmodern intellectual climate in which the meaning of the pornographic can be remade, and its perverse pleasures recognised. In the 1990s, even if it was not directly present in mainstream media, pornography became a popular cultural phenomenon. Consequently, and at another level of the cross-referential lattice which is the media in postmodernity, there has been a proliferation of television programmes and press and periodical articles which talk about pornography – and about porno-chic – without necessarily trying to look like it. Through these various forms of journalistic media, pornography has migrated from the pornosphere to what Jürgen Habermas called the public sphere – that region of mediated space in which the members of a society come together to learn about and discuss issues of importance to them. Historically, pornography was not regarded as the appropriate subject matter for such debate, remaining on the margins of legitimate public discourse, but as porno-chic emerged in the late 1980s and early 1990s, the media of reportage, analysis and debate began to take an interest.

This pornographication of the public sphere took place alongside the media's growing fascination with what the next chapter calls 'striptease culture' – broadcast and press material based on various forms of sexual self-revelation and bodily exposure – and is thus a sub-set of a broader sexualization of mainstream culture. But porno-chic in the public sphere is distinctive in treating as a legitimate subject of intellectual and journalistic inquiry what has hitherto been the forbidden zone

– the secret museum – of pornography. The print media led the way in this regard, with a growing editorial interest in pornography evident from the early 1990s. In *Mediated Sex* I noted that in the first half of that decade the explanatory framework structuring a large proportion of this coverage shifted from the generally hostile (based on moral conservative or anti-porn feminist paradigms) to the inquisitive and non-judgemental (McNair, 1996). Since that time press interest in talking about pornography has persisted on both sides of the Atlantic, with critical, condemnatory pieces greatly outnumbered by those more interested in the cultural and sociological meanings of pornographication. An exception to this trend was Martin Amis's high-profile piece for the *Guardian* newspaper in March 2001, which focused its critical gaze on the notorious American producers Max Hardcore and Rod Black (see previous chapter).[32]

Television and porn

TV also embarked on an exploration of the pornographic. The period 1998–9 saw a peak in televisual porno-chic and sexually oriented programmes in general, as the Royal Television Society observed in May 1999. 'In the last year there seems to have been more sex on British television than ever before'.[33] In Britain, which has featured proportionately more of these programmes in its schedules than most countries, including the United States (where, though pornography is freely available, free-to-air television is more tightly regulated), the majority have been commissioned and broadcast by Channel 4, which pioneered the trend with 1995's *Red Light Zone* – a season of forty-two programmes dealing with pornography and sexual culture in general. The ratings success of the *Red Light Zone* at a time of intensifying competition for audience share in the television sector encouraged further exploration of the sexually transgressive by British broadcasters. Channel 4's post-*RLZ* output ranged from the self-deprecatingly 'trashy' and ironic (*Eurotrash*), to historical and sociological documentaries located firmly in the British public-service tradition. 'Themed' nights and weekends like *Censored* functioned as rubrics under which the channel could 'explore the boundaries of how far you can go on British screens'.[34]

Some critics condemned this project as the product of naked (literally) commercialism, and the channel's chief executive Michael Grade was famously dubbed 'Britain's pornographer-in-chief' by the conservative tabloid *Daily Mail*, but Channel 4's motivations were honourable. The aim of giving cultural space to previously marginalized communities was part of C4's remit from its establishment and in September 1998 the channel broadcast two female-authored programmes exploring the role of explicit sexual representation (pornography and erotica) in advancing women's rights. *Erotica: A Journey into Female Sexuality* examined the sexually explicit art of women like performance artist Annie Sprinkle and photographer Phyllis Christopher, while *Susie Bright: Sex Pest* followed up the *Red Light Zone*'s transmission of Bright's short film *How to Read a Dirty Movie* with a longer documentary by the leading US sex-radical. In a neat postmodern twist the

Australian pop singer and queer icon Kylie Minogue was enlisted to introduce the two programmes, defining their ethos thus:

> Renegade TV. Independent, rebellious messages. Counter-culture breaks through into the mainstream.

In 2000 Channel 4's pay-per-view offshoot Filmfour transmitted *Sex: the Annabel Chong Story*, a feature-length video documentary about the career of the Singapore-born porn star Grace Quek, who achieved a measure of porno-celebrity by having sex with 250 men in one day. She was also presented as a university student who had chosen to move into porn as a kind of artistic and intellectual experiment. Alongside the story of how this record-breaking event was organized and conducted, therefore, the film examined the ethics of pornography, and Quek's challenge to what she characterized as the anti-porn orthodoxy of American academia. At the same time as giving its subject the space to articulate her porno-aesthetic, however, the film did not avoid the disturbing ethical questions raised by her participation in the 250-man session – was she as much in control of her own decision-making as she claimed to be? Was there something in her strictly religious Singaporean upbringing against which she was rebelling? Was Grace's participation in the porn industry evidence of a sex-radical intelligence, or a damaged psyche?

Regardless of the ethical dimension, of course, sex sells in this medium as much as anywhere, and whether it is packaged as counter-cultural or not there can be little doubt that the opportunity to present viewers with sexualized, mildly transgressive imagery at a time of growing competition fuelled the growth of porno-chic on British television. Channel 4 pioneered the trend, and has pushed its transgressive content further than any other UK broadcaster, but ITV and the BBC were not excluded. Channel 4's *Censored* seasons were preceded by BBC2's *Empire of the Censors*, while the same channel's *Doing Rude Things* presented a tongue-in-cheek historical account of the British pornographic film industry. Channel 5, which came on air in 1997 and had a particular budgetary interest in 'sexy', audience-friendly programming of the type that porno-chic almost always delivered, rivalled Channel 4 in the attention it devoted to all things porno. The previous chapter referred to Channel 5's introduction of soft-core pornography (as some critics categorized it) into the United Kingdom's free-to-air television in series like *Red Shoe Diaries*. C5 also gave us *Sex and Shopping*, a curiously titled series (because while there was plenty of sex, there wasn't really much shopping going on) about the pornography industry. In thirteen half-hour episodes *Sex and Shopping* covered in unprecedented detail and explicitness straight, gay and lesbian porn, and porn on the internet. It profiled leading performers and producers, with (naturally) many hours of illustrative on-set footage.

Channel 4 further indulged growing mainstream interest in the mechanics of the pornography industry with *Boogie Nights in Suburbia*, broadcast in February 1999. The subject of this documentary was the same as that of an article published in *Company* magazine of January 1995[35] – the 'do-it-yourself', semi-amateur pornography business in which non-professional models are used. The film was a mixture of the sleazy and the sociological, in which the predatory activities of the pseudonymous Ben Dover and other 'producers' (leaping on his models at the end of a shoot appeared to be a habit of Ben's) were set against the clear financial benefits which some women accrued from their participation in the films.

Also in this tradition was a 1998 episode of *Louis Theroux's Weird Weekends* (BBC2) dedicated to the porn industry in the San Fernando valley. Theroux's distinctive documentary style – a kind of televised gonzo journalism in which he immerses himself in whatever sub-cultural community he is interested in that week – was applied to San Fernando's community of porn performers and producers. Porno-chic was clearly recognized as the rationale for the programmes as Theroux's 'guide', the porn industry publicist Susan Rinetti, provided the sub-text:

Theroux: Is porn an exciting place to be right now?
Rinetti: The public is at a time and a place where they're open to hearing about this. Hollywood currently has four movies in the works about the adult entertainment industry.
Theroux: So they [the porn industry] are actually making a conscious effort to bring themselves into the mainstream.

What followed went a step further than *Sex and Shopping* or *Boogie Nights in Suburbia*, as Theroux declared his intention to 'try out porn as a lifestyle'. In keeping with this ambition, the film was punctuated by his meetings with, and employment by, porn producers, including one company specializing in videos for the gay market. It was all presented as good, cutting-edge fun, with only one producer, Rod Black, who specialized in bondage imagery producing any hint of unease from Theroux.

> As Rod Black's vision came to life, I thought I'd seen enough. Maybe more than I wanted to see.

In general, however, Theroux's film, like most of the examples of documentary porno-chic viewed for this book delivered a non-judgemental, frequently sympathetic account of what it's like to be 'in' pornography from the perspectives of performers, producers, agents and their supporting casts. One notable exception was *Hardcore*, broadcast by Channel 4 in April 2001. The film told the story of 'Felicity, an English girl who came to Los Angeles to become a porn star', following her through induction into a career in the industry. While allowing Felicity to stress that her involvement in porn was wholly voluntary, and to give her reasons (economic), the film, like Amis's *Guardian* article (see above), focused on her reluctant participation in the productions of Max Hardcore. Although she entered his studio as a consenting adult, the film revealed Felicity's growing discomfort at the degrading nature of what she was being asked to do, culminating in a tearful bedroom scene in which the documentary-maker himself felt obliged to intervene.

In depicting the most deeply misogynistic sector of the American porn business *Hardcore* presented a useful corrective to the generally non-judgemental, frequently celebratory content of televisual porno-chic.

At the more self-consciously 'serious' and public service-oriented end of the televisual spectrum were the several programme strands devoted to weighty, academically inflected explorations of twentieth-century sexual culture, such as BBC2's *Sex Bomb*, broadcast in October 1998. In four programmes covering the period from the 1960s through to the 1990s, *Sex Bomb* examined the impact of the post-World War II social and sexual revolutions on British society. The similarly themed *Sexual Century*, produced by Carlton but never actually broadcast on terrestrial television, explored what the book of the series characterized as 'the thrusting of sex into the mainstream as a cultural force' (Hickman, 1999, p. 7). *Pornography – A Secret History of Civilisation* on Channel 4 was, as its title suggests, the most directly focused of these series on pornography proper. It was also the most sophisticated in sociological terms, locating what it characterized as a centuries-long debate around the nature of the obscene firmly in the context of religious and patriarchal control regimes. The illustrations and examples provided in the five programmes were highly explicit, passing the watchful eye of the regulator only because they could be classified as science/documentary rather than porn. In his introduction to the book of the series producer Fenton Bailey gave an account of how his original idea was passed from one broadcaster to another for six years, before being commissioned by Channel 4 at a time when 'pornography was edging its way from the margins into the mainstream' (Tang, 1999, p. 10).

One further category of televisual porno-chic deserves mention – the humorous, innuendo-laden magazine show best typified by *Eurotrash*, broadcast on Channel 4 since 1987 and presented by the French TV personality and style guru Antoine de Caunes, with involvement in its early years by Jean Paul Gaultier. In its title and content *Eurotrash* played on the high culture/low culture elitism of the European intelligentsia, specializing in pseudo-journalistic 'investigations' into the cheaper and rawer end of the pornography business, while indulging a fascination for the seemingly infinite variety of sexual perversions being practised across the continent (and by the Germans in particular, it seemed). At this level *Eurotrash* belonged to the category of 'tasteless' expository television pioneered by the sadistic Japanese game shows of the 1980s and brought to the United Kingdom by *The Word* and other programmes. *Eurotrash* stayed just on this side of 'chic', however, through the involvement not only of the supersexy de Caunes but Gaultier too, whose haute couture designs had of course been instrumental in the emergence of fashion fetishism and s&m chic. A less explicit televisual sex magazine played for a time on Rupert Murdoch's Sky One satellite channel, under the title of *British Sex*. Like its Channel 4 counterpart *British Sex* presented an ongoing narrative on the mainstreaming of sexuality – part-journalism, part-entertainment in the British 'nudge, nudge, wink, wink' tradition. Items included the making of 'messy sex' magazines (illustrated, of course), reports from the 1999 UK Festival of Erotica, and discussion of the growth of the sex aids industry.

The *Guardian* columnist Charlotte Raven placed the material contained in these programmes on a continuum somewhere between porn and erotica. They were sexually explicit, she observed, but 'none have anything to do with masturbation'.[36] Precisely. They are not porn, but porno-chic, referring to pornographic texts in their content and style, but not singularly dedicated to the task of sexual arousal in the manner of true porn. Their proliferation at the end of the twentieth century reflected a broad collective ease with the public exploration of sexual culture; a popular interest in consuming, through the media of the public sphere, sexuality in all its forms (while maintaining the continued segregation of the truly pornographic from mainstream culture).

Like the other categories of porno-chic examined in this chapter the historically dominant anti-pornography perspective was largely absent from the great majority of these programmes, replaced by a stance of detached matter-of-factness (*Sex and Shopping*), postmodern irony (*Eurotrash*), or quasi-academic intellectualism (*Pornography – A Secret History*). When porno-chic addressed the ethics of pornography this was done most frequently in the context of the censorship debate. Here too, though, the tone of most of the material was far from that of distaste or moral rebuke, with a stress instead on the difficulties posed for established censorship regimes by the internet and other new technologies. BBC's *Panorama* strand covered the subject in a programme called *Porn Wars*, contrasting the situation in Britain with that of its near neighbours.

> In Europe pornography is upfront, legal and glossy. In Britain most porn is under the counter, seedy and illegal. Britain has the toughest porn laws in the western world, but can they really stop the tide of foreign porn?[37]

References to 'tides' of foreign porn and, later, 'armadas of porn invading our shores' may suggest a sensationalistic approach, but if the lurid language was a necessary prime time concession to lingering anti-porn sentiments the programme generally avoided moral panic and focused instead on the business aspects of the European porn industry, portraying performers and producers alike as normal human beings doing an unusual, but essentially professional job of work. This image of business-as-usual was then set against the UK government's stern approach to censorship, and the home secretary's long-standing hostility to porn, which was in turn contrasted with the observation that

> Britons are increasingly owning up to having sexual desires and fantasies, just like everyone else.

Viewers were thus encouraged to draw the conclusion of the previous chapter – that for technological and cultural reasons, the age of censorship was coming to an end in Britain.[38]

Conclusion

The emergence of porno-chic in 1990s popular culture reflected a broad public interest in the pornographic which it was in the economic interests of an increasingly commercialized and competive media to satisfy. Porno-chic was (and continues to be) a further stage in the commodification of sex, and the extension of sexual consumerism to a broader mass of the population than have previously had access to it. Unless one subscribes to the religious notion of sex as sacred, however, and the notion that commodification is by its nature 'theft', it is not self-evident that this is always and everywhere a bad thing.

Porno-chic has on occasion been tacky, often humorous, sometimes deeply serious. Some 'serious' explorations of pornography have been the cover for the straightforwardly competitive tactic of putting tits on television (rarely dicks). Others, to their credit, have presented to the public gaze opinions and sexualities rarely, if ever, granted visibility in mainstream culture before. Like the expansion of the pornosphere itself, porno-chic would not have happened in the absence of popular demand for access to and participation in sexual discourse. Porno-chic has been the occasion for important public debate around issues like censorship and sexual identity. From Koons to Madonna to Paul Thomas Anderson it has also inspired some art, popular and avant-garde, of great originality and power (see also Part III). Porno-chic, from that perspective, might be viewed as an index of the sexual maturation of contemporary capitalist societies, rather than a measure of their degeneration into sleaze. Blanket criticism of porno-chic as 'barren titillation' or sexploitation arises from the application of a set of elite aesthetic criteria for evaluating the public sphere which, as the popularity and ubiquity of porno-chic shows, are no longer shared (if they ever were) by audiences as a whole.

5

STRIPTEASE CULTURE

The sexualization of the public sphere

Striptease culture is the name of this book, and also the label I give to a third strand in the broad cultural sexualization which is the subject of Part I – the media of sexual confession and self-revelation. Though rooted in the same political, economic, and technological processes which led to the expansion of pornography and porno-chic, this form of cultural sexualization is distinctive in one important way. Where pornography and porno-chic almost always involve professionals (actors, artists, advertising 'creatives'), striptease culture is often the outcome of media activity by people who are, at least when they start out, amateurs and non-celebrities – 'ordinary' people, to use that label of convenience for the moment. To that extent, if there *is* a democratization of desire underpinning the sexualization of contemporary culture then this is where it is most obvious. Striptease culture frequently involves ordinary people talking about sex and their own sexualities, revealing intimate details of their feelings and their bodies in the public sphere. It is all those forms and contexts in which people outside the starry world of celebrity claim or are given space in the media to engage in sex talk. Unlike the stripped naked performances of Jeff Koons or Madonna, what they say and do with those spaces is rarely 'art' in the recognized sense. And although striptease culture involves forms of exposure and self-exposure which refer to the sexual, and which may at times be sexually explicit, neither can it accurately be described as pornographic.[1] The words and images one encounters in striptease culture are not necessarily erotic, although they may well be about erotic*ism*. They may contain nakedness, self-exhibition and self-revelation, of a literal and metaphorical kind, but they will rarely aim for sexual arousal in the audience. They are closer to anthropology than pornography in their focus on the discovery and explanation of sexual phenomena.

Striptease culture, in this specific sense, will be found in confessional talk and debate shows; documentaries and 'docu-soaps' (as a particular sub-genre of obser-vational documentary became known in the late 1990s); in print media and on the internet – in all those mediated spaces, indeed, where people talk about or otherwise reveal aspects of their own and other's sexualities. In the 1990s these forms of 'sex talk' proliferated across the western media. Mark Simpson refers to the 'sex-confessional imperatives of the late twentieth century' (1996, p. 15). This chapter considers why they came into being and what they mean. Why do people choose to go naked into the public arena? Why are audiences attracted to the resulting texts? Why do media organisations devote so much of their resources to producing them?

Striptease culture: conditions and causes

The emergence of what I am calling striptease culture presupposes, firstly, that there is an audience whose members are, to some extent, voyeuristic; who are relatively comfortable adopting the position of spectators of other's confessional performances. A senior producer for the company which makes *Eurotrash* acknowledges that 'voyeurism is one of the staples of all television',[2] even that of the public service BBC. That there *is* such an audience of voyeurs is shown by the consistently high ratings achieved by these programmes.

If the phenomenon of striptease culture in mainstream media indicates a broad streak of voyeurism in western audiences (I focus on the UK here, but the forms of striptease culture discussed in this chapter are also present in the United States, western Europe, and the advanced capitalist societies of the Far East and Australasia), it also implies a sub-group within the population who are prepared to step forward and indulge the demands of mass voyeurism with confessional words and self-revelatory deeds. That there are many such individuals is shown by the sheer number of confessional programmes on western television, all dependent on voluntary participants. For the *Big Brother* series broadcast in 2000 there were 40,000 UK applicants for ten available places. The conceptually similar *Survivor* series, broadcast in the United States around the same time, provoked a comparable level of interest from the American public.

Striptease chic

A third precondition for the emergence of striptease culture, apart from the availability of the basic elements needed to make the production viable – audiences and participants/performers – is a regulatory environment, and a taste regime, receptive to the spectacle of ordinary people stripping off, physically or emotionally. Such a climate had been established by the mid-1990s, as part of the broader cultural sexualization explored in Chapters 3 and 4. Porno-chic and various forms of celebrity erotica sexualized the advertising and entertainment sectors of mainstream culture in the 1990s, as we have seen, and one dimension of these trends was a pop cultural interest in striptease. Paul Verhoeven's *Showgirls* (1996) and Alan Bergman's *Striptease* (1996) were big-budget cinematic products of this fascination, though the makers of both misjudged the extent to which merely showing the act of striptease could persuade cinema audiences to forgive poor film-making.

Striptease starred Demi Moore as a stripper, and though neither a critical nor commercial success, sparked much speculation on the cultural significance of the fact that Hollywood's then leading lady should be prepared to get her tits out for the lads, as it were. More so than *Showgirls*, which was received as a rather old-fashioned,

89

over-hyped product of the patriarchal male gaze (see previous chapter) Moore's aggressive championing of *Striptease*, and the display of her own body which was at its promotional heart, signalled a heightened mainstream interest in what had hitherto been perceived as the sleazy, sad world of strip clubs. Part of the reason for this interest was the reappraisal of sexualized female exhibitionism by feminists familiar with *Sex* and its related artefacts. These were prepared to view strippers as feisty independent souls rather than exploited victims, and to accept sympathetic portrayals of them in fictional and non-fictional contexts, even when authored by men. The leading character in the Carl Hiassen novel on which *Striptease* was based is unambiguously the romantic heroine of the story, and a figure meriting largely unreserved admiration on the part of the reader. Parallelling the positive reappraisal of porn industry performers implicit in porno-chic Hiassen's stripper, in the book and as played by Demi Moore, is doing a difficult job for decent money, in conditions which, if clearly not ideal, are hardly worse than those faced by the average worker. Her club-owning employer is not a vicious exploiter but, like Burt Reynolds's character in *Boogie Nights*, a benign protector. What sleaze there is in *Striptease* arises chiefly from the harassment of Moore's character by the drunken, sexually inadequate male spectator (again played by Burt Reynolds, in the second of his late 1990s cameos) who never looks like emerging triumphant from the narrative's twists and turns. The stripper in *Striptease* is a feminist, in short, who chooses the life she leads and makes no apology for it.[3]

Around the same time as *Striptease* was in the news Moore appeared on the front cover of *Vanity Fair*, naked and pregnant, setting off a vogue for public celebrity nakedness which carried through the rest of the decade and saw Sylvester Stallone and others adopting similarly exposed positions. In 2000 the rising Broadway star Alan Cumming pastiched the trick by posing naked in the edition of *Out* magazine in which he 'outed' himself. Throughout the late 1990s, too, the 'new lad' magazines like *Loaded*, *FHM* and *GQ* made increasing use of celebrity pin-ups on their front covers and photospreads. Television, movie and pop stars (usually female, of course) queued up to bare themselves in these magazines, aware that their huge circulations were a direct route to enhanced fame and fortune. In these titles posing nude lost its 'top shelf' stigma, and the resulting images were largely spared categorization as pornography (though the magazines were criticized for their contribution to the patriarchal 'backlash' – see Chapter 8).

Popular culture's love affair with striptease was cemented with the surprise cinematic hit of 1997, *The Full Monty* (Peter Cattaneo). Here, in a clever exploration of the 'men-in-crisis' mood of the late 1990s, striptease was, for the first time in mainstream cinema, presented as something which men did – reluctantly, at first, then with undeniable pride, despite the humiliations and objectifications experienced at the hands of their female spectators. In *The Full Monty*, like *Striptease*, stripping for money was framed as nothing to be ashamed of, but a rational choice in a culture where public nakedness has commercial value.

In the 1990s striptease also became something which artists did, and not just in the context of porno-chic (see previous chapter). A March 2001 British newspaper article profiled the 'stripping academic' Dr Cathy Macgregor, who for several years combined her career as a college lecturer with performing in English strip clubs, where she presented shows like 'Scarlett's Story: Part One'. Eventually, she emigrated to Florida and adopted lap dancing as a full-time occupation. For Dr Macgregor striptease made economic sense (she claimed to earn more in two days of performance than in a month of lecturing), but it also had political significance. As she put it, 'lapdancing is a logical step from my intellectual, feminist work. You are empowered. You choose where you work. You leave if you don't like it'.[4]

Political sleaze, celebrity scandal

If stripping became chic in the 1990s, that decade also saw an unprecedented degree of elite sexual exposure in the journalistic media. In Britain, as the Conservative government of John Major staggered through the years 1992 to 1997 it was engulfed in a wave of sex scandals which, because of their fundamental irreconcilability with Tory 'Back to Basics' propaganda, contributed substantially to the electoral success of Tony Blair's New Labour party in 1997.[5] Inevitably, the progress of these scandals brought into the public domain, through political journalism in both the elite and popular media, unfamiliar talk of autoerotic asphyxiation, love triangles, bi- and homosexuality, and children conceived outside of marriage. There had always been sex scandals in British politics, of course, but never had they been so visible or widely reported. Ironically, given its public commitment to a particular kind of family values, the 1992–7 Conservative government occasioned an unprecedented sexualization of the British public sphere.

In the United States a little later the Monica Lewinsky scandal flooded the media, not just in America but across the world with explicit references to, among other things, allegations of rape and sexual harassment, semen stains on a blue Gap dress, oral sex techniques, and the appropriate definition of 'sexual relations'. As I noted in my Introduction, Clinton's sexual misadventures were not different in kind from those of previous US presidents, most notoriously John F. Kennedy, but they *were* the first to be exposed to the full glare of media publicity, thence to become part of the real time news agenda as each episode in the saga unfolded (Figure 5.1).

The sexualization of political culture illustrated most dramatically by the Clinton–Lewinsky scandal was one consequence of the emergence of the internet, which by the late 1990s had seriously undermined the capacity of political elites to keep information secret. I have argued elsewhere that the construction of the internet ushered in an era of 'rapid and chaotic information flow, in which something as innocent as a White House blow job can be whipped into a major political crisis within hours' (McNair, 2000, p. 125). This was possible because, in the era of the internet, news reports of scandal (as of everything else) are spread around the world at the speed of light, bypassing official attempts at suppression or censorship. With the emergence of politically independent, anarchistically inclined websites like the Drudge Report, iconoclastic and irreverent, the private

Figure 5.1 Bill and Monica 1

lives of presidents and politicians, as well as other public figures hitherto protected from such scrutiny, became in the 1990s a staple of mainstream news and journalism in the capitalist world. The Starr Commission report on the Lewinsky affair received millions of hits when it was posted on the internet, and the book version was a bestseller.

Video technology also played its part in facilitating this expanded culture of voyeurism. In 1999 Bill Clinton's videotaped testimony before the Starr Commission became a global media event when, despite the president's understanding that it would remain confidential, it was transmitted in its entirety. In more than three hours of interrogation, shown more or less unedited (Figure 5.2), Clinton was stripped of his privacy and dignity before the entire world, obliged to disclose details of his relationship with a White House intern which he might reasonably have presumed to be forever their own private business. In an attempt to end the scandal in the summer of 1999 Clinton confessed his sins before the American people on television, providing another set of powerful video images and giving the narrative of sexual self-revelation in which he was the central character another plot twist.

Public interest in the sex lives of the rich and famous is not new, of course, and the journalistic indulgence of it dates back at least as far as the eighteenth century's scandalous news coverage of the affairs of European aristocrats. John Hartley observes that in early modern Europe 'sexual sensationalism [was used] above all in a tireless effort to prove that the old ruling classes were unfit to survive into the new age' (1996, p. 118). The modern form of tabloid celebrity journalism was pioneered in the 1920s gossip columns of Walter Winchell, and is similarly justified with reference to the democratizing power of elite exposure.[6] I leave the reader to judge for her or himself whether such news is empowering for audiences or not. Either way, journalistic exposures of the private lives of public figures have always sold newspapers and attracted television audiences. In the late twentieth century, as proliferating news outlets became more aggressive in their pursuit of those audiences, their reliance on celebrity scandal increased, culminating in such spectacles as Diana and Dodi's much-covered romance in July–August 1997, and the tragic paparazzi-provoked car crash which killed them both.

I will distinguish between the above examples of *involuntary* elite exposure and striptease culture in general, for one simple reason. The journalism of political sleaze and celebrity scandal can, as its victims often claim, be compared to a kind of rape, in so far as its subjects are not volunteers, and their appearances in the public sphere are the end product of unwelcome journalistic violation of their privacy. Although many celebrities play a mutually beneficial game of cat-and-mouse with the journalists, exchanging images of their naked bodies and private intimacies in return for the publicity on which celebrity is built, many others have not courted exposure, and their nakedness before the public is justifiably viewed as an unacceptable intrusion on their privacy. If it is true (and I think it is) that the news coverage of the Monica Lewinsky scandal can be defended with reference to the public's legitimate interest in the personal morality of the United States' president, such

Figure 5.2 Bill and Monica 2

justifications are not applicable to tabloid exposure of a British cabinet minister's homosexuality or a television soap star's parents' marital difficulties.[7] Journalistic exposure of private affairs can, in certain circumstances, be viewed as contributing to the maintenance of democratic accountability. In others no such defence is convincing, and there is no reasonable excuse (apart from the nakedly commercial) for making public what anyone, celebrity or not, has a right to expect to remain private. My advocacy of the democratizing potential of striptease culture is qualified by ethical considerations, therefore, and does not extend to the *involuntary* intrusion into private lives which is the staple of some news media.[8]

These forms of expository journalism are not striptease culture as I am defining it here, although the increased incidence of the former has been one of the environmental factors in which the latter became so noticeable a feature of contemporary media. In both, it is true, the line between public and private is eroded, indeed disappears – an erosion made more acute by the introduction of information technologies which evade official mechanisms of state censorship and control of knowledge. The same technological innovations which have made the pornosphere an increasingly unregulatable zone make the maintenance of a certain kind of privacy problematic. The increased prominence in the late twentieth century of a journalistic culture in which private, sexual affairs became part of public debate about entertainers, artists, politicians, leading business people – became carnivalesque spectacle, indeed, before a mass audience – is one manifestation of the same movement toward sexual self-revelation and confession which underpins the other forms of cultural striptease examined in this chapter. Crucially, however, the latter represent voluntary excursions into the public sphere by individuals who know – or should know (see below) – what they are getting into, and why they are getting into it.

The economics of striptease

None of this would have gone so far as it has done without the additional factor of increased competition between proliferating television and print media channels. As more television channels have come on air in the United States, Britain and elsewhere, and as more lifestyle magazines have been launched, the intra-media struggle for audience share has intensified. The 1997 arrival in Britain of the relatively low-budget Channel 5[9] raised the barriers of what was acceptable across the range of British television, and at the same time further fragmented the audience. Channel 4, which from its launch in the 1980s established its identity by claiming the terrain of the sexually transgressive, was now joined by the more conservative ITV (*Vice – the Sex Trade*) and BBC (*Naked*) in scheduling programmes which exploited the vogue for sexual self-revelation. Sex usually sells, we recall from the previous discussion of porno-chic, especially when it is perceived to be transgressive and taboo-breaking sex. 'Television's obsession with sexuality', wrote one critic, 'however perverted or salacious, is clearly ratings driven, because this stuff gets viewers'.[10] The economically driven sexualization of television was further fuelled by the introduction of new programme-making technologies such as lightweight digital cameras. These enabled the production of broadcast quality material involving an unprecedented degree of close-up intimacy between producers of documentaries and their subjects, and providing new possibilities for voyeurism by the audience. It was in this climate that the discussion of sexuality and its display moved decisively into the public sphere.

The people posing

One strand in striptease culture applied the fashion for celebrity nakedness and sexual self-objectification to the representation of 'ordinariness'. In 1999 the British Women's Institute – an organization not previously known for its interest in sexual controversy – published a calendar in which its members posed naked. The calendar's aim was to raise money for charity, which it did with considerable success. Though far from explicit, and photographed with sensitivity to the novelty of the experiment, the images were nonetheless unprecedentedly sexualized representations of 50-something, conservative Englishwomen, posing nude and looking quite at ease in their birthday suits. The calendar secured voluminous press coverage for its sexually transgressive qualities while signalling, perhaps more than any other single example of striptease culture in the 1990s, the nonchalance with which mainstream society – even its more conservative elements – now viewed public displays of nakedness.

In December 1999 Channel 5 broadcast *Naked London*, a documentary profiling the work of the American photographer Greg Friedler. Friedler specializes in nude images of ordinary people – 'all ages, shapes and sizes' – and had already produced *Naked New York* (1997) and *Naked Los Angeles* (1998). Those books confirmed that striptease culture was an international trend, which by 1999 had become the subject of mainstream televisual fare in both the United Kingdom and United States. In America, writes marketing economist D. Kirk Davidson, 'the popularity of such shows and such topics is beyond question. Competition among networks and among the production companies has become a matter of which show can introduce the most outlandish and the most titillating subject matter' (1996, p. 95). The documentary on Greg Friedler's work focused on his efforts to recruit 200 volunteers, and followed him into the studio so that those who were stripping off for his *Naked London* book were also appearing naked on British television. Friedler's demystificatory project, as revealed in the documentary, was to 'strip his subjects of their protective clothing. By contrasting the public image with the private, he hopes to reveal an inner truth.'

> Hopefully, it says the way you dress and what you do doesn't necessarily define who you are. It's all about humanity. It's all about showing the public the private side of people.

This aim was reflected in finished photographs which, like those of the Women's Institute, were closer to documentary than erotica in their flawed ordinariness; more anthropological than pornographic in their unflinching representation of the naked human form, unmanipulated and relatively unencumbered by cosmetic distortion.

The culture of confession

Encouraged further by the 1990s growth of self-help philosophies, therapeutic counselling and a general 'outing' of the self the trend toward self-revelation, both psychological and physical, found its natural home in the form of the confessional talk show. This genre, exemplified by the *Jerry Springer Show* in the United States and *Kilroy* in Britain, earned its label because its *raison d'être* was to secure from participants details of their lives which had until that point been secret. The talk shows encouraged people to reveal their feelings about what they and others had done – to confess with shame and repentance in some cases, to be defiant and proud in others. Not all of these confessions were sexual in content but the potentially risqué, often taboo nature of sexual revelation made it a staple of the heavily ratings-driven talk show format from the beginning. In America the *Jerry Springer* and *Ricki Lake* shows rarely talked about anything else, intensifying the tension inherent to the programme format by exposing participating members of the public to surprise revelations from their nearest and dearest. A man would 'come out' live on air, in front of his unsuspecting girlfriend; a woman would reveal that she was having an affair with her sister's husband, or her mother's boyfriend. Sometimes the subject matter was darker – sexual abuse and domestic violence were frequently addressed, for example. The genre's combination of voyeurism and surprise (what would the 'confessors' say? How would the recipients of the revelations react?) made the shows volatile and raucous, and highly successful in ratings terms. Many of them were exported abroad, or inspired imitations in overseas markets, like *Tricia* in the United Kingdom.

At the end of the 1990s questions were raised about the ethics of confessional culture when two American examples of the genre – presented by Jennifer Jones and Jerry Springer respectively – were linked to murder cases where revelations on the show were followed by fatal crimes of passion. On an edition of the *Jenny Jones Show* produced in 1995, a gay man's revelation of his sexual attraction to an unknowing straight acquaintance provoked a subsequent homophobic shooting. Then, in July 2000, on the *Jerry Springer Show* a no more than usually bad-tempered on-air argument between three members of a love triangle provoked an off-air murder. On the convincing evidence of these cases, it was suggested by critics, commercial criteria were being permitted to override the programme-makers' responsibilities for the welfare of their participants.

These examples are undoubtedly disturbing, and indicative of the consequences of an under-regulated culture of confession in a gun-worshipping society where individuals tend to shoot first and ask questions later. Elsewhere in the universe of the talk show, fortunately, sexual revelation has rarely been accompanied by such catastrophic results. On the contrary, a strong defence of the form is the space it provides for ordinary people to talk about issues of considerable (human) interest to them, and sex talk in particular; and its capacity, when sensitively directed, to give representation to the previously under-represented – to publicize that which has been not just private, but suppressed, repressed or oppressed into invisibility.

The concept of the public sphere as set out by the German sociologist Jurgen Habermas in his classic writings (1989) has rightly been criticized for its patriarchal bias. His public sphere is an arena of debate practically monopolized by men, whose political, economic and social superiority are reproduced in public discourse and media representation. The confessional talk show represents one programme format where male dominance has been much less obvious, and where the normatively preferred agenda of 'serious' politics and public life is replaced with popular human interest themes. While the production teams who make these shows retain the structural biases in favour of men which still characterize the media generally, there are many women involved at all levels, including in the frontline presentational roles. More importantly, the briefs within which these shows operate leads inevitably to those areas of experience in which females in patriarchal society can speak with acknowledged authority – the family and domestic environment; relationships with children, men, other women; emotional life. Where the traditional public sphere has focused on the male worlds of politics, economics and foreign affairs ('male' in the sense only that they have hitherto been dominated by men), the confessional talk show has prioritized the domestic worlds of women.

As women have moved out of the domestic sphere into the commanding heights of patriarchal society, raising issues about the reconcilability of paid work and motherhood, for example (see Chapter 2), or the appropriate sexual etiquette for women in a post-feminist world, the confessional talk show has addressed those subjects too. One edition of the *Scottish Women* series, for example, made by Scottish Television and broadcast in 1995, was devoted to the subject of female sexuality. At a time when such discussions were virtually unknown on mainstream television (or anywhere else in the non-feminist media for that matter), *Scottish Women* and its presenter Kaye Adams assembled one hundred female participants for what was at one and the same time a private (women only) and public (several hundred thousand viewers were watching) discussion of what turned women on; of what they could buy to spice up their sex lives, and where they could buy it. The programme provided space for and made visible hitherto marginalized voices and perspectives, and achieved this in its discussions of dozens of subjects over a period of years, of which only a small proportion were about sex and sexuality. In this sense, striptease culture is a sub-set of a wider culture of confession and public intimacy which spread through the western media in the 1990.

Scottish Women was the product of what was in the 1990s the still relatively protected environment of British public service broadcasting. Elsewhere in the televisual marketplace, however, and even where commercial pressures have been more acutely felt, the confessional talk show still constitutes a distinctively accessible, non-heterosexist, feminized discursive space. In the United States, Rikki Lake often uses her show to introduce issues of gay sexuality, child abuse, and other taboo topics. Talk shows of this kind, in short, have been just as much about the public exposure of things which should not have to remain hidden, as they have been about the commercially driven revelation of things better left unsaid. The mediated discussion of sexuality on talk shows has been the vehicle for a substantial feminization of the public sphere, and an enhanced presence within it of the voices and discourses which must, all other things remaining equal, contribute to the societal dissemination of progressive sexual politics. The presence of women speaking about women, or about their relationships with men – watched and listened to by audiences of men and women – cannot but add to the stock of knowledge and ideas used by people in their own personal lives. More recently, on 21 November 2000 Channel 4 broadcast a one-hour documentary on the subject of vibrators, consisting of women talking openly about their sexualities, and the benefits they had obtained from the use of dildos. The programme presented another space for female sexuality to be publicly recognized, discussed, and given voice. It also confirmed Channel 4's intention of providing a platform for the dissemination of 'sexual culture and other taboo subjects' to its niche audiences.[11]

Reality television

If sex became a staple subject of television talk shows in the late 1990s, documentary makers also found the subject of increasing interest. During this period British television broadcast dozens of documentaries with sex-related themes. There were documentaries about pornography, as the previous chapter noted, and about striptease itself. Echoing the reinterpretation of striptease led by Demi Moore and others, a wave of late 1990s documentaries about strippers and lap dancers applied a similarly revisionist approach to the subject. *Fantasy Club*, broadcast by Channel 4 in December 1999, followed the fortunes of six striptease artists working at a club in the northern Scottish city of Aberdeen. Mixed up with footage of the girls at home and work was a narrative about why people become strippers, how they were treated by employers and customers, and how they related to each other. Not since Roland Barthes's famous essay on the semiotics of the form[12] had striptease attracted so much serious critical attention.

Fantasy Club was one of the first products of new digital video recording technologies introduced by production companies in the late 1990s – lightweight cameras which allow fly-on-the-wall documentaries and docu-soaps to be made with the minimum number of human operators actually present in the space under observation. Digital video cameras have made documentaries cheaper to make, and they have also allowed greater flexibility and intimacy on the part of programme makers. In *Fantasy Club*, for example, the cameraman – one individual who filmed the lives of his subjects over a period of weeks – followed the girls into their bathrooms, bedrooms, and changing rooms, eavesdropping on conversations about sex and breast size, and recording the girls' interactions with each other. From inside the Fantasy Club itself, CCTV cameras provided footage of the strippers' performances, which were mixed in with the digital video footage throughout the documentary.

Fantasy Club's non-judgemental take on striptease was a part of the ongoing reappraisal of traditionally stigmatized individuals and activities which has accompanied the sexualization of contemporary capitalist culture. In a post-*Full Monty* environment *Fantasy Club* staked its claim as old-fashioned, fly-on-the wall documentary, giving voice and visibility to a group of workers usually excluded from access to the media in anything other than their objectified role as strippers. They talked, explained their motivations, criticized their bosses, clients and each other, fought and fell out. On the face of it, there is no good reason why the phenomenon of striptease should not be exposed to the attentions of documentary makers, using the same techniques as were applied in docu-soaps throughout the 1990s to hotels, airports, cruise ships and other working environments. *Fantasy Club* delivered new information about the nature of striptease as a profession, and if some of that information was combined with nudity, that is in the nature of striptease.

Of course, the opportunity to transmit nude and semi-nude footage of attractive young women for what could have been expected to be a predominantly male audience is a powerful motive in the making of a programme like *Fantasy Club* (and the many others about various aspects of striptease which have followed it[13]). Scenes such as those shot in the girls' bathtub were 'titillating' by any standards, and were presumably intended to be. For this reason *Fantasy Club* and other documentaries with a similar content have been condemned as voyeuristic, on the assumption that the encouragement of voyeurism is in itself sufficient to justify condemnation. As we have seen, however, this can no longer be a taken for granted foundation stone of mainstream cultural criticism, nor even of that coming from the feminist movement, substantial elements of which have advocated the re-evaluation of striptease and the sexual objectification which it literally embodies. The equation of sex worker with 'victim' or 'exploited' no longer holds true, whether it be in a Hollywood movie like *Striptease*, a short film about a New York strip club for lesbians shown as part of Channel 4's *Red Light Zone* in 1995 or in published accounts like *Sex Work* (Delacoste and Alexander, eds., 1988). An interview with the manager of Fantasy Club revealed that strippers could earn many hundreds, indeed thousands of pounds on a good evening, a degree of renumeration which stands in sharp contrast to the pittance wages paid to many workers in less stigmatized jobs. In the case of *Fantasy Club* and the other programmes mentioned here, the film-makers appeared to be acting with the full and informed consent of their subjects. In documentaries of this type, the degree of power extended to participants by producers must be a factor in how they are read by critics.

Similar arguments apply to the more ambitious *Fetish*, directed by Nick Broomfield and given a cinematic release in 1997. A television showing followed in 1998, in one of Channel 4's frequent late-1990s slabs of 'adult' programming. *Fetish* was similar in style and tone to Louis Theroux's *Weird Weekends* on the pornography industry, placing the documentary-maker firmly at the heart of his subject, and even participating in it. In the end, Broomfield chickened out of the good thrashing that his s&m specializing subjects wanted to give him, but otherwise his personal involvement in the narrative was characteristically enthusiastic. In *Fetish*, footage of men being strung up, whipped and generally abused (all consensually, of course) was integrated into a serious examination of why they did so, and why these women were prepared to indulge sexual fantasies of this kind. A hitherto secret world was exposed and explored. Beeban Kidron's 1994 film *Pimps, Hookers, Hustlers, and their Johns* adopted a similar approach to the more down-market world of low rent prostitution, exploring the motivation of all the participants in the sexual transaction. In contrast to Broomfield's funny, non-judgemental film, Kidron's study portrayed a sordid, exploitative world populated with sad, pathetic men and crack-addicted prostitutes.

The darker, deviant side of human sexuality (as defined by comparison with what mainstream culture had traditionally presented as 'normal) was also addressed in British television series such as *Vice – The Sex Industry*, an examination of prostitution and the men who use it, and *Adult Lives*, a similarly themed trawl through the sexual deviations of the average Englishman. A 1995 BBC2 documentary looked at paraphilia – the term given to 'bizarre' sexual perversions such as necrophilia. The *Bangkok Bound* series, transmitted on Channel 4 in 1999, contained a series of short segments about various forms of sexual deviance, all linked by their connection with Thailand. One programme followed a middle-aged, middle class English jeweller to Bangkok, where he rendezvoused with his male lover. His wife, also filmed, sent him happily on his way and waited patiently at home in England, apparently unconcerned by her husband's need for this regular break from heterosexual normality in the exotic east.

The internet

The coming of the internet, I noted above, made the private lives of elites public in new and sometimes unwelcome ways. It also provided new ways for non-celebrities to voluntarily make their lives public. From the mid-1990s onwards, the accessability of cheap web cameras allowed internet sites to be constructed which included live, moving images of a person going about his or her daily business, which were then fed into the growing global community of internet users. Some of these sites were straightforwardly pornographic, in so far as they functioned as masturbatory aids for those who paid for access to them. Women (and less often, men) performed striptease before the camera, or provided a specific sexual performance at the request of the user. Others stressed their asexual ordinariness. One might see a woman taking her clothes off, or strolling around her bedroom in bra and knickers, and there may well have been an erotic charge to those images, but the pornographic content, if present at all, was complementary to the broader aim of showing life 'as it is lived'. Webcasts typically lacked narrative and plot, offering instead an ongoing real-time eavesdrop on the intimate environment of its subject, or 'star', as many of them became. And why not? As one writer puts it:

> Exhibitionism used to require leaving the house dressed in such a way
> as to increase the risk of being spat at in the street – or at least booed

at by a studio audience. Exposing yourself in the safety and comfort of your own home is something different: it is the nearest ordinary people have ever come to documenting their own lives alongside those of kings, queens and the previously under-challenged writers of history.[14]

The first, and still most successful of these sites was www.jennicam.com, which was launched in 1996 and in 2000 was promoting itself as

A real-time look into the real life of a young woman; an undramatized photographic diary for public viewing.

Opening on to Jenni's page the user finds a gallery of video stills depicting scenes from her domestic environment – Jenni in the shower; Jenni sleeping; Jenni eating. While there is a certain amount of nudity in these images, they are not obviously erotic, and certainly not pornographic. Along with the written version of her journal, the images simply give an account of this woman's life, in all its ordinariness. Some sites, like UK Dolls,[15] build an elaborate architecture of pay-per-view watching which may be intended to culminate in masturbation. Others, like Jenni-cam, exist on the basis that watching what other people do in their private space is inherently interesting. The proprietor of one site, UK Cam Girl (www.ukcamgirl.org), recounts how its popularity grew (800–1,000 hits per day as of September 2000) as 'it has become the norm for workers to watch webcams in the office on those long, boring afternoons'.[16] By the year 2000 there was even a Top 100 Girls with Cams listing.[17]

Fly-on-the-wall reality television

In 2000 the interactive power of the internet was extended to a new type of television programme, which combined use of the live webcam with elements of the docu-soap and game show formats. In America, NBC broadcast *Survivor*, and in Britain, Channel 4 showed *Big Brother*. Originating in Holland before exporting to Spain and the United Kingdom in the summer of 2000, *Big Brother* placed ten people in a controlled, rule-governed environment – 'Big Brother house' – and then asked them to live with each other for ten weeks, pausing only to nominate two of their number for eviction every seven days, until one emerged triumphant to claim the £70,000 prize.

Daily updates covered the progress of the group, summarizing their evolving relationships and interpersonal dynamics with footage edited by the producers. Some of this footage had a mildly sexual content – members of the household were filmed taking showers; taking their clothes off or putting them on; flirting with each other – but sexual revelation was only one, incidental element of a show which was really about individual and group psychology. The game show elements of *Big Brother* resided in the contestants' efforts to avoid nomination by their peers, and in the audience's power to vote on nominations and to decide who would stay or go.

The originality of *Big Brother* lay in its use of live cameras, connected to the internet, which allowed members of the public to eavesdrop on events in real time, accessing footage which was unedited by the production team. Events happening on web camera acquired a value and interest of their own (as when 'Nasty Nick' was shown being ejected from the house for breaking the rules, several hours before the event was shown, in edited form, and with added commentary, on television), and the programme series was the first in Britain to exploit something of the potential of the internet when used in conjunction with television. In doing so, it highlighted the prominence of striptease in the British media, and prompted another wave of critical commentary on the evils of confessional culture. One observer complained of revelatory television in general that 'instead of becoming famous for doing something, these outings in self-exposure grant their participants the consolation prize of becoming famous merely for being'.[18]

The ethics of confessional culture

The motivations of those who participate in public access programmes of this type, whether they contain a sexual dimension or not, have been examined in research carried out at Stirling University for the Broadcasting Standards Commission.[19] This found that while straightforward exhibitionism, often linked to the possibility of becoming famous (even if only for Warhol's fifteen minutes), is a motive for some, many participants wanted the opportunity to raise awareness of an issue, or to increase the public visibility of a hitherto marginalized social group. In *sex*-oriented public access programming in particular (a sub-set of reality television), the desire to talk about one's own or another's 'deviant' or little understood form of sexuality, and thus to increase societal tolerance or acceptance of it, is often a powerful motive. The finding that non-celebrity participants in media 'performances' have mixed motivations, most of which are non-pecuniary, civic-minded and altruistic, is supported by the experience of the photographer Greg Friedler whose work (nude images of ordinary people, assembled in volumes like *Naked New York, Naked Los Angeles*, and *Naked London*) was profiled in one of the documentaries defined as striptease culture above.

> A lot of people told me they did it [answered his advertisements and stripped for his camera] for the sake of art, and they supported what I was doing. Other people did it because they were exhibitionists and somehow got a rise out of it. A lot of people did it because they were lonely, and wanted to know that someone cared, even in the oddest way.[20]

The frank, self-revelatory confessions contained in striptease culture provoked another criticism: that in their encouragement of hasty self-revelation and self-exposure, such spectacles endanger their participants as well as degrading those members of the voyeuristic audience who become engrossed in them. Even if the participants in striptease culture are consenting adult volunteers freely choosing to participate for reasons of their own, it is argued, it is not necessarily in their best interests to allow them to do so, and the producers of the programmes have a responsibility to intervene where necessary. In an attempted exposé of *Big Brother* (it is probably only coincidence that the Channel 4 series was the undisputed broadcasting event of 2000, in contrast to the relative failure of the BBC's more conventionally worthy version of striptease culture, *Castaways*) the BBC's *Panorama* current affairs strand quoted one academic who suggested that 'it damages them [the participants] as much as it damages us [the viewers]'.[21] In fact, participation in *Big Brother* benefited both the careers and bank balances of the lucky few who made it through the application process. Book-writing, television presenting (both Nasty Nick), pop music (Craig), and modelling for style magazines (Mel and Anna) were just some of the opportunities coming the way of the *Big Brother* participants after the conclusion of the show.

Both this programme and a subsequent documentary on confessional culture broadcast by Channel 4[22] presented anecdotal testimony from participants on *Big Brother* and other shows which accused the programme-makers of manipulation and dishonesty. Such allegations are a common reaction to the experience of media exposure by individuals who do not feel that they came over quite as well as they had expected. On the other hand, the homicides associated with the *Jenny Jones* and *Jerry Springer* shows present more persuasive evidence in favour of caution around confessional culture, illustrating in the most dramatic form how televised revelations can have substantial negative effects on the lives of participants once they return to the world beyond the media. As already noted, the presence of firearms in the mix makes the American experience distinctive. In Britain the example of 'Nasty Nick' from *Big Brother* might be cited as a less tragic illustration of how an individual can reveal more about themselves than hindsight might deem wise. In Nick Bateman's case, post-*Big Brother* opportunities to make money from tabloid newspapers, advertising and others willing to pay to capitalize on his brief fame may have been sufficient to compensate for his media-fuelled status as a national hate figure. The prostitutes and their clients featured in the documentaries discussed above received no such compensation. They may have agreed to be involved, but should they have been allowed to offer themselves up to so intimate a public examination?

Previous research in which the author was involved approached this question with regard to British public participation programmes in general (i.e., not only those with a sexual content), and concluded that there were no legal, ethical or moral grounds on which to prevent consenting adults from appearing on screen to talk about themselves, *unless* third parties (such as children, other relatives and friends) were involved without *their* consent (Hibberd *et al.*, 2000). Exhibitionism, emotional or physical, as much as the desire to claim space for hitherto under-represented communities and identities, are motivations for participation in striptease culture with which we can agree or disagree, approve or disapprove. It is paternalism of the worst kind, and untenable in the twenty-first century, for self-appointed moral regulators to claim the right to police that participation, and even to prevent it, merely because it is felt that participants need 'protection' from themselves.

The research also concluded, however, that programme-makers had a clear responsibility to ensure that consent was genuinely *informed* – that is, that participants were adequately briefed in advance of their appearances as to the nature of their contribution and its function within the programme to which they were contributing. Assurances should be given, preferably in writing, that contributions made for one purpose would not be used for another. Participants should know what to expect, in other words, when they agreed to take part in such displays. They should also be given the opportunity to change their minds, if they decide after due consideration that this particular form of self-revelation is not for them. And they should be fully briefed on the potential consequences, to themselves and others, of appearing on television (or radio, for that matter). One of the key findings of the Stirling research was that, due to increasing competitive pressures on producers and broadcasters – the same pressures, we recall, which have given these programme formats much of their attractiveness – the resources required to deliver informed consent in the way I have defined it are not always available. There is, in short, evidence of corner-cutting in the production of at least some of these programes which could lead to participants putting themselves and others at risk of emotional or even physical harm. There is a role for regulation in these forms of striptease culture, then – not the regulation of an individual's choice as to whether he or she appears or not, but the regulation of the production process so that those who do appear know what they are getting into, and what the consequences of their appearing 'naked' in the media might be.

Watching the defectives?

And what, finally, of the voyeuristic audience, without whom these programes could not exist? *Does* watching reality television damage us? And even if it does not, do we have the right to eavesdrop on what are often painfully intimate displays, offered up by individuals who may (and with the best will in the world) not be in full possession of sound judgement as to their own best interests? One of the programmes referred to above – *Adult Lives* – was described on its transmission as 'a freak show that adopts the language of the porn business'.[23] The choice of language reveals the disgust often provoked among critics at both the participants in, and the spectators of, these programmes. The BBC presenter Anna Ford cited the following as evidence of the tasteless excesses of some of these programmes, and put the question asked by many critics of confessional culture.

> Recently, ITV, in *Vice – The Sex Trade*, featured prostitutes at 9p.m. One, a woman who treated men as babies, dressed them in nappies and breastfed them. She worked from home, happy to let her own child share her ample breasts with her odd clients. A wet-nurse to the

emotionally damaged, whose husband runs the business and, I presume, takes the money. But the powerlessness of this pathetic sex-slave was not the subject of the programme. Pure peep-show voyeurism showed her on the phone, telling a client that she could fill a pint glass from her breasts, and later feeding him.

There was a beautiful 18-year-old, rigid with tension as she described the utter revulsion she feels for the men who use her. Abused when in care, her only solace comes from the things she can now afford, bought with the money earned from sexual services sold in an alleyway. What was the justification for a series that appears to have no aim beyond peering at these sad victims of an already unpleasant and exploitative life?[24]

The same question might be just as validly be asked of documentaries about starving nomads in Africa, however, or news coverage of atrocities in the former Yugoslavia. What is the justification for our being exposed to those images of dead and dying human beings, other than to raise our awareness of their plight beyond what any individual sitting at home can realistically do to alleviate it? Does the fact that we are powerless before the spectacle of mass starvation or racist war crime mean that we should be prevented from seeing it?

Some critics seemed unsure of whether they should welcome striptease culture as a significant democratizing phenomenon, or condemn it as offensive trash. Anna Ford expressed this ambivalence in her comments, recognizing that, on the one hand:

Perhaps it's all part of the struggle to be free of the embarrassment and pain of Anglo-Saxon inhibitions. In this, the media may be acting as the brutal advance guard for a society in the throes of great changes, and its genuine wish to be more open about our sexual natures.

And on the other:

Are we on the right track, and simply struggling through the primeval slime before we emerge into the sunlight? Is it a cleansing process to hear the worst words, witness the crudest sex, and giggle at the worst perversions, before switching off having found a new maturity? Or should we now stand up and say, 'Enough'? We, the public, will no longer buy, read or watch this corrosive stuff.[25]

Presenting the choice as an either/or one is misleading since 'we, the public' can already 'switch off' by simply choosing not to consume striptease culture. As it is, programmes like *Vice* and *Adult Lives* are watched by significant, but not huge, audiences. Many viewers are either insufficiently interested in the subject to make time for it in their viewing schedule, or too embarrassed to watch, and they are clearly under no obligation to do so. Few, it would appear from the Broadcasting Standards Commission's *Sex and Sensibility* report, are actually offended. Consistent with public attitudes to film censorship noted in Chapter 3 the BSC's own 1998–9 *Monitoring Report* found that portrayals of sex on British television were of less concern to viewers than images of violence and the use of bad language. The prime-time, full-frontal image of a naked male actor in the BBC's *Tom Jones* drama series broadcast in 1997 attracted only ten complaints to the regulator. Even the images of a naked Keith Chegwin on a Channel 5 game show, itself an attempt to pastiche striptease culture, passed without adverse critical commentary from any but the most predictable of sources. The BSC's 1999 survey of viewers found that, although complaints about sex had increased by 60 per cent since 1998, they amounted to only 22 per cent of all complaints made to the regulator (693 of approximately 3000). Not only did 78 per cent of viewers think the portrayal of sex was acceptable; 64 per cent of the BSC's sample believed it was a *necessary* element of contemporary cultural life. The former director of the British Board of Film Classification James Ferman argues on the basis of this and other evidence that:

> Our society has moved in the direction of being relaxed about sex. Sex is not a big hang-up anymore, as it was twenty or thirty years ago, and as people have begun to be relaxed about it they've begun to be relaxed about portrayals of it. I think this is simply a fact of life. It's happened not only in Britain, it's happened in every country in the western world.[26]

In this context the explosion of striptease culture can be viewed as a marker of changing social attitudes and tastes, democratizing not only in its opening up of the public sphere to a broader set of perspectives and interests than have traditionally found representation there, but also in its challenge to the censorial paternalism which characterised the regulation of British broadcasting for the previous seven decades of its existence. To this extent, striptease culture has been a means of allowing television's social power and influence to be employed in a positive direction. The documentary producer John Willis argues that:

> Sex is a central feature of our lives and needs to be portrayed as an integral part of our relationships. It would be retrograde to turn the clock back to the secretive world of the past where sex was sordid and swept under the television carpet. Broadcasting has played a wonderful role in de-stigmatising areas of sexual behaviour, particularly homosexuality [see chapter on 'The Mainstreaming of Gayness'], and contributing to open debate about a whole range of issues.[27]

Striptease culture has been controversial, not because it bears any comparison to what Chapter 3 defined as pornography (although, like porno-chic, it has frequently been denounced as 'pornographic') but principally because of the challenge it poses to a demarcation just as important in western societies as that which has separated the obscene from the not-obscene. Striptease culture makes public that which has traditionally been restricted to the private sphere, and opens up a space hitherto monopolized by male, heterosexual elites to women, gays, and other once marginalized groups. To characterize that as 'dumbing down' or some other species of cultural degeneration is a familiar reaction to that opening up by precisely those elites who have seen their exclusive right to define the shape of the public sphere questioned.

Controversy may also be a product of the fact that the amateurishness of the performances in striptease culture lend the voyeurism they encourage a heightened quality of transgressiveness, since we are seeing things which it may not be decent for us to see – imperfect, ageing bodies in the case of the Women's Institute and *Naked London* photos, as opposed to the glossy, air-brushed displays of Madonna, Koons or Demi Moore; the naïve, unrehearsed revelations of ordinary people on talk shows or on *Big Brother*, as opposed to the PR-honed, market-tempered confessions of the stars. Striptease culture is the real thing, and it can be difficult and uncomfortable to watch, in a way that the pleasing images of porno-chic, or the anonymous writhings of the truly pornographic may not be. Striptease culture is not the occasion for parades of gamine supermodels and designer-trained Adonises, but of imperfectly ordinary people with perfectly ordinary perversions and sexual idiosyncrasies, no more real but certainly more representative of humanity in general than the idealized stereotypes which populate large tracts of our sexual culture. We want those pleasing stereotypes, to be sure, and they have their place in our aspirational sexual culture, but they no longer monopolize it.

More than that, though, striptease culture has been a vehicle for what John Hartley calls 'the democratisation of the public sphere', a process conducted, in his words, '*through the media* of feminisation and sexualisation' (1998, p. 14) (his emphasis). Part of a wider late twentieth-century trend towards the prioritization of 'human interest' in the media, striptease culture is one specific manifestation of the *privatization* of the public sphere; the turning over of at least some of its discursive space to the human interests of the people, as opposed to its long-standing monopolization by the public interests of elites. We may not always like what the people do with that access when they get it, but such is cultural democracy. Get used to it.

Part 2

Sexual representation

Introduction

If, as I have argued, the sexualization of culture is as much related to broad social change as it has been a product of ground-breaking new technologies and commercial imperatives; if it is as much evidence of progress in sexual politics as it is a vehicle for patriarchal backlash and reaction, then one would expect to see that reflected in the representations of gender disseminated through the media. These are structured by ideas about how men and women, gay and straight, do and should relate to each other and themselves.

My assumption in the three essays which make up Part II is that media representations have a triple function. First, they reveal what sexual and behavioural norms are in a given society at a given moment, even if these norms are more or less removed from how people actually live. They are to that extent also a source of aspirational fantasy.

This leads to their second, more didactic, function as bearers of ideology. We learn from media culture (alongside school, the family, and the pressures to social conformity emanating from our peers) something of our roles, rights and responsibilities in the sexual as in other arenas. This learning does not take place in a vacuum, of course, but in an environment shaped by the twists and turns of sexual politics and their cumulative effects on all aspects of our lives. In both of these functions the media are promoters of sex and gender roles, demonstrating what *is* and modelling what *might* be.

And third, in their existence as commodities, media representations distribute ideas about sexuality. They circulate in a cultural marketplace of relatively well-informed, politically sophisticated, choice-rich consumers who will not respond favourably to images of themselves they regard as offensive or patronising. Representations have an ideological function, but must also resonate with where we are as individuals, as sexual communities and as societies (and not necessarily where establishments, patriarchal or otherwise, would like us to be). They communicate ideas not only in a top-down direction, but bottom-up and side-to-side. The media, in short, both *affect* and *reflect* social relations, and do so in an environment where we have the power to endorse, reject, or modify their messages according to 'decoding' responses conditioned by our individual circumstances. They engage us in an ongoing negotiation between the real (how we live) and the ideal (how the media portray us as living); between the normative and the representative, the humdrum and the fantasy.

Resolving these tensions leads to ambivalence and contradiction in media content, and the following essays generally avoid the discussion of representation in terms of 'good' or 'bad' where 'good' is defined as the positive (but just as unreal) counterweight to the negative stereotype (the 'bad'). Endless images of nice, gentle queers victimized by cruel homophobes are just as unrepresentative as the legions of limp-wristed, double-entendre-cracking poofs who used to populate telly sitcom land. Likewise, portrayals of relentlessly predatory men placed alongside saintly women bear scant resemblance to the complexities of masculinity and femininity as experienced by people in the real world. Recognition of this ambivalence, and an assumption that the contemporary audience has the capacity to be aware of and even take pleasure in it, informs my critical strategy. Rather than seeking to demonstrate by tortuous textual analysis that the symbolic dice are always and everywhere loaded against the subordinate strata of patriarchy I look for the cracks, the moments of quiet subversion, the cultural echoes of the sexual realignments I have previously identified in the discussions of pornography and porno-chic, in striptease culture and in art.

Bell hooks put it well, I think, in an essay accompanying the 1994 exhibition *Black Male: Representations of Masculinity in Contemporary American Art*, so let me end this brief introduction with her appeal for imagination and daring in the critical project.

> For those of us who dare to desire differently, who seek to look away from the conventional ways of seeing . . . the issue of representation is not just a question of critiquing the status quo. It is also about transforming the image, creating alternatives, asking ourselves questions about what types of images subvert, pose critical alternatives, transform our worldviews and move us away from dualistic thinking about good and bad.[1]

6

'WOMEN, KNOW YOUR LIMITS!'

As recently as 1995 influential culture analyst Richard Dyer could argue, with little fear of contradiction from his academic peers, that the representation of women in the mass media amounted to 'a relentless parade of insults' (p. 1). Dyer's choice of language was overdone (things have never been so black and white as his phrasing suggests), but the essence of the argument will be accepted by most students of the media: that depictions of women in patriarchal culture have reflected their subordinate sexual, political and socio-economic status. So common-place has it become that now, in the parodic-nostalgic style of postmodernity, the feminist critique of patriarchy culture has become part of prime-time culture. A comic pastiche by the British comedian Harry Enfield of the post-World War II public information film refers to the crude sexism of an era still well within the memories of many women alive today. The scene opens around a middle-class dinner-party conversation. The men are discussing the merits of 'the gold standard', as their wives listen silently. Then one of the women dares to make a contribution.

Daphne: I think the government should stay off the gold standard, so that the pound can reach a level that would keep our exports competitive.

Narrator: The lady has famously attempted to join the conversation with a wild and dangerous opinion of her own. What half-baked drivel! See how the men look at her with utter contempt.

Husband: Daphne, we're going home.

Narrator: Women, know your limits! Look at the effect of education on a man and a woman's mind. Education passes into the mind of a man. See how the information is evenly and tidily stored. Now see the same thing on a woman. At first we see a similar result, but now look. Still at a reasonably low level of education her brain suddenly overloads. She cannot take in complicated information. She becomes frantically and absurdly deranged.

Look at these venomous harridans. They went to university. Hard to believe they're all under twenty-five. Yes, over-education leads to ugliness, premature ageing, and beard growth. Women, know your

113

limits! In thought be plain and simple, and let your natural sweetness shine through.

The joke works – and my female students laugh as much as their male counterparts when I show them this clip – because the audience understands that, if this is how things used to be, the world is now a very different place. By the beginning of the twenty-first century the achievements of second-wave feminism had created a climate in which women could enjoy the flirtation with base sexism frequently engaged in by Enfield and other comedians, both male and female. Images which twenty years ago would have provoked a riot in the lecture theatre, or pickets at the doors of the BBC, were now accepted as belonging to an era which had gone and at which, from this distance, women and men alike could safely chuckle.

Enfield's sketch exaggerates for effect, of course. Even in the period when it is set, and long before the influence of fully formed feminist ideas came to be felt on the media, rumblings of discontent were beginning to be heard about the cultural prejudices and social expectations imposed upon women as more and more of them entered the world of paid employment. Two contributions to the letters page of *Woman* magazine on 10 June 1950 illustrate the misgivings experienced by many.

Well-groomed brain
Why is it people believe that women who take an interest in clothes are bound to be nitwits? I am twenty-one and pride myself on being something of an intellectual. Yet I have learned that some of my middle-aged colleagues consider it damaging to my hopes of a career that I am also clothes-conscious. They say that an interest in clothes indicates a *typically frivolous feminine mind*. Since I devote most of my evenings, as well as my working day, to literary pursuits, it seems hard if I can't spend a lunch hour nylon-hunting or hat-chasing without being called a moron. If I want to be a career woman must I also be an old frump?
(Miss M.C., Sidcup) (my emphasis)

The plain truth
By the time I was eight years old I knew I was a plain child, and by the time I was eighteen, I had already asked myself, 'What man will want to marry me?' – and answered by becoming a career girl. When I was twenty-one I was married, six weeks after our first date. Even my husband never said I was pretty, but he had a way of looking at me that made me wish I had been a raving beauty, just so I could deserve such a look. I'm still plain, but at over thirty it doesn't matter so much – nothing I can do will basically alter my face, and if people don't like it, well, it's just too bad. As one plain girl to another, I would say: 'Don't set the value on yourself too low – there is nothing as unattractive as lack of confidence'.

(Jane, Croydon)

These letters anticipate 'Cosmo woman' by ten years. They are written by women who work and want to look good, and resent the societal expectation that they can't do both; women who expect to be allowed to spend money on their appearance, yet still be taken seriously; who are aware that their lack of confidence may be just as much of a handicap as anything men might do to or think about them. By the 1950s, if these letters can be taken as any kind of evidence, the growing economic power of the female wage labourer was coming into conflict with her subordinate social status, leading to still muted but significant expressions of discontent. As that discontent intensified over subsequent decades, the designers and manufacturers of goods and services for which women made up substantial markets were required to adapt to a quite different competitive environment from that to which they had been used. Changes at the socio-economic level had to be reflected in those spheres of capitalism which were sensitive to the resultant changes in tastes and desires. As women became consumers not merely of household cleaning products and foodstuffs but clothes, cars and holidays, advertising 'had to adapt itself to the effects of feminism, for the simple reason that its mission in life is to sell things to people – particularly women, and including feminists' (McKenzie, 1998, p. 85).

In the 1950s advertising still projected a notion of femininity as a precious mix of the fragrant and the chaste. By the late 1960s and early 1970s it reflected a more liberal, if still pre-feminist environment, where women's bodies were frequently displayed in poses combining both passivity and sexual availability. During this period, as Chapter 2 noted, the feminist critique of advertising as a key vehicle in the dissemination of patriarchal ideology (second in offensiveness only to pornography) first developed, in response to images which seemed to signify women's sexual and social subordination while at the same time freeing men to be more aggressive predators. Women in these advertisements were allowed to be sexy, but remained as much a thing to be owned by men as the commodities they were associated with. The social anthropologist Erving Goffman's forensic analysis of the representation of gender in 1970s advertising noted the use of the sexualized female body, and also identified what he called 'the ritualisation of subordination' typical of the era.

> Elevation seems to be employed indicatively in our society, high physical place symbolising high social place. . . . In contrived scenes in advertisements, men tend to be located higher than women. The resulting configurations can be read as an acceptance of subordination, an expression of ingratiation, submissiveness, and appeasement.
>
> (1976, p. 47)

As feminist ideas circulated and gained influence, however, images began to be more closely policed. The critique of sexism began to register on the advertising industry (as in due course, and for the same reasons, would the critique of racism), which recognized that such spectacles as semi-naked females being used to sell everything from mustard to cars and window frames no longer resonated with the young, affluent, professional women (or men, for that matter) to whom they were directing their campaigns (the character played by Mel Gibson in the hit movie *What Women Want* (Nancy Meyers, 2000) goes through this self-revelation, assisted by the device of having him read women's minds). By the late 1980s straight commercial advertising (that which wanted to be perceived as cutting edge, at least) was obliged to reflect the fact that women now had an improved economic, social and political status within patriarchal society. More women than ever before were wage earners as well as housewives, persons of independent economic means who could spend and consume with relative freedom; active participants in a burgeoning leisure and sexual culture, free of the reproductive constraints of their mothers and grandmothers; increasingly likely to be aware of sexual politics and feminism (even if they were not activists), and expecting to be accorded appropriate respect. No longer were cars sold with images of luscious lovelies draped across their bonnets, but with ads in which high-kicking, sexually demanding women were holding the keys or behind the wheel, reminding us that 'size matters' and warning their male partners to 'Ask before you borrow it.'

This didn't mean that the use of the sexualized female body in advertising disappeared; only that its meaning changed. Echoing trends in other branches of popular culture, advertising in the late 1980s and 1990s increasingly deployed women in a manner which sought to reconcile the commercially important truism that sex sells with the representational sensitivities demanded by a new political environment. Paralleling Madonna's use of her body to flirt with the conventions of pornography (and provoking the same debates as to the meaning and 'correct' interpretation of the images) women in these ads were often portrayed as assertive, even aggressive sexual animals. In contrast to the unreflexive objectification of the 1970s women were represented in these images as active and even dominant; the proud bearers of both sexual citizenship and consumer sovereignty.

These ads objectified the female body, then, but in a reception environment where the target audience could be expected to know what sexism was, and to agree that it was in general a bad thing. They declared that in a culture familiar with the feminist critique of sexism a new context had emerged in which sexualized looking was permitted, and that the women thus looked at were not necessarily the victims, actual or potential, of predatory masculinity. They were ironic, assuming a media literate audience able to take a joke.

Some didn't see it that way, however. Late 2000 saw British magazines and billboards adorned with the nude, airbrushed figure of supermodel Sophie Dahl, promoting Opium perfume. In the photograph, taken by Steven Meisel, one hand is placed over her left breast (the right, with nipple barely visible, is exposed). Her legs are raised and slightly parted. She wears expensive jewellery and gold, high-heeled shoes. The whiteness of her skin contrasts with a shock of red hair, green eye shadow and red lips, the latter opened and conveying a sense of sexual self-absorption. A standard semiological reading would recognize here the attempt to transfer this quality to the perfume, and thus to associate it with the promise of sexual pleasure for the women who will wear it. Although Dahl was being widely praised around this time as a positive counter-balance to the ultra-thin look favoured by many of her professional colleagues (see below), critics read the image as old-fashioned sexism. After receiving several hundred complaints from women claiming to be offended by the ad, the Advertising Standards Authority ordered it to be withdrawn, leading Libby Brooks of the *Guardian* to wonder what all the fuss was about.

> Compare Dahl's hungrily parted legs with the Barbie doll blankness of Claudia Schiffer [in an ad campaign for the Danish department store Hermes, where she appears before the viewer in various sets of lingerie] the embodiment of female sexual passivity. In her pretty pastel bra and knickers she is slutty, but not too slutty, eager to please, eager to satisfy – and as challenging as a blow-up doll.[1]

The Opium ad, on the other hand, was 'genuinely erotic . . . it reminds us that desire is a vivid, transformative force.'

Referring to the readiness even of some feminists to defend what would once have been denounced unreservedly as sexist trash, the *Guardian* culture critic Jonathan Freedland warned of:

> a danger here that women should be aware of: by trading in the currency of sexism [or, what was more likely, allowing men to trade in it], they may end up giving it new life. To them [those who thought they *could* see the joke] words like 'bitch', along with images of submission, work as clever, ironic devices – because they play off the experience that went before. But a new and younger audience, which does not remember life before feminism, or even feminism itself, is much more likely to take such messages neat, stripped of all allusion.[2]

Wherever one stands in this debate (and the many others which have been provoked by similar campaigns, such as the infamous Wonderbra ads featuring Eva Herzegovina), it nicely illustrates the impossibility of universal agreement amongst the members of a viewing or reading public on the meaning of any image. As Chapter 1 suggested, media representations can and do generate a potentially infinite variety of decoding responses, and despite the efforts of some critics to assert a 'right' reading (i.e., theirs) next to which everyone else is wrong, the polysemic potential of a nude Sophie Dahl is obvious from the diversity of comment her image attracted on this occasion.

It is worth noting at this point that as sexualized looking lost its negative associations advertisers calculated that selling sex could be extended to the objectification of men as well as women. At the same time as overlaying the familiar image of the sexualized female body with post-feminist irony, therefore, advertisers and magazine editors turned their attention to the *male*. Brylcreem's 'Masterpiece', produced by Grey Advertising in 1991, in which a man disrobes before a group of female art students, was one example of this 'shifting dynamics in the sexual politics of advertising',[3] and there have been many more, for products ranging from perfumes and denim jeans to Diet Coke and ice cream. In this period, observed Lisa Tickner in 1987, 'the glamourised nude [became] accepted by both sexes as part of the natural language of the media' (p. 237). The sexualized gaze was being transformed from something that men 'do' to women, into one element of a post-feminist sexual culture in which women as well as men could participate.

New women's magazines

In women's magazines too, from *Woman* in the 1950s to *Marie Claire* and *Company* in the 1990s, we can observe the gradual replacement of the prim, domesticated, willingly submissive reader satirized in Harry Enfield's sketch by an altogether less inhibited, more assertive type. Chapter 2 noted the radicalizing impact of *Cosmopolitan* on an emerging mass of women workers in the 1960s, and subsequent decades saw a further sexualization of the 'Cosmo girl' culminating in the highly sexualized 'new woman' magazines of the 1990s. Like their 1960s predecessors, but embracing a much more explicit verbal and visual language, these magazines assumed a reader who was economically empowered and sexually competitive – 'out there' in the world, spending her wages on clothes and boyfriends (and sometimes girlfriends, as 'lesbian chic' took hold in the 1990s – see Chapter 7). They assumed a sexually active reader, and routinely advised her on the best methods of giving and getting sexual pleasure, within or outside of a steady relationship. In a 1987 essay Janice Winship recognized that these magazines 'express less the customary passive sexuality of women than an assertive strength. . . . Maybe it isn't a sexuality which wholly breaks from the oppressive codes of women as sexual commodities, but neither does it straightforwardly reproduce them. The conventions of gender and sexuality are being actively tampered with' (1987, p. 127). In these magazines, she continued, feminism is present, if not actively championed.

> Not overtly political around feminism, there is still a cultural level at which feminism *is* taken for granted. The magazines don't so much assume that the feminist case has been won as that it goes without saying that there is a case.
>
> (ibid., p. 136)

As with recent trends in advertising, however, objections have been raised to the images of women – and young women in particular – which the new generation of magazines contain. A 1999 study commissioned by the Health Education Board of Scotland found that magazines were 'bombarding the young with images of sexually active teenagers'.[4] If that was stating the obvious, the HEBS went on to draw the conclusion that the magazines in question (and television too) were contributing to rising levels of sexual activity among children and young adults, and the associated negative effects of unwanted pregnancy and single parenting which frequently followed.

Although the HEBS study was informed by a feminist political agenda moral conservatives shared its concerns and many of its conclusions. Anderson and Mosbacher argued from *their* 1997 study of women's and girls' magazines that the images contained in them promoted a dangerous and deeply damaging view of women as sex-obsessed, predatory and selfish. The director of the UK children's charity Kidscape, interviewed about the potential impact of a new magazine for young girls called *Mad About Boys* argued that it would encourage not only promiscuity but paedophilia (this was in the period following the moral panic around paedophilia started by the *News of the World* tabloid in 2000[5]):

> The pressure on young girls reading this will be to think: I should be sexy, I should be flirting with boys and I should be wearing make-up. But by encouraging young girls to be sexual you don't only open them up to the possibility of older boys taking advantage of them, you open them to the possibility of paedophiles. They will say, 'She's ten, but she's asking for it.'[6]

Once again we encounter the debate not just about media effects but the meaning to be attached to particular representations of female sexuality and sexual behaviour. Do magazines have the power to 'cause' increased levels of sexual activity in girls and young women? If so, does proactive, even promiscuous female sexuality reinforce the patriarchy or undermine it? For Anderson and Mosbacher, ascribing to a notion of femininity rooted in moral and religious conservatism, it was clearly the latter. Public health bodies like the HEBS, on the other hand, working to a social agenda informed by feminist notions of the predatory male, fear with good reason that increased levels of sexual activity will leave at least some young women vulnerable to unwanted pregnancy and premature dependence on feckless men.[7]

The culture of thinness

Apart from their alleged effects on the sexual behaviour of young females, it has also been argued that advertising, fashion and style magazines promote a culture (perhaps cult is a better word) of *thinness* which is oppressive to women in general. In the vast majority of advertising and fashion images an unhealthily, unnaturally narrow range of body types is on view. These representations are deeply *unrepresentative* of 'real' women – that is, the average woman, in statistical terms. They promote a body type which has been linked to a perceived rise in the incidence of eating disorders amongst young women in the late twentieth century. A report by the British Medical Association in 2000 noted that 1–2 per cent of the female population in Britain suffer from anorexia, and 1–5 per cent from bulimia. It also noted that about 50 per cent of adolescent girls regularly read fashion magazines and that 15-year-olds watch, on average, 3.2 hours of television per day. For the

BMA 'society's aesthetic preference for thinness in women is a significant factor in the aetiology of eating disorders', and to the extent that the media promote or reflect this preference they '*may* influence young people's perceptions of acceptable body image' (my emphasis).

> The media obviously have a role in perpetuating the culture of thinness in contemporary Western societies, as they are a major source of our ideas about fashion and desirable body image. . . . The media *may* contribute to low self-esteem in young women by promoting slender-ness as the path to social, sexual and occupational success. (BMA, 1999, my emphasis)

The BMA report was careful not to say that the media *cause* eating disorders; only that they are a highly visible element of an environment in which some young women are driven to anorexia and bulimia,[8] and in which more women than need to do so for health reasons are compelled to diet obsessively. The qualification is important since without it one is unable to explain the fact that only 1–2 per cent of girls and young women suffer from anorexia, and not the other 98 per cent, most of whom will be exposed to at least some of the offending images in their everyday lives. Moreover, the allegedly pathological effects of a culture of thinness are difficult to reconcile with the fact that obesity amongst women (and men) is on the increase throughout the western world, and especially in those countries (like the United Kingdom and the United States) where thinness in women is said to be most worshipped.

Whether there is a cause and effect connection here or not, it is a fact that the *extra*ordinary, emaciated body types which have been favoured in much advertising and other media for years now are perceived as offensive to many women, saying as they do that extreme thinness has a higher value than other, more natural body shapes. The oppressive force of this idea is seen even in the statements of A-list celebrities like Kate Winslet and Drew Barrymore, both of whom have found themselves the target of journalistic sniping about their allegedly excess weight. Kate Winslet complained bitterly in 2001 that she felt herself obliged to shed the kilos in order to secure movie roles of the quality she enjoyed in *Titanic*. Sophie Dahl, who came to prominence as a supermodel of above average (for a supermodel) build and weight (i.e. size 14) was criticized by many young feminists when she was observed to have slimmed down for the controversial Opium ad discussed above.

In response to the persistent criticisms of this female version of 'body fascism' there has been a conscious effort on the part of at least some magazine editors and 'creatives' in advertising to acknowledge the fact that not all women are, or want to be, as thin as the typically waif-like supermodel, and to incorporate alternatives to that stereotype in their publications. Susan Sontag observed in 1999 that although 'the identification of beauty as the ideal condition of a woman is, if anything, more powerful than ever, today's hugely complex fashion-and-photography system sponsors norms of beauty that are far less provincial, more diverse, and favour brazen rather than demure ways of facing the camera'.[9] In September 2000 the British retail chain Marks & Spencer nicely illustrated Sontag's point with its 'normal' women campaign, using models of size 16. One test of my argument that the producers of cultural commodities must respond to the demands and aspirations of their target audiences (including those informed by feminist theory and politics) will be the extent to which the thinking behind Marks & Spencer's campaign is seen in other companies' advertising in the coming years. It may be significant that the release of *Bridget Jones's Diary* in 2001 was dominated by publicity surrounding its star's (Renee Zellweger) attempts to put on weight for the role (this extending to the eating of three meals a day plus snacks), and the visible podginess which she displays in the film. Whether this was evidence of a sustained assault on the culture of thinness from within mainstream cinema, or a temporary gesture of tokenistic defiance, remained to be seen.

Girls on film

This brings us to cinematic representations of femininity. Linda Grant has observed, with good cause, that 'film is overwhelmingly a male industry, about the projection of male fantasies'.[10] In Peter Greenaway's *Eight and a Half Women* (1999) one of the lead characters remarks that most directors make films to satisfy their sexual fantasies. And, Greenaway would surely agree, to explore their sexual anxieties. Cinema then, is an arena where the changes in sexual politics which have taken place since World War II are inevitably reflected and dramatised. But if films 'consume, transform and shape popular discourse', as Sharon Willis puts it, 'they inevitably do so ambivalently, offering up possibly progressive impulses and indicating points of resistance as well as managing resistance and anxiety' (1997, p. 55). As in advertising, fashion and style magazines the images of women one finds in popular cinema cannot but tell the story of feminism's advance through, and subsequent residence in, the very heart of patriarchal culture. Filmic representations, like those others, must resonate with the changes taking place in women's lifestyles and values to succeed in the emerging marketplace of empowered female audiences. Tasker's *Working Girls* analyses how 'women's entry into previously restricted areas of work in the 1980s produced a "new" stereotype and a "new" look – crystallized in the phrase "power dressing"' (1998, p. 35). Sigourney Weaver's performance in *Working Girl* (Mike Nichols, 1988) is cited as an example of the persona, while Nicole Kidman's psychopathic weather girl in *To Die For* (Gus Van Zant, 1997) is another. For Tasker, however, these representational changes are limited. Cultural resistance and male anxiety ultimately punish these characters in so far as, though they *are* strong roles, they are set against more sympathetic female characters and in the end meet their downfall. The patriarchy is reasserted.

Other key films – *Fatal Attraction* (Lyne, 1987), *Basic Instinct* (Verhoeven, 1992) and *Disclosure* (Levinson, 1994) – are argued by feminist critics to share the features of what Sharon Willis calls 'a new kind of "women's film", shot through with [masculine] anxiety about the price of women's power, preoccupied with women's aggression and violence' (1997, p. 60). In *Basic Instinct* the character played by Sharon Stone conforms neatly to Michelle Aaron's argument that 'the connection between women's deviant or independent sexuality and her deadliness is so strong that it haunts all representations of strong women or of strong relationships between women' (1999, p. 74).

And yet, for all that their work carries the stamp of its authorial origins, leading directors like James Cameron (*Aliens*; *Titanic*; the *Terminator* series), Steven Soderbergh (*Erin Brockovich*; *Out of Sight*), and John Dahl (*The Last Seduction*) have embraced post-feminist models of femininity with something like enthusiasm, creating positive icons like Ripley. Sure, she's deadly, but it could be argued that she has to be, in a movie like *Aliens*. She's an action heroine, after all. The significant feature of the *Aliens* series is that it is a woman who triumphs, outlasting not just the sexually charged alien but the expendable men who pad out the cast.

Having put the Ripley character on screen, Ridley Scott's *Thelma and Louise* celebrated two women's determination in dealing with more earthbound predators – first the male whose killing sets off the chase at the heart of the narrative; then Brad Pitt's devious drifter (straight out of a Levi's ad in which his is the sexualized, objectified body); and then the massed forces of patriarchy as represented by the police. So powerful was the film's feminist message (albeit one authored by a man) that it became an acknowledged icon of the new sex-political environment. The film ends with the heroines' self-sacrifice (martyrdom is a frequent ending to male-centred road movies also – see *Easy Rider* and *Two-lane Blacktop* for good examples) but it is, within the narrative conventions of a generic mainstream movie, a broadly sympathetic portrayal of two women pursued to their deaths by the forces of patriarchy.

And despite the criticism of its alleged misogyny, even Sharon Stone's Catherine Trammell in *Basic Instinct* (Figure 6.1) was read by many viewers as a positive role model for femininity. Focus group research on how men viewed violence in the media carried out by the author for the Broadcasting Standards Commission produced the following responses.

> She's manipulative and she plays games with people, but she's great!

> She's cold, calculating, yeah. She's great, isn't she!

> She is the exact opposite from the stereotypical female who's at home doing the washing, and the ironing.

> She's the one that's in control. You saw it when she was there with the policemen. You know they are attracted to her, and she knew that, and she was playing on that and calling them by their first names and watching them sweat.

> [She] could be a role model for women. It teaches them to take control I suppose. She is obviously a woman who is very, very confident in what she does, and she is always in control, very intelligent.
>
> (McNair *et al.*, 1998)

Figure 6.1 Basic Instinct

Paul Verhoeven is not a feminist (no man can be a feminist, in the same sense that no white man could have *been* a black power activist: a man can, of course, support feminism), and there is much that is disturbing in the film – the 'did he, didn't he' rape scene, for example, in which Curran (Michael Douglas), frustrated by Trammell's manipulation of him and his colleagues, forces himself on his ex-lover, who at the last moment submits. Despite that and other manifestations of 'male anxiety' when faced with the new woman Catherine Trammell's toying with and eventual victory over Michael Douglas' hapless cop was a significant break with the masculinist conventions of the detective thriller genre. His 1997 film *Starship Troopers* also shows Verhoeven engaging with the new sexual politics in its portrayal of female troopers who are every bit the sexual and fighting equals of the men alongside whom they fight. In contrast to the much-criticized *Showgirls*,[11] when in *Starship Troopers* his camera lingers on naked butts and bulging biceps they belong to women and men both, creating an unusually subversive vision (for mainstream Hollywood, at least) of a military future where gender difference has become irrelevant (Figure 6.2).

'Ambivalent' images, then, but telling echoes of an evolving sexual culture. Sometimes they are undermined by lazy stereotyping, as in the dyke-coded female lawyer counterposed to Erin Brockovitch's feisty heroine in Soderbergh's otherwise much praised film. And as the overdone figure of Julia Roberts highlights in that film, the new type of strong Hollywood woman is hardly more representative of 'real' women than the cinematic stereotypes of the past. Today's screen woman can be strong, but still has to be a certain kind of sexy. She can be dangerous and dominant, as in the two big 'girl power' movies of 2000, *Coyote Ugly* and *Charlie's Angels*, but she also has to be cute. There has to be something in it for the guys, after all.

Girls *in* film

Most of the films discussed thus far were directed by men, and even if we allow that many male directors have incorporated significant elements of the new sexual politics into their work it is beyond argument that deep and permanent change in the structure of sexual representation requires much greater involvement of women in film production. There is now evidence of slow but steady progress in just that direction. That said, cinema remains a sub-sector of the media where women have made relatively few inroads as compared to journalism, for example. A remarkable statistic cited by Christina Lane in her study of the US film industry is that of all the films produced by Hollywood between 1949 and 1979, only 0.2 per cent – one in five hundred – were directed by women. As recently as 1990 only 5.6 per cent of Hollywood movies – one in twenty – were directed by women. Though hardly cause for celebration, one in twenty is considerably better than one in five hundred, suggesting that successive generations of women directors are making inroads into what has always been a deeply masculinist industry because, like the art world described in Chapter 11, involvement in it has not been easy to reconcile with

Figure 6.2 Starship Troopers

traditional notions of femininity. The industrial processes and big capital investments involved in cinema have made it one of those art forms from which women have been excluded. Recently, however, Lane observes 'a massive entrance of women into powerful roles within the world of commercial cinema' (2000, p. 37).

A pioneer in this respect, and one who also highlights the problems historically faced by women in this field, is Kathryn Bigelow, who achieved her status as a mainstream director by avoiding overtly 'women's themes', gravitating instead to genre pictures in which women feature prominently like *Near Dark* (horror), *Point Break* (heist movie), *Blue Steel* (police thriller), and *Strange Days* (science fiction). Her films have certainly contained unconventional representations of strong women (Angela Bassett in *Strange Days*), and sometimes positioned them as the leading protagonists (Jamie Lee Curtis in *Blue Steel*), but they have not been (in Bigelow's own words) 'feminist' films, even if they are films made by a feminist director. Of *Blue Steel* she has said that 'I subscribe to feminism emotionally and I sympathise with the struggles for equality. But I think there's a point where the ideology is dogmatic. So I'm not saying that *Blue Steel* is a feminist tract, per se. But there's a political conscience behind it' (quoted in Lane, 2000, p. 102).[12] Bigelow exemplifies that small group of women who have made it as directors in mainstream cinema by careful avoidance of overtly feminist themes.

Given the rarity of female directors in Hollywood, and the even greater rarity of female directors addressing feminist themes with anything like the directness of Ridley Scott in *Thelma and Louise*, the question has inevitably been asked: can women work to expand the possibilities of mainstream cultural production from within (and the question is equally applicable to other media), or must they stay on the avant-garde margins if they are to preserve their artistic integrity? The difficulties historically faced by women in penetrating the popular cinema industry leads some to the conclusion that there is no place for them there – or not, at least, for women with a directly feminist approach to their craft. Christina Lane paraphrases this view, and the Mulveyesque theory of the invincibility of the male gaze from which it is derived, in the following terms.

> If Hollywood is governed by a patriarchal system of operations . . .
> women would do better to challenge mainstream representation from
> an avantgarde perspective rather than from within the Hollywood
> industrial complex.
>
> (ibid., p. 15)

Laura Mulvey's influential work was written in the 1970s, when the institutional domination of the male gaze was virtually total. But recent developments give grounds for some optimism about the ability of feminist directors with feminist projects to break into the mainstream from the independent sector, and that a substantial audience exists for their films when they do. Kimberley Pierce's *Boys Don't Cry* (1999) – an uncompromising true-life account of homophobia and hate crime – made few concessions to the mainstream that this viewer could discern, and still won two Oscars. Jane Campion's *The Piano* (1992) is a powerful feminist statement about oppressive masculinity which achieved commercial and critical success all over the world. Her *Holy Smoke* (2000) provided mainstream audiences with another feminist-informed exploration of the difficulties faced by women when they seek to escape from the constraining expectations of family and social etiquette. Mary Harron's *American Psycho* (2000), while not principally concerned with the representation of women, had an interest in sexual politics, and followed her *I Shot Andy Warhol* indie-crossover hit into the multiplex, confirming her emergence as a potential 'A-list' director.

The careers of Campion, Pierce and Harron show that in cinema, as in other spheres of cultural production, the passage from avant-garde innovation to mainstream acceptance is now a viable route for female directors to pursue. If the directorial 'A-list' has till recently been closed to women, the successes of these directors prove that there is a space for feminist auteurs on stage on Oscar night. The question may then be asked: 'have women directors subverted, revised or exaggerated patriarchal codes of cinema from within Hollywood? And to what extent have their oppositional discourses been betrayed, negotiated, uncontained (not recuperated by the status quo) or embraced by mainstream, commercial production?' (Lane, 2000, p. 55). Readers will have their own views on that. My own is that all artists are required to make concessions to the demands of the mainstream if they wish to succeed there, and feminist artists are no exception. Films such as *The Piano* and *Boys Don't Cry* show that within those constraints it is possible to make popular feminist films for international audiences of women and men.

Such films *are* now being made, and in greater numbers than ever before. A very few women are playing on the same level as the leading male directors, although they do not necessarily identify themselves as the makers of 'women's films'. In Britain female directors such as Antonia Bird and Lynne Ramsay are emerging. These trends, and their parallels in other sectors of the culture industries, are bound to influence the content of representation. The continuing predominance of men in the culture industries means that there have been important limits to that change, but these are increasingly being tested by a new generation of female writers, producers and directors, willing and able to work within the mainstream, in the language of the popular, in the cultural marketplace. We await with anticipation the results of their efforts in the years to come.

Bad girls on the box

For those women not prepared to wait for the film industry to fully open its doors to them, television drama has provided another kind of space for the presentation of sexually assertive, socially confident, intellectually dominant women. Cinema's loss has been television's gain in this respect, and the resulting programmes have been a route along which, as Lane sees it, 'feminist discourses have been appropriated into the commercial mainstream' (ibid., p. 62). Susan Seidelman moved from feature film direction to successful television (*Sex In the City*).[13] In Britain female-authored series like *Prime Suspect, At Home with the Braithwaites* and *Bad Girls* have significantly expanded the range of images of women available to the mass audience. *At Home with the Braithwaites*, in particular, was a ground-breaking, witty, and politically sophisticated (but never preachy) prime-time depiction of a lottery-winning woman who uses the money and the power it gives her to seize control of her life in the face of a weak, philandering husband. In the end she gets to keep both her money and her man. *Prime Suspect*'s Tennison (Helen Mirren) was the first of many highly successful female TV detectives.

A recent collection of essays about US television concludes that, whether written by women or men, this particular medium 'has given us complex and contradictory female characters who reflect, direct and occasionally critique America's fantasies and anxieties about historical roles and gender norms' (Helford, ed., 2000, p. 1). The 'tokenism of the past', as this observer describes it, 'has given way to a recognition of a significant and appreciative audience for programming that includes images of strong, independent women' (ibid., p. 5). Characters like *Xena the Warrior Princess* and *Buffy the Vampire Slayer* are read by these authors as strong, independent embodiments of the feminist ethos, often with ambivalent sexualities,[14] 'riding the wave of contemporary girl power discourse that is part of an even larger US media fascination with popular feminism' (Ono, 2000, p. 164). Of *The X-Files*' Scully (Gillian Anderson) Lynn Bradley argues that she 'has challenged television's portrayal of women and changed the way we think' (2000, p. 66).

Mention of these tele-heroines brings us back, however, to the argument that, strong and independent though they are, these are inappropriate role models for young women. Ally McBeal is too thin to be real, it is argued; Marcia in *Sex and the City* is too sex-obsessed; Courtney Cox and Jennifer Aniston in *Friends* are too oppressively beautiful. All true, as is the fact that popular film and television have always been spaces for the articulation of aspirational fantasy as much as gritty realism. Julie Burchill has written an excellent book-length essay on the cinematic representation of women, *Girls On Film* (1986), which pays homage to the screen goddesses of the past whose mystique lay largely in their aloofness and unreachability. She reminds us that film (and latterly television) have never represented 'the real woman' in an unmediated sense and probably never will, preferring to depict versions of aspirational femininity judged to be appealing to male or female audiences, or both. That may be regrettable, depending on what social role one wishes the media to perform, but it is unlikely ever to change. Now, at least, a growing number of those fantasies are being authored by, and targeted at, women.[15]

7

THE MAINSTREAMING OF GAYNESS

An attractive woman slides up to the bar of a trendy night club somewhere (Figure 7.1). A good-looking young man catches her eye, offers to buy her a drink. She accepts, reluctantly, obviously impatient with him. Kronenbourg will do nicely, thankyou. He wants her to stay and talk awhile. She declines with a pout and walks off to join her partner, who happens to be – another attractive woman. From the balcony above they look down at the hapless hettie and smile sympathetically. The man smiles back, resigned to his place in this brave new world of polymorphous perversity.

In 1991 American culture analyst Larry Gross wrote that women and gays 'share a common fate of relative invisibility and demeaning stereotypes' (p. 61), within a mainstream culture that is 'the embodiment of a dominant ideology'. That was then. Five years later, the gay writer Mark Simpson could identify what he called a 'fin-de-siècle obsession with same-sex desire and its trappings' (1996, p. 3). In 1997 the *Guardian* reported that 'Britain is becoming a place where gayness increasingly provokes curiosity from outsiders rather than hostility, commercial enthusiasm rather than anxiety'.[1] By 1998, observed Andy Medhurst in *The Face*: 'the world's gone gay. From politics to pop, tabloids to peak-time TV and high-street marketing, this year gay culture has been more visible than ever before'.[2] Steven Capsuto's history of homosexual representation in American broadcasting, published in 2000, notes that 'things are better than they were in 1990, and far better than the near invisibility of the 1950s and 1960s' (p. xiii). The Kronenbourg advertisement, broadcast on British TV in 1999 as part of a promotional campaign for what is perhaps the archetypally masculine product, nicely illustrates these points, and signals the extent to which by the end of that decade it had become cool to be gay in western culture; when homosexuality had come to signify style, elegance and desirability rather than badness, madness or sadness.

So if Capsuto and the others are right, how did we get there from the invisibility and the 'demeaning' stereotypes identified by Gross little more than a decade ago? And having got there, how can gay artists, entertainers and performers 'occupy a place in mass culture, yet maintain a perspective on it that does not accept its homophobic and heterocentrist definitions, images, and turns of analysis' (Creekmur and Doty, eds., 1995, p. 2)? To answer those questions suggests others:

Figure 7.1 Kronenbourg film advertisement

what is the goal of gay liberation (to achieve equality within mainstream hetero-sexual society, or to win acceptance for a separate gay sphere outside of it)? What is the role of culture in the articulation of homosexual identity and gay rights, and how can that role best be realized? What relationship to, or distance from the mainstream, should gay culture have?

Before trying to answer those questions let us recall that a major factor in the representation of femininity has been, and remains the predominance of men in the culture industries. A comparable structural constraint has shaped the evolution of images of homosexuality. Although there have always been many more gay men in positions of power and influence in the culture industries than there have been women (straight or gay), they have until recently been required to remain 'in the closet', their sexual orientations hidden from public view. The great Soviet director Sergei Eisenstein was gay. Rock Hudson was gay, we discovered as he lay dying from AIDS in the 1980s, as were Cary Grant, James Dean, Montgomery Clift, and many other leading stars. So have been many more directors, musicians, advertisers, and artists than is generally known. Even less is generally known of lesbians in the media, now or in the past, although we know there have been many. Such were the negative associations of homosexuality that not even the wealthiest and best-loved of celebrities could afford to have their sexual identities publicised until very recently. In the late 1990s celebrities were still being mercilessly pursued by rumours and tabloid allegations of their homosexuality, often sparked by the 'outing' activities of radical gay groups like Outrage.

The desire of those in public life to retain privacy in this aspect of their lives (and also the readiness of some to fake heterosexuality) is understandable, given the homophobic history of western culture in the twentieth century. It means, however, that the following discussion of images of homosexuality is complicated by the fact that the distinction between gay and straight authorship of them is not always clear, and cannot be taken as given in the absence of a clear public statement one way or the other. This matters, because if one is to condemn a particular image as homophobic one should know if its creator is gay him- or herself and if so, why he or she has created such an image. Additionally, the decision of an artist not to out him- or herself often has to do with their desire to avoid being pigeonholed as a 'gay artist', rather than an artist who merely happens to be gay. Some of the most successful (in terms both of commerce and critical praise) mainstream images of (or skilfully-nuanced references to) homosexuality have been produced by artists such as the Pet Shop Boys, whose singer and lyric writer Neil Tennant revealed his sexuality only after a decade of public work had already established him and musical partner Chris Lowe as major international pop stars.

Before Stonewall: mad, bad and sad

The immediate effect of the Oscar Wilde libel trial, as we have seen, was to drive a then-tentatively emerging homosexual identity deeper underground, where it stayed until the sexual revolution of the 1960s allowed some limited liberalization of the law governing same-sex relationships and lifestyles. During this period the popular media's acknowledgement of the existence of homosexuality, whether male or female, was restricted to occasional, and usually comic, innuendo built around the stereotypes of effeminate limp-wristedness (in the case of men) and parodic mannishness (for women). Censorship regimes in the United States and Britain were hostile to the depiction, even the mention, of homosexuality, and film directors and producers who might have been inclined to address the theme in their films were unable to do so directly. Steven Capsuto records that on radio, until the 1950s 'gay imagery reached listeners implicitly, mostly in the form of swishy male comic-relief roles. So long as no one actually *said* that a swishy character was homosexual, the network censors allowed him on the air' (2000, p. 3). Public television followed the same codes when it began after the Second World War, where the camp, but not explicitly gay, comedian, compère or game show host became a regular feature.

By 'camp' in this context I mean the appropriation and feminization of images and symbols from the heterosexual parent culture, leading to the transformation of their meaning so that they come to connote gay identity and style. Camp is 'a gay version of irony and critical distance' in which there is always 'the collision of two or more opposing sets of signals' (La Valley, 1995, p. 63). Its presence alerts the viewer to the possibility of an artist's or performer's gayness but does not publicly declare it. The adoption of camp traditionally functioned as a way of signifying gayness without coming out, and has thus been associated with 'closet' queens working in mainstream culture. Larry Grayson, John Inman, more or less the entire cast of British sitcom *It Ain't Half Hot Mum*, exemplified the type – effeminate, precious, specialists in sexual innuendo. Gay performers of this type were 'a comic caricature of themselves', as Jacques Perretti puts it, 'often cranking up the ooh-missus act to an absurd degree of self-mockery'.[3]

Because the adoption of camp implies a certain 'safeness', and a desire to be accepted by mainstream heterosexual society, it has been criticised by some queer critics and activists as a betrayal. Camp was seen, and still is by many, as a collaborationist cop-out, a means of avoiding uncomfortable confrontation with heterosexism. Others, though, have defended camp's place as a distinctively gay style in art and culture – the first, indeed, 'to indicate the potential for gays, lesbians, or bisexuals to reverse, or at least question, the terms of dominant cultural production and reading' (Creekmur and Doty, eds., 1995, p. 2). Richard Dyer argues that camp is 'just about the only style, language and culture that is distinctively and unambiguously gay male' (1992, p. 135). Though rarely 'political' in the narrow sense, 'camp offers a subversive response to mainstream culture, and provides both in-group solidarity and an opportunity to express distance from and disdain for the roles most gay people play most of the time' (Gross, 1992, p. 39). The pastiching and comic subversion of parent culture that is at the heart of camp has been and remains an important resource for the gay community, in short. Before Stonewall and the rise of gay rights it was, indeed, an essential 'survivalist strategy' (Cleto, 1999). As we will see, it has continued to function as an important vehicle for the penetration of mainstream culture by homosexuals.

Not all the nod-and-a-wink gay characters who appeared in the media before Stonewall were playing it for laughs, though. Alfred Hitchcock's *Rope*, made in 1948, depicts two murderous homosexuals, as morally weak as they are sadistic and cruel. Though it is never made explicit in the script, by various devices the audience is invited to infer both the homosexuality of the decadent duo, and the connection between their sexuality and the vicious crime which icon of American hetero-masculinity James Stewart eventually uncovers. Lesbians, too, on those rare occasions when they appeared in film and television during this period were usually portraying murderous freaks.[4]

More transparent representations of homosexuality began to be permitted in the 1950s, when the Kinsey report and other developments in sexology opened up public debates about the condition – how extensive was it (Kinsey estimated that 10 per cent of the population had some experience of homosexual behaviour)? What caused it? Could it be cured? Discussion of these questions interested the journalistic media, of course, and the issue-oriented, mildly sympathetic views of homosexuality which they encouraged were reflected in well-meaning films such as the appropriately titled *Victim* (Basil Dearden, 1960). This British film, the first mainstream production to address gay issues head-on, dared to say the 'h' word. It also introduced the stereotype of the gay male (played by Dirk Bogarde) as a pathetic creature consumed by guilt and self-loathing. An advance, then, on the invisibility of the previous sixty years, and an honourable attempt to make serious drama from the problems then being experienced by homosexuals – principally blackmail – as they tried to work around illegality and social stigma. *Victim* established the sub-genre of the 'gay issue' movie.

A break with representational convention was attempted by Stanley Kubrick in *Spartacus* (1960) when, from his bath, senator Crassus (Laurence Olivier) addresses slave Antoninus (Tony Curtis) on the moral virtues. As the slave washes his back Crassus engages him in a conversation laden with sensuality and double meaning.

Crassus:	Do you eat oysters?
Antoninus:	When I have them, master.
Crassus:	Do you eat snails?
Antoninus:	No, master.
Crassus:	Do you consider the eating of oysters to be moral, and the eating of snails to be immoral?
Antoninus:	No, master.
Crassus:	Of course not. It is all a matter of taste, isn't it? And taste is not the same as appetite, and therefore not a question of morals, is it?
Antoninus:	It could be argued so, master.
Crassus:	My taste includes both snails and oysters.

With this coded reference to bisexuality Kubrick was ahead of his time. This part of the scene was cut from the version of the film released in 1960 and seen publicly for the first time in a remastered edition released nearly forty years later. As the

1960s progressed, however, it became easier to address the theme of homosexuality openly, if only in ways which conformed to current thinking on the 'problem'. In John Schlesinger's *Midnight Cowboy* (1969) Jon Voight stars as a straight man down on his luck in New York city and forced to mix with homosexuals, who are depicted without exception as either weird or depraved. He becomes a male prostitute, and at one point is provoked into battering one pathetic male customer over the head with a lamp stand. Although Voight's character – blonde, blue-eyed, muscular – can be read as a figure of gay male fantasy (and director Schlesinger was himself gay) the dominant mood of the film is better summed up by the critic who wrote that it 'presents homosexuals as crazy; as guilt-ridden; as prissy. The homosexuals are cartoons, and their world is presented as loathsome, intolerably isolated . . . as foul and self-denying' (Hirsh, 1976, p. 202).

William Friedkin's *The Boys in the Band*, on the other hand, released a year later, was considered a major advance by some critics[5] because 'it presents the homosexual in his own environment and not just as a misfit in the heterosexual world' (Phillips, 1976, p. 166). Freidkin's is today seen as a landmark movie in its successful attempt to challenge the stereotypes purveyed in *Midnight Cowboy*[6] and elsewhere. That it appeared at the cusp of the 1960s is no accident, since this was the moment when a 'gay liberation' movement was being born. Homosexual support groups like the Mattachine Society and the Daughters of Bilitis had existed for several years, but the Stonewall riots in June 1969 were the catalyst for the emergence of what became a politicised and proactive gay community, out and proud (in some cases, at least), confident in its right to exist and with a developing infrastructure of services centred on the big American and European cities. *The Boys in the Band* captured something of that 'gay scene', as in a more contentious way did Friedkin's later *Cruising* (1978). Made after *The Exorcist* and *The French Connection* had made Friedkin an A-list director, *Cruising* uses the 1970s gay leather scene in New York as the location for a serial killer thriller starring Al Pacino as a straight undercover cop who has to pretend he's gay (and may have suppressed homosexual tendencies). *Cruising* was less well-received than *The Boys in the Band*. Because both killer and victims were members of the gay community the film was accused of negative stereotyping and was, indeed, the first film to be picketed by gay activists. Like *Basic Instinct* two decades later the association of homosexuality with violence and sexual perversion was read not as a by-product of the plot or the beginnings of a pop cultural integration of gayness into generic narratives like detective movies, but as gay-bashing.

Friedkin denied that the film was homophobic – 'I wasn't thinking about what [*Cruising*] might or might not say about the gay movement – I was just using that world as a background to a murder mystery, pure and simple'.[7] It disappeared from public view nonetheless, not becoming available on video in the United Kingdom, for example, until the late 1990s. By then, ironically, its relatively realistic depiction of the New York gay bar scene, complete with references to fisting, rimming and all the hedonistic excess of the post-Stonewall, pre-HIV era, was welcomed as a celebration of that moment in gay history captured by Robert Mapplethorpe in his

1970s and 1980s photographs (see Chapter 10). John Greyson's foreword to Tom Waugh's *The Fruit Machine* (2000) fondly recalls a time when 'a combative and diverse gay Left picketed *Cruising* and thus forever changed our passive relationship to dominant cinema'. Ten years later, he recalls with bemusement, 'my queer film class watched *Cruising* with uncritical awe; for them it was an ethnographic account of a distant culture that had gone with the wind' (p. x).

As *Cruising* was bringing pickets out to cinemas throughout the western world the lifestyle it depicted was receiving a different kind of exposure in the hit singles of the Village People, whose 'YMCA' and 'Go West'[8] stand to this day as popular classics. Where *Cruising*'s homosexuals were reviled as sinister and dangerous Village People's were embraced by the mainstream as camp parodies of leather-clad hypermasculinity. Edmund White recalls in his introduction to Mapplethorpe's *Altars* (1995):

> Soldier, cop, construction worker – these were the new gay images, rather than dancer or decorator or ribbon clerk. A new tribalism replaced the isolation of the self-hating queer individual; a kind of body fascism came into vogue, a muscular bulk took precedence over boyish slimness, as the weathered thirty-five-year-old man instead of the hairless ephebe became the beau ideal.

Village People embodied this tribalism, and brought it to the pop charts shorn of its negative s&m associations. In doing so they were only the campest product of a popular music industry which, in the 1970s and thereafter, provided a key platform for the mainstreaming of gayness, and male homosexuality in particular. Men have historically dominated pop music of course, as they have dominated other sectors of the creative industries, and it was not until the rise of kd lang and a handful of others in the 1990s that 'out' lesbian performers were accepted in the pop charts. Gay men, on the other hand, found the music industry to be a relatively sympathetic environment after Stonewall. Constrained until the 1970s by the same institutional homophobia that prevented homosexuals in other culture industries from outing themselves[9] the first decade of gay liberation was accompanied by the rise of glam rock – a theatrical application of the camp aesthetic adopted by musicians who, if they were not themselves gay (and most claimed not to be), saw the route to both artistic credibility and commercial success in flirting with the signifiers of gayness in their visual imagery. David Bowie, for example, in establishing his identity as a new kind of space-age pop star – neither hippie nor rocker, but a blend of *Clockwork Orange* and *2001*, seasoned with a dash of Marlene Dietrich – declared himself to be gay in a 1972 *Melody Maker* interview, although he was at the time both married and a father. He had already been photographed in a dress for the cover of his *Man Who Sold the World* album,[10] and taken to wearing feather boas and knee-length boots in live performances, reportedly at the instigation of his wife Angela (Buckley, 1999). Throughout the life of his Ziggy Stardust alter ego (1972–5, approximately) Bowie advocated sexual experimentation and androgyny, including the public avowal of his own, at least partly homosexual, preferences. He was also one of the most successful artists of that decade (with six albums in the UK charts at the height of Ziggy mania); and successful, moreover, with straight audiences, male and female, who copied his image faithfully.

Whether homo or hetero (today of course he is very much the latter, and father of two children to his second wife), Bowie pioneered a wider adoption of gay style by major British artists like Elton John (gay but not fully out until the 1990s), Sweet, Slade (both comprised of working-class heteros, but happy to wear earrings and lipstick as if it were going out of fashion) and Roxy Music. In America 'glam' was pioneered by underground acts like the New York Dolls, and later embraced by megastars like Alice Cooper, before the style metamorphosed into punk and new wave.[11] Subsequent eras of rock and pop music in Europe and America carried the glam heritage in more or less subtle ways, allowing the music industry to act as a permanent bridge between the gay and straight worlds (see for example the careers of The Cure, the Human League, The Smiths, Suede and Pulp in the United Kingdom, or Marilyn Manson and the homoerotic heavy metal bands of the United States). Although as late as the 1990s a genuinely gay artist like George Michael could still be reluctant to 'out' himself (doing so, in his case, only after being caught in flagrante delicto with an undercover cop in a Los Angeles lavatory), glam and the atmosphere of studied decadence and sexual experimentation which permeated much pop music thereafter contributed significantly to the breaking down of homophobic and masculinist stereotypes among young people (I speak here from personal experience. To a straight, 14-year-old Bowie fan in 1974, the notorious cover of *Diamond Dogs*, and the 'Rebel, Rebel' lyric from that album seemed like the most natural thing in the world).[12] The spirit of gender-bending inclusiveness which that record (and the glam movement as a whole) embodied was reflected in the styles of subequent generations of rock stars such as the Simple Minds and Japan.

Glam is today cited as a key influence by many contemporary gay and queer artists. Film director Todd Haynes's *Velvet Goldmine* (1998) – 'a deliciously queer reading of the glam-rock years'[13] – fictionalizes the Ziggy Stardust story with the reverence of a true believer. For Haynes and other prominent late 1990s queers like Michael Stipe of REM (producer of *Velvet Goldmine*) glam, like queer culture itself, was 'about blurring boundaries between gay and straight, between men and women'.[14] Although glam achieved this through the work of artists who were not all themselves gay it created the conditions for the emergence of more overtly camp performers like Village People, and then for the appropriation of disco culture by the flowering gay scene.

Emerging from that scene, and building on the success of Village People (and with the first intimations of a 'gay plague' on the horizon), early 1980s bands like Bronski Beat, Frankie Goes To Hollywood, and Culture Club no longer bothered to hide their sexuality. Where Queen's Freddie Mercury, until the day of his death from AIDS in 1991, never publicly acknowledged that he was gay, a younger generation of politicized pop stars wore their identities on their sleeves. Pioneers in this respect were Bronski Beat, who broke through to the mainstream charts with an openly gay voice in 1984. A 1999 assessment of Bronski Beat founder Jimmy Somerville's career argued that 'in the days before *Queer As Folk*,[15] Gay Exchange and the Pink Pound, homosexuality had a hard time of it in the cultural consensus: the choice was basically John Inman or the Village People. Somerville was among the first musicians to make a clean breast of the fact and to bring the gay aesthetic into the mainstream'.[16]

An exception to this trend were the Pet Shop Boys, who released their first album in 1985, after Bronski Beat and others had proved the commercial viability of being out in public. Despite that example, for many years Neil Tennant and Chris Lowe resisted media attempts to label them as gay, preferring to adopt a stance of aloof detachment from the outing debates which accompanied their rise. Their distinctive electronic dance music, accompanied by lyrics about 'Rent', 'Shopping' and 'Sin' made sense read either as gay- or straight-authored texts, and appealed equally to both markets. But their production work for artists like Liza Minnelli and Dusty Springfield, and their collaborations with the queer film director Derek Jarman more than hinted at their sexual orientations, as did camp covers of U2's 'Where the Streets Have No Name' and Village People's 'Go West'. Their ambivalent sexual identities were part of their act, integral to the aura of sophisticated discretion which underpinned their global commercial success. If the Pet Shop Boys contributed to the mainstreaming of gayness they did so by insinuations, puns and camp borrowings rather than direct declarations of sexual preference or political commitment. This made them unpopular with some critics, such as John Gill, whose book on *Queer Noise* complains that:

> When asked about influences and traditions, they have often invoked the figure of peekaboo queer Noel Coward, who got away with murder in his work while maintaining a vigorously straightlaced public visage. The Pet Shop Boys may fall short of Coward's wit and sophistication, but they very much fit the bourgeois English tradition of discreet perversion and collusion with the establishment.
>
> (1994, p. 9)

Whether their 'collusion', and the huge commercial success they have enjoyed has been good or bad for the development of broader societal attitudes to homosexuality – and whether it is a valid alternative to the pink-triangle-adorned approach of bands like Bronski Beat – is for the reader to judge. For better or worse, their rise reflected the fact that by the mid-1980s gay liberation had generated an affluent market for consumer goods and services, and an active sub-culture based on clubbing. A further phase of crossover began when that subculture was discovered by straight film producers like the late Don Simpson, who, according to Peter Biskind's history of Hollywood in the 1980s, 'discovered in it a series of signifiers and motifs that he would allow to infiltrate his works'. Biskind argues:

> Simpson was to gay culture what Elvis Presley was to rhythm and blues, ripping it off and repackaging it for a straight audience . . . he took gay culture, with its conflation of fashion, movies, disco, and advertising, and used it as a bridge between the 'naïve' high-concept pictures of Spielberg and Lucas in the 70s, and highly-designed, highly self-conscious high-concept pictures of the 80s.
>
> (1998, p. 404)

Despite rumours and speculation about his sexuality Simpson was not a closet gay, according to his biographer Charles Fleming (1998). On the contrary, he emerges from that book as a heterosexual predator of the worst kind. Nevertheless, Simpson-produced films like *Top Gun* (Tony Scott, 1986) are now acknowledged as vehicles through which at least some elements of a homoerotic gay style[17] passed unannounced into the mainstream.

By then, of course, the gay community was engaged in serious self-examination, and being targeted by evermore explicit safe sex education messages produced by the parent culture. State-sponsored and private advertising increasingly addressed homosexuals as consumers, and also as priority targets in public health campaigning. At the same time, and in direct response to perceptions of official neglect of the HIV/AIDS epidemic, gay campaigners were developing more militant tactics for combating homophobic prejudice, such as outing. At this point, as HIV/AIDS wreaked havoc on the gay community (and prompted by the death of Rock Hudson) Hollywood began to explore the gay experience in more tolerant, sympathetic terms, reviving the 'gay issue' movie with Jonathan Demme's *Philadelphia* (1993). Made after Demme had been criticized by gay activists for allegedly stereotyping gays in his portrayal of the serial killer Buffalo Bill in *The Silence of the Lambs*, *Philadelphia* starred Tom Hanks as an AIDS-affected lawyer who suddenly has to confront the institutionalized homophobia of his blue chip partners. Hanks won a best actor Oscar for the part, and in an emotional acceptance speech proceeded to wax with inappropriate sentimentality (or so the critics thought) about his love and respect for gays.

This incident was later fictionalized in the comedy *In & Out* (Frank Oz, 1998), where 'straight' schoolteacher Kevin Kline is outed by an award-winning Matt Dillon, playing a straight actor playing a gay man in a film-within-a-film pastiche of *Philadelphia*'s liberal worthiness. *In & Out* is a very funny film; an example of the late 1990s sub-genre of gay movie which sought to embrace 'the revolutionary power of laughter' and move beyond the well-intentioned but over-sentimental victimology of *Philadelphia*. Although dealing with the ethics of outing (and the consequences of outing someone who is: a) unaware or unsure of his gayness, and b) working and living in a homophobic environment), *In & Out* played its politics for sophisticated laughs, assuming a mainstream audience's awareness of the significance of Barbara Streisand and Bette Midler to the male homosexual, for example, and able to take this and other in-jokes in a spirit not just of tolerance but wholehearted acceptance and celebration.

In & Out, and comparable films like *The Birdcage* (Norman Jewison, 1997) advanced the 'gay' movie beyond its early 1990s focus on HIV/AIDS, allowing A-list actors like Kevin Kline and Robin Williams to portray gay characters who were neither sad, mad, bad or diseased. These films celebrated gay sub-culture with genuine affection, while at the same time poking satirical fun at homophobia in American society (exemplified by Gene Hackman's conservative congressman in *The Birdcage*, transformed by the end of the film into a reluctant transvestite).[18] They were followed by films – also mainly comedies – which, though not with homosexual characters at their narrative centres, placed them prominently in the lives of heterosexual protagonists. In *My Best Friend's Wedding* (P.J. Hogan, 1997) Julia Roberts comes to rely on Rupert Everett's gay protector for support in the campaign to win back her boyfriend from Cameron Diaz. Everett's homosexuality is associated throughout with his sensitivity, compassion and wisdom as a friend, and his gayness never becomes the 'issue' at the heart of the movie. His homosexual traits – exquisite dress sense and grooming; the ability to access his feminine side – are no more stereotypically realized than a mainstream Hollywood script requires any character's to be. Everett's gayness is also a device which allows for high comic moments, as when the Roberts character asks him to pretend to be straight, and to act as her fiancée, in the hopes of making her real love interest jealous. In these ways the film explores the dynamics and positive potential – because of the lack of an obvious sexual tension, the script implies – of friendships between gay and straight people, and between straight women and gay men in particular.

My Best Friend's Wedding was enormously successful (taking $300 million at the US box office alone), confirming the receptiveness of the mainstream audience to films in which gay men were allowed to play characters who were neither victims nor predators, but quasi-romantic leads. Others in a similar style followed, such as *The Object of My Affection* (Nicholas Hytner, 1998) starring Jennifer Aniston, and *The Next Best Thing* (John Schlesinger, 1999), which again put Rupert Everett on screen as leading man to a heterosexual female icon – this time Madonna.

Madonna, as we have already seen, was a key figure in the mainstreaming of gayness with her late 1980s/early 1990s work. The hit single 'Vogue' (and the accompanying video promo) was full of camp references. The documentary *In Bed With Madonna* (Alek Keshisian, 1991) gave prominence to her gay dancers, and the *Sex* book contained several images of the star with gay men and lesbians, including those of the s&m-practising variety. Her relationship with the lesbian 'bad girl' Sandra Bernhard was widely publicized. Although it seems clear (marriage and two children usually being reliable indicators) that Madonna is essentially heterosexual, her engagement with gay style and same-sex sexuality was an important moment in the mainstreaming of gayness.

The Next Best Thing was a relative critical and commercial failure, however, primarily because of a weak script, but is significant nonetheless for its illustration of how far mainstream US cinema had progressed in its treatment of gay themes from the era of Schlesinger's *Midnight Cowboy*. The film places Everett as a straight girl's best friend (again) who assists in fulfilling her dream of having a baby. The baby is duly born, and the trio form an unconventional (and platonic) household until Madonna's character eventually falls in love with a straight man and moves out, taking the child with her. At this point the film turns from the light comedy of its first half to a more serious, and less successful, examination of the ethical issues involved in tug-of-love situations. A rather too melodramatic courtroom sequence highlights the prejudices which continue to exist in relation to gay men fathering or parenting children.

The Next Best Thing was a flawed, if honourable, attempt to address current sex-political themes while cashing in on both the success of the earlier Everett–Roberts collaboration and the long-standing real-life friendship between Madonna and Everett. Described (with a nod to the pioneering gay-themed movie of that title) as 'longtime companions' in a March 2000 *Vanity Fair* feature, the film contained many references to their real-life relationship, and to Madonna's current situation (by then she was romantically involved with her future husband Guy Ritchie).[19] Notwithstanding its flaws, the film reflected a growing public consensus around the validity and general acceptability – even desirability, within limits – of the gay lifestyle.

This transformation in the cultural climate was also signified by the mainstream success of Don Roos's *The Opposite of Sex* (1998), in which the peace and tranquillity of an 'ordinary' gay couple are threatened first by the arrival in their lives of Christina Ricci's toxic femme fatale, followed by false allegations of sexual abuse by a former pupil of the lead character (Martin Donovan plays a school teacher). In this film too – described by one reviewer as 'a radical assault on sexual and social pieties'[20] – the forces of heterosexism (personified by Ricci and her manipulative white trash ways) and homophobia (represented by the members of the schoolboard which suspends Donovan's character from his job) are constructed as the problem. The characters' sexualities are incidental to what is a film about relationships and the destructive power of desire.

On television, too, representations of homosexuality changed both quantitatively and qualitatively in the 1990s. A Broadcasting Standards Commission report published in 1992 noted of British television that homosexuality 'was not reflected in the symbolic universe of the everyday presentation of sex' (Hargrave, 1992, p. 87). There had up until that point been a handful of pioneering exceptions, such as the gay magazines *Gay Life*, produced by London Weekend Television in the early 1980s, and Channel 4's *Out On Tuesday*. Jeanette Winterson's *Oranges Are Not the Only Fruit* was successfully adapted for television in the late 1980s. The more recent prison drama *Bad Girls* has included lesbians among its fictional inmates. *At Home with the Braithwaites* also featured a strong lesbian character. All three series were written by women, illustrating the impact which more women at higher levels in the creative industries is having on representation in general. The mould-breaking US sitcom *Ellen* was also creatively led by a woman who was herself a lesbian.

As the 1990s progressed the representation of both male and female homosexuality in a wide variety of contexts became commonplace, even fashionable. In

1994 Channel 4 produced, to critical acclaim and respectable ratings, a four-part adaptation of Armisted Maupin's *Tales of the City*, praised by Steven Capsuto as 'one of the very few programmes that shows gay, straight, transgender, and bisexual characters living peacefully side by side and forming warm friendships across those sociological and sexual boundaries' (2000, p. 318). 1999 brought the first 'gay soap opera' to British television in the shape of *Queer As Folk* – 'gay' in the sense that it was unapologetically centred on the Manchester gay scene and its tangled, promiscuous relationships, rather than having gay characters play minor roles like *EastEnders'* Colin and *Brookside's* Beth Jordache (both caused flurries of media coverage in the 1980s). *QAF*, like *Tales of the City*, was successful amongst both gay and straight audiences, and secured a commission for a second series.

Elsewhere on television out gay presenters like Graham Norton became major UK stars, and those who were reluctantly outed, like Michael Barrymore, found their careers strengthened rather than destroyed by the experience.[21] The proliferation of docu-soap, 'reality TV' and lifestyle formats also made homosexuality more visible by highlighting, as in the hugely successful *Changing Rooms*, the existence of stable gay relationships between both men and women, and signalling their equality with straight couples. A docu-soap about expatriate Brits on the Spanish costa followed a gay couple trying to set up a drag club. Most famously, Anna in *Big Brother* was the vehicle for a ten-week-long exposure to unsensational, matter-of-fact, everyday lesbianism, and emerged from the experience as a close runner-up to the laddish Craig. Watching these programmes, one was struck by the presumption implicit in them that living a homosexual lifestyle is no longer remarkable. When public debate *is* provoked it more often than not involves condemnation of homophobia (as in the occasion on *Big Brother* when Nasty Nick was criticized for his association of male homosexuality with paedophilia).

Gay magazines appeared on both BBC and Channel 4 (*Gaytime TV*, *Dyke TV* and *That Gay Show*[22]), and much of what Chapter 5 called striptease culture addressed aspects of the homosexual experience in documentary mode. These programmes reflected the growing need of media organisations, faced with a fragmenting market of sexually oriented niches, to supply tailor-made content.

In the United States, too, by the end of the 1990s *USA Today* could report that 'gay and lesbian characters are popping up all over prime time these days'.[23] From the pioneering Jodie in *Soap* (played by the straight Billy Crystal) to the trail blazed by *Ellen* (the running narrative of which increasingly focused on star Ellen DeGeneres' real-life lesbianism) gay characters were becoming ever more visible on television, and by 2000 appearing routinely in sitcoms like *Dawson's Creek* and *Will & Grace*, not just as special guests and bit parts (such as Sandra Bernhard's cameos in *Rosanne*) but as major characters in ongoing narratives. Gay representation in these formats was no longer tied to currently newsworthy issues like AIDS and the ethics of gay marriage,[24] although the presence of such issues in public debate can still provide incentives for sitcom and soap opera writers to include them in storylines.

Back in Britain, the shifting consensus was also reflected in former bastions of homophobia such as the British *Sun* newspaper. In June 1999 Boyzone star Stephen Gately revealed that he was gay to the hitherto homophobic *Sun*, leading one observer of the British press to concede that even 'the *Sun* has moved with the times'.[25] Although the *Sun* will always be a fairweather friend to the gay community, as seen in its attempt to put in place a 'gay mafia' narrative framework for covering the early years of the New Labour government, the failure of that campaign suggested that something in the cultural environment had indeed changed, and that even the tabloid newspapers had to move on from knee-jerk gay-bashing. Chapter 2 discussed the issue of Section 28 which featured prominently in British public life in 2000, and noted that many newspapers, especially the *Daily Record* in Scotland where the debate was most fierce, lent themselves to the most ignorant and prejudiced homophobia. They lost the debate, however, and the true state of British public opinion around the 'promotion of homosexuality' issue was more accurately reflected by the loudly applauded appearance of Boy George on the flagship *Question Time* debate show, where he ran rhetorical rings around the lead campaigner against the repeal of Section 28, millionaire Brian Soutar.

Designer dykes and killer queens

The picture painted so far here suggests a popular media system responsive to, and even in the vanguard of, progressive sex-political change beyond the television studio or film set. But the manner in which the western media embraced homosexuality and inserted it into the cultural mainstream in the 1990s produced some unease and resentment among many gay critics and activists. I have already quoted John Gill's dismissal of the Pet Shop Boys as collaborationist traitors to the queer cause. The same author condemned Boy George as the 'not-queer queer you could take to tea with your mum, about as threatening as Big Bird from Sesame Street' (McNair 1996, p. 153). For Gill and others, these non-threatening personae merely replayed the negative stereotypes of the past. Others viewed the main-streaming of gayness as the betrayal of an authentically radical sexual sub-culture, and its replacement by a commercialized gay chic driven, especially in the representation of gay women, by heterosexual voyeurism. Becker *et al* point out that 'the most explicit vision of lesbianism has been left to pornography, where the lesbian loses her menace and becomes a turn-on. Men maintain control over women by creating the fantasy images of women that they need. Pornography 'controls' and uses lesbianism by defining it purely as a form of genital sexuality that, in being watched, can thereby be recuperated into male fantasy' (1991, p. 27). Most mainstream images of lesbians, it was argued, were authored by men and structured by the perspectives of the male gaze.

This criticism was made, for example, of Paul Verhoeven's *Basic Instinct* (1992), a film which as well as being a landmark in the pornographication of the mainstream (Chapter 4), and in the debate about changing representations of women (Chapter 6), also featured two gay characters. Sharon Stone's Catherine Trammell is a bisexual – successful, beautiful, and murderous. Her lover Roxy is a murderess too, though less sympathetically drawn, who ends up as plot fodder for Michael Douglas's detective. Echoing the critical response to *Cruising* in the late 1970s the film was attacked for its alleged stereotyping of homosexuals as violent psychopaths, and for those moments when the script tips into casual homophobia. These criticisms are most valid when they apply not to Verhoeven's portrayal of a bisexual killer (we do not, after all, say that movies are 'anti-men' because the vast majority of criminals depicted are male) – but in the recurring sniping by the film's straight male characters at gayness. Having slept with Catherine, Curran taunts the gay lover with his conquest. Catherine is described as 'the fuck of the century', and the direction of the scene clearly implies that what Roxy really needs is a man, and a man like Michael Douglas in particular. The frustrated Roxy can do nothing except turn homicidal as a prelude to getting conveniently killed. Elsewhere, when discussing Curran's accidental shooting of gay tourists in San Francisco (part of the background to Curran's man-in-crisis persona), his down-to-earth, feet-on-the-ground sidekick seeks to comfort him with the observation that 'there's too many fairies here anyway'. This throwaway line is not delivered ironically, nor context-ualized in a manner suggesting that we might be surprised by or question its homophobic premise. One is tempted to think that, in this case, the comment reflects the film-maker's as much as the character's views.

But it is also possible to read *Basic Instinct* as a positive representation of homo-sexuality, given the genre conventions within which it works. Sharon Stone's lesbian lover gets it, certainly, but in the end her own bisexual character emerges victorious from her sexual deviance and destructiveness. She may be monstrous, as Barbara Creed characterizes the stereotypical screen lesbian (1995), but she gets her man, if she wants him (and it's not clear even at the end that she does). It is Michael Douglas's Curran whose weaknesses are most exposed and pored over by the script. In the process bisexuality is given unprecedented visibility in a popular cultural context. One reviewer on the internet observed that Sharon Stone in *Basic Instinct* was like

> a Madonna who can act. She's aggressively sexual, stylish, hip, mocking and smart. Ironically, her character, the one that is attracting a lot of protest energy, is the best defence of the movie's intentions (as non-homophobic); her bisexuality is unapologetic, taken for granted, and celebrated as a strength. Michael Douglas' character is not particularly attractive or a very compelling apologia for heterosexuality, by contrast.

The US critic J. Hoberman, reflecting on the allegations of homophobia, considered that the lesbians are 'the film's most positive characters' and that 'Stone is the ultimate bad girl. . . . In every instance [she] flaunts her transgressive power.' Bad, in this sense, is good, and at any rate, better than invisibility.

A similar defence can be mounted in the case of the Wachowski brothers *Bound* (1996). The film, made before the brothers broke into the A-list with *The Matrix*, was received by many critics on its release as another example of 'lipstick lesbianism' – the mainstream realisation of male fantasy rather than authentic lesbian identity. According to *Sight and Sound*'s reviewer the directors were 'in the business of exploiting lesbianism for kicks. The erotic scenes are cartoons of heaving passion, which the brothers linger over with unabashed heterosexual glee [in a] porno fantasy treatment'.[26] On the other hand *Bound* was unconventional (to this viewer at least) in being a neo-noir thriller where not only are the two central characters lesbians,[27] but they emerge victorious from their tussle with a group of psychopathic male gangsters. The sex scenes, however one interprets their function in the movie (i.e. as wank fodder for the voyeuristic male or as ground-breaking depictions of lesbian desire[28]) occupy only a small proportion of the running time (they were made, as it happens, with the consulting input of Susie 'sexpert' Bright, whose views on pornography were discussed in Chapter 3).

Lipstick lesbianism, it is true, had by the time of *Bound*'s release become a trendy media slogan in the wake of the notorious August 1993 cover of *Vanity Fair* depicting kd lang being shaved by supermodel Cindy Crawford, and was almost universally dismissed by gay activists and queer theorists as a commercial sell-out. Deborah Bright argued that 'such appropriations of queer signs effectively "de-gays" them and transforms them into safe consumer style choices any woman, queer or straight, might make' (1998, p. 10). Linda Dittmar was more ambivalent in her assessment, recognizing the perverse pleasures which lesbian chic could provide for both gay and straight in the audience. In particular, 'it opened up for lesbians – notably middle-class and upwardly mobile white lesbians – a hospitable new space for self-definition' (1998, p. 320). Ultimately, however, Dittmar considered lesbian chic to be the product of a conspiracy against uppity women. 'The coining of "lesbian chic" responds to a felt need by designers, advertisers, journalists, entertainers, and some working in the sex industry to neutralise an assertive new woman they saw entering the public sphere.' To endorse it would be to the cost of 'our [lesbians] collective, interdependent political well-being'. The British critic Joan Smith saw what she acknowledged as 'the current media's fascination with lesbianism' to be 'a manifestation of sexual anxiety rather than an affirmation of gay identity'.

> The fascination with lesbian chic is primarily an anxious response on the part of straight culture to the disruptive, dangerous aspects of sex per se. It validates voyeurism, reinforces stereotypes and ultimately tries to domesticate sex with the proposition that something as complex as desire is really just a question of fashion.[29]

Same old same old, then; a dismissal which was extended to mainstream representations of homosexuality in general. The appropriation of gay iconography by Don Simpson, Madonna, the glam rockers, or the makers of the Kronenbourg ad with which I opened this chapter – all are interpreted within this framework as the neutering and devaluing of a radical style for suspect ends. Underpinning that reading is the assumption that commercialization (or commodification) is of itself a Very Bad Thing, incompatible with progressive social change. Gay chic, designer dykes, lipstick lesbians – all mean that the homosexual can no longer be an outsider or a rebel, but is locked into mere consumerism like the rest of us, and any gay man or woman who participates in that process is a traitor to the cause.

On another front, the continuing presence in popular culture of the camp – or 'swishy' – persona which, as already noted, dominated representations of homosexuality for much of the pre-Stonewall era, was also attacked. 'Are such figures simply licensed jesters', asked Andy Medhurst, 'permitted to poke fun at the straight world but kept safely at its margins as little more than amusing pets, or do their barbs carry the seeds of a real exposing?'[30]

The question is relevant to a programme like the late 1990s BBC sitcom *Gimme, Gimme, Gimme*, where a camp-as-knickers gay man shares a household with a single, straight woman (herself a ridiculous caricature of a sex-starved spinster). But unlike the limp-wristed stereotype of the past, Tom in *Gimme, Gimme, Gimme* is allowed to be 'out', and even proud. Indeed, he is given all the best lines with which to defend himself against demeaning or homophobic statements when the plot throws them up. The queen is dead, the programme says, but long live the queen who knows himself and asserts the right to be whatever kind of poof he feels comfortable in being. In this respect, the postmodern reclaiming of the camp gay stereotype parallels the Wonderbra and Opium ads discussed in the previous chapter – it looks, superficially, like something that used to be read as insulting and oppressive. Now, it *means* something else; can mean, indeed, defiance and resistance. Andrew Sullivan notes: 'the irony is that homosexuals have delighted in playing with the constructions that define and constrain them, showing in their ironic games with the dominant culture that something in them is ultimately immune to its control' (1995, p. 72).

The Birdcage, too, widely attacked by gay critics for its reproduction of camp cliches, is equally capable of being read as a celebration of a certain kind of actually existing gayness. *In & Out*, on the other hand, was praised for its use of gay in-jokes, but attacked for its conditionality and its sexism. One reviewer, on watching the film, identified 'an unspoken rule of liberal films about male homosexuality – the securing of gay men's self-esteem requires women to be made marginal and ridiculous. In the ideological map of films like this it's permissible to vilify homophobic individuals, but not to attack homophobia as a systematic form of oppression.'[31] This is certainly true of *In & Out*, in which Kevin Kline's unknowing fiancée is left stranded and humiliated at the altar. But she gets her moment of redemption with Matt Dillon, and is not treated unsympathetically by the script. As for the larger point – is it really possible for a pop cultural text to dissect systematic homophobia in the manner suggested by this critic? And is it not permissible to vilify gay characters, or for homosexuality to be represented negatively, in any context whatsoever? *Cruising*, as noted earlier, was one of the first films to raise the issue of what 'positive' images of homosexuality in mainstream culture should look like. Could representations of gayness be allowed to reflect negative as well as positive aspects of the lifestyle? Were the media to be required to act as social engineers and propagandists on behalf of a specific group (given that this was a group which deserved some special treatment after such a history of repression and invisibility), or to provide a space for the honest representation of lived realities? In the 1970s the gay liberation movement was still too young and angry to permit the latter, but as time passed and the community gained confidence the notion that gay people can never be portrayed as flawed, as 'bad' or even, if a plot requires it, as vicious killers, has increasingly been acknowledged as restrictive and counterproductive. If gays are people too, then they are endowed with the normal mix of personality characteristics. To suppress 'negative' representations on the grounds of combating homophobia merely detaches homosexuals in popular culture from what people know to be the truth.

This is recognized explicitly in what Ruby Rich has defined as 'new queer cinema' – 'films that celebrate an anti-integrationist stance, or a dissident sexuality'[32] such as Todd Haynes's *Poison* (1990) and *Velvet Goldmine* (1998). Kimberley Pierce's *Boys Don't Cry* is a more recent example. These films are clearly not intended to function as pro-gay propaganda. Rather, they construct the bearers of 'dissident sexualities' as problematic and damaged, if also capable of happiness and contentment.[33] And they are increasingly finding crossover success in the mainstream cultural marketplace. As Chapter 6 noted in another context, *Boys Don't Cry* won two Oscars, including Best Actress for Hilary Swank's portrayal of Teena Brandon. Predictably, perhaps, this very success was condemned by the critic who coined the term. For Ruby Rich, faced with the fact that general audiences can enjoy and understand films made by and for homosexuals, 'the New Queer Cinema has become just another niche market, another product line pitched at one particular type of discerning consumer'.[34] To which one might reply: and what, exactly, is wrong with that?

Conclusion

Richard Dyer wrote a few years ago that 'the power relations of representation put the weight of control over [it] on the side of the rich, the white, the male, the heterosexual' (1994, p. 2). This remains true, on balance, but white, male, hetero-sexist hegemony in the sphere of sexual representation is fragmenting, if the products of popular culture discussed in this and the previous chapter can be taken as reliable evidence. Partly because of the persuasive power of equal rights ideology on a relatively liberal professional group (media workers); partly too because of the challenges posed to traditional sexual culture by HIV/AIDS and other STDs; partly because of the irresistible economic power of sexual consumerism, and the emergence of women and gays as economically empowered groups; and partly because of the technology-driven fragmentation of cultural markets into quite precise niches[35] – the representation of homosexuality in mainstream culture has changed qualitatively, and not merely tokenistically, in the last two decades.

Support for this conclusion comes not least from the views of those conservative critics who complain, as *USA Today* put it in 1999, 'that the matter-of-fact depiction of gay characters on TV amounts to a tacit endorsement. The Christian Action Network said its members are "disgusted" by the "more than two dozen homosexual characters portrayed weekly on network television alone."'[36] Similar views have been expressed in the United Kingdom. And the conservatives are right. Mainstream culture *has* become, not just more sexually explicit, but also more sexually deviant, perverse, radical.

One important question remains unanswered, and may be unanswerable – have the changes in popular culture described here positively impacted on social attitudes more generally? Does the spectacle of Kevin Kline playing a gay schoolteacher make a heterosexual person more sympathetic to gay schoolteachers in real life? Might this performance, like that of Robin Williams in *The Bird Cage*, or Rupert Everett in *My Best Friend's Wedding*, help to erode the prejudice which drives such campaigns as that mounted against the repeal of Section 28 legislation in the United Kingdom, or against the right of declared homosexuals to serve in the US military? Do these films, and the many other pop cultural contexts in which positive images of homosexuality have been presented to mainstream audiences, merely reflect the slow but steady advance of gay citizenship rights in western societies, or have they contributed to those changes?

The answer must be – a bit of both. In the model of the media–society relationship I am using in this book social change is not something which the media on their own can be said to *cause*, or which they can prevent from happening. But they *do* play an important role in shaping the environment within which certain ideas gain or lose ascendancy. Referring to the self-outing in a 1999 newspaper interview of the man then being touted as the next Conservative prime minister, a senior documentary-maker argued that

> Broadcasting has played a useful role in de-stigmatising areas of sexual behaviour, particularly homosexuality, and contributing to open debate about a whole range of issues. It is inconceivable that Michael Portillo could have come out about his past without the change in social attitudes encouraged by television.[37]

After decades of exclusion and negative stereotyping television and the other mass media, for a variety of reasons, *have* entered a phase where they are contributing to a virtuous spiral of progressive change in sexual culture. They have done this by making homosexuality more visible than ever before, and by allowing representations to become more diverse and representative of the reality of lived (gay) experience, in all its flawed and imperfect complexity. The media in the 1990s have disseminated images of homosexuality which have created admiration as much as fear, and affection as much as anger. In that context, debates about the political correctness of this or that representation miss the point. Steven Capsuto retells Vito Russo's anecdote concerning Nicholas Roeg's 1976 film *The Man Who Fell to Earth*. Failing to see what relevance homosexuality had to the plot, the actor Buck Henry (playing Thomas Jerome Newton's lawyer) is reported to have asked the director, 'Why is my character gay?' 'Why not?' Roeg replied. 'There are homo-sexuals.' In his quiet recognition of this fact Roeg was unusual in the 1970s, but the presence of homosexual characters in all manner of contexts, many transcending the 'gay issue' or problem of the day, has become commonplace. And that, surely, is progress.

8

MEN BEHAVING SADLY

The crisis of masculinity?

The Sunday Times's television critic A.A. Gill complained in 1998 that 'the old pre-feminist stereotypes of women have been transposed to men'.[1] In the same newspaper Bryan Appleyard asserted that the sexual revolution has left us with 'a mass culture in which nothing good can be said about men and nothing bad about women'.[2] These are good examples of 'backlash', gestures of male resistance which arise from the perception that the changes described in this book have gone too far; that feminism and gay rights are all very well, but, hey – give us some slack here! They protest too much, of course, and their sweeping generalizations misrepresent the scale of cultural change just as much as those who dispute that there has been any change at all.

Men *have* been neglected, including by academics. In media sociology and gender studies the application of a feminist paradigm to the analysis of sexual stratification led to a focus on images of women and their role in the reproduction of patriarchy; or, in the case of gay and queer theorists, on the media's homophobia. This gap in the study of sexual representation is now being filled, largely in response to the perception which became widespread in the 1990s of an ongoing 'crisis of masculinity' in capitalist societies. Susan Faludi's *Stiffed* (1999), the successor publication to her *Backlash*, is illustrative of how many feminists are now attempting to redress the historic imbalance in scholarly and journalistic writing about sex and gender, and to make room for discussion of the specific problems of hetero-sexual men.

The 'crisis of masculinity' is not new, though. In 1977 Andrew Tolson wrote that 'the sexual tensions of the 60s, and the effects of the permissive society, undermined the masculine presence . . . sexuality [was] publicised, criticised, compared. It [was] not so easy for men to maintain the pretence of sexual bravado' (p. 16). Few men could live up to the 1960s ideal, suggests Tolson, even if they had wished to. The crisis he identifies in the late 1970s was one born of what we would today call 'performance anxiety', arising from the gap between social and cultural expectations of a hyper-masculinity relatively unaffected by feminism (and embodied in such oversexed figures as Warren Beatty and Robert Redford) and the reality experienced by men in their everyday lives (a gap explored in Ang Lee's 1997 film *The Ice Storm*).

The contemporary crisis of masculinity is more serious than that, questioning as it does long-established assumptions about what masculinity actually *is*. When the sexual revolution was followed by feminism and gay rights, and the traditional superiority of men came under not just economic but ideological attack, agreed notions as to what masculinity was and should be began to fragment. The status of women in the labour force, and within the family, improved. Images of male homosexuality, with their alternative models of the masculine (in at least some forms of gay identity) were integrated into the cultural mainstream. All this forced straight men to re-examine the assumptions and practices into which they had been reared. Capitalism was evolving, leaving behind the sexual stratification system which had served it well since the industrial revolution.[3] The 1990s saw an explosion of public debate around the consequences of this crisis for men in particular, and social stability in general. Many commentators perceived these as likely to be more negative than positive, and blamed the media for amplifying them.

Some of these objections – and they came from both men and women – were justifiably dismissed as knee-jerk reaction to progressive social change. Others articulated the growing realization that amidst the remarkable advances being made by feminism and gay rights the needs and interests of straight men were being ignored. To her credit, Faludi's follow-up to *Backlash* acknowledges that the progressive reform and eventual replacement of patriarchy with a more humane and egalitarian system of sexual stratification will require, after all, the *consent* of its former 'ruling class'; a voluntary relinquishment by men of at least some of their historic privileges, and their acceptance of less oppressive models of masculinity. This means a broad recognition of the difficulties many men are experiencing in a changed sex-political environment, and some understanding of their attempts to negotiate these through culture. In a press interview to promote *Stiffed* Faludi argued that 'it's essential now not to just sit around complaining about male behaviour but to try and understand it. So much of feminism has been about showing women to be not just products of their biology but of society and culture, but we don't do that for men'.[4] That is the spirit in which this chapter approaches the 'crisis of masculinity', and its representation in a range of media forms. Previous chapters have looked at how men represent women and gays. My concern here is with the images which men make of themselves, and what these tell us about their changing status in the world.

The death of the patriarchal hero

Among the myths perpetuated in much critical writing about the media and sexuality is that it is only women who have been objectified and stereotyped in patriarchal culture. The critique of objectification often implies that men are not themselves routinely subjected to sexualized looking. Rudolf Valentino, Cary Grant, Clark Gable and a hundred other heart-throbs of the past prove otherwise, and remind us that a quite narrow range of ideal types have been just as dominant in media representations of masculinity as they have been to femininity. What changes, in images of men as of women, are the contours of those stereotypes. Masculinity (like femininity) is not a fixed quality, but a set of gender-specific behaviours which adapt over time to changing material realities (in particular, men's place in society, and the relationships which flow from that). It is a fluid category, rather than a rigid structure, socially constructed as much as biologically determined.

If there is no single masculinity, however, there are, at any given time, in any given culture, a hierarchy of masculinities, some dominant, others subordinate; some rewarded, others punished. One might speak of a *dominant heterosexual masculine* – a set of normative characteristics to which real world variants are encouraged to approximate, but are unlikely ever to match (see Figure 1.1). Representations of masculinity in the media have always articulated and promoted these ideals. They tell us at any given time, not necessarily what men are, but what a society expects and wants its men to be. And by studying those representations we can trace the changing nature of the expectations placed on men by patriarchy as it adapts to broader political trends.

Images of male heroism, for example, have always been an important element in the cultural construction of masculinity (particularly in time of war, or at periods of heightened ideological tension, when movies may be consciously directed at the mobilization of patriotic-national values). But the constituents of that heroism, and the way in which it is expressed, have changed over the decades, along with change in the broader political and cultural environments. In the pre-cold war era of the classic Hollywood western, rugged individualists like John Wayne and Gary Cooper made and defined America as a mythical landscape ready for colonization by white Anglo-Saxon civilization. They were *pioneering* heroes, confronting lawlessness and savagery in films like John Ford's *Red River* and *The Searchers*. During the cold war this model of American manhood was depicted making the world safe for freedom and democracy in the iconic figures of such as James Stewart and Henry Fonda. From the late 1960s, on the other hand, as the counter-cultural critique of the Vietnam war introduced a note of uncertainty to the American dream, cinematic heroes embodied a more hesitant masculinity, morally ambiguous and anti-authoritarian. Clint Eastwood embodied this *existential* hero in Sergio Leone's spaghetti westerns, and in the Dirty Harry series. His strength and power were never in doubt, but his silent, violent persona reflected a moment in American popular culture when innocence and unquestioning obedience to authority were replaced by cynicism and the possibility of rebellion.

After the humiliations of Vietnam and Watergate came the *neglected* hero – Rocky, Rambo and the many imitators spawned by Stallone's rise to fame in the late 1970s. As a cinematic sideshow to the rise of Ronald Reagan's revanchist administration Stallone's neglected hero was frequently a victim of official incompetence and corruption, seeking revenge against well-meaning liberals at home as much as baby-eating commies abroad. Still patriotic, the neglected hero no longer believed in the infallibility of the state or justice system even as he prepared to die for his country.

In time the action hero exploded into absurdity (and in figures like Ripley, his attributes became part of the repertoire of the screen female, or action hero*ine*), to be replaced by the rise of the *ironic* hero – a man of action, certainly, but increasingly aware of the changing political and cultural environment within which he was doing his heroic stuff. Mel Gibson's performances in the *Lethal Weapon* series exemplified the combination of traditional toughness, self-mockery and sensitivity to issues such as racism and sexism which characterised the type. Bruce Willis's *Die Hard* series was full of self-referential jokes about the hyper-masculinity central to the action hero genre. Arnold Schwarzenegger parodied his own absurd persona in films like *Kindergarten Cop* and *The Last Action Hero*.

The above are all American examples, but the popular cinemas of every country contain their own distinctive trajectories of evolving masculinities, the parameters of which trace out their specific political and cultural histories (compare, for example, the asexual, stiff-upper-lip hero of the 1950s British World War II movie with Sean Connery's James Bond in the 1960s). My point here is simply that masculinity and its representation *do* change, over time and across cultures. Much of that change can be interpreted as responses to, or reflections of, political trends such as the rise of feminism and the mainstreaming of gayness.

That Michael Douglas moment: the masculinity-in-crisis movie

A fascinating illustration of this can be seen in the film work of Michael Douglas, whose characterisations of men-in-crisis over a period of nearly twenty years reveal at various times both resistance to and acceptance of the need for men to reposition themselves in the sexual stratification system. Douglas's iconic role in this respect is made more resonant by his father's status as an exemplar of an earlier model of relatively unproblematic American masculinity (see Kubrick's *Spartacus*, for example, in which Kirk Douglas embodies the qualities of heroism and physical courage, as well as the advocacy of freedom and democracy over un-American tyranny).

In Adrian Lyne's *Fatal Attraction* Michael Douglas is confronted, in one-night-stand partner Alex (Glenn Close), with the emasculating personification of toxic feminism. She is the avenging angel sent to punish the wayward American male, and to threaten his comfortable nuclear family. Some critics have viewed Alex as a metaphor for the destructive impact of HIV, and a stern moral lesson for men on the dangers of sexual promiscuity in the time of AIDS (Singer, 1993). That is a credible reading, but the film is also intelligible as a straightforward dramatization of the challenge posed to conventional masculinity by the post-feminist sexual assertiveness of (some) women. Alex's blood-splattered fate – though consistent with the generic conventions within which the film worked – allowed it to be cited as a backlash text by Susan Faludi and others, but the script also makes room for a sustained critical commentary on men's sexual selfishness and weakness. Michael Douglas's character prevails in the struggle for survival, but he is seen to be responsible for his own troubles, and is forced to go through painful confession and self-examination of his own flaws before the story's end.

Four years later Douglas starred in *Basic Instinct* (Paul Verhoeven, 1992), a key men-in-crisis film already discussed in other contexts. In Chapter 7 I noted that while *Basic Instinct* was criticized for its misogyny and homophobia[5] it is far from being just another 'slasher' movie in which illicit sex is accompanied by violent death. On the contrary, it is distinctive in at least three ways from the conventional serial killer thriller. Firstly, while a woman is the principal sex object of the film (this being its most conventional feature, and one which places it firmly in the history of patriarchal cinematography), this same woman is also the perpretrator of the violence, with (mostly) men positioned as victims. The main male protagonist (Michael Douglas as Nick Curran) is pursued sexually from the start of the film to its end. This is a film in which a woman dominates men intellectually, sexually and physically. She teases them, harasses them, murders them, toys with their masculinity, and lives to tell the tale.

The film is full of masculine anxiety, however, which as Chapter 6 noted, explains its place (for some) in the repertoire of backlash movies. Inevitably, having created a serial killer in Catherine Trammell (although her status is not confirmed until the final shot) it is the bisexual deviant whom the film constructs as 'bad' – murdering, monstrous, and manipulative. Catherine is beautiful, but beastly too, reinforcing (as some gay activists saw it) the deep-rooted popular myth that homosexuality and sexual kinkiness are ultimately forces for evil. And if this on its own could be read as a consequence of plot rather than authorial prejudice, there are other, more obvious signifiers of the film-maker's attitudes to sexual politics. At the heart of the film is a scene in which consensual sex between Curran and an ex-girlfriend (herself positioned by the script as a suspect killer) becomes rape. Beth (who has just realized that she has been raped by her ex-boyfriend) says: 'You weren't making love then,' before the scene moves to a close. The rape is real (she says no, and resists him, but he fucks her anyway), but our response as viewers is manipulated so that decisive moral judgement becomes difficult. Did that really happen? And why? It is too brutal and calculated a scene to be accidental. Was the writer/director making a point about the complexity of power relationships, and the ease with which love becomes hate? Are we being told that 'date rape' happens, and it's no big deal? Are we being invited to think that Curran is so frustrated with Trammell's manipulation of him that he takes it out on the only person he can? And if so, are we being invited to sympathize with his frustration? Were the film-makers trying to stimulate precisely the kind of uncertain audience response which most viewers of *Basic Instinct* manifest? *Basic Instinct* is a deeply ambivalent film, then, which in its own way displays the unease with which men in the 1990s were confronting a new sexual culture and politics. Its flaws are undeniable, but the glimpses it provides into a masculinity under pressure, and not coping very well with it, are in the end what makes the film significant.

Less ambivalent, more directly hostile to the rise of the post-feminist woman, was Barry Levinson's *Disclosure* (1994), in which Douglas played an executive in a hi-tech electronics company subjected to sexual harassment by his new boss Demi Moore. Based on Michael Crichton's novel, the story turns the traditional feminist analysis of workplace politics on its head and positions men as the victims of predatory, power-hungry women, although a key speech by Moore's character makes the feminist case for her amoral behaviour quite persuasively. When a lawyer says to Meredith Johnston (Moore), 'the only thing you have proven is that a woman in power can be every bit as abusive as a man,' she responds:

> You wanna put me on trial here? Let's at least be honest about what it's for. I am a sexually aggressive woman. I like it, Tom [Michael Douglas] knew it, and you can't handle it. It is the same damn thing since the beginning of time. Veil it, hide it, lock it up and throw away the key. We expect a woman to do a man's job, make a man's money and then walk around with a parasol and then lie down and let a man fuck her like it was still a hundred years ago. Well, no thankyou.

There is no doubt by the end of the film, however, as to whom we as viewers are expected to sympathise with. Unlike Catherine Trammell in *Basic Instinct*, this strong woman is firmly put in her place.

Douglas also starred in Joel Schumacher's *Falling Down* (1994), playing a newly unemployed defence worker lashing out at those around him as he makes a richly symbolic journey across Los Angeles to the home of his estranged wife and daughter. Women are at least partly to blame for this man's plight, the film suggests, and Douglas' D-Fens character is ultimately martyred to what might be read as the combined forces of feminism, multiculturalism and an uncaring capitalism. In all of these roles, and in other performances not discussed here (his characters in *Wall Street* [Oliver Stone, 1987], *The Wars of the Roses* [Danny De Vito, 1986] and *Wonder Boys* [Curtis Hanson, 2000], for example) Michael Douglas's career emerges as an extended narrative on the developing crisis of late-twentieth-century American masculinity. For nearly two decades his characters have negotiated their way through a changing political landscape, ambivalent about feminism and its implications for men, but obliged to respond to and deal with it, even if that means, as in *Falling Down*, martyrdom and self-annihilation.[6]

Auto-critique

Douglas's films tell us much about what was happening to western men in the 1980s and 1990s, even if they were somewhat confused about whose fault it was. During the same period, away from mainstream cinema, young male directors embarked on a much more direct critique of masculinity, exemplified by Neil La Bute's *In the Company of Men* (1997). La Bute's film tells the story of two men working away from home for the same company – one a rather mild-mannered manager, the other fiercely competitive and utterly ruthless – who decide to have their way with a female, any female, and then drop her. Around this spare plot the film describes with excruciating detachment the worst attributes of contemporary masculinity, including the cruelty and contempt with which some men treat not only women, but each other. The film is a portrayal of men at their least sympathetic and rage-inducing; a nihilistic, neo-Darwinian account of what men are, for better or worse (or a certain kind of corporate man, at least); or perhaps a portrait of what the system forces men to be. As one reviewer put it, the film is 'a vision of patriarchy in all its pristine ugliness'.[7]

Labute's follow-up to *In the Company of Men* was *Your Friends and Neighbours* (1999), a more luxuriously produced but equally bleak and self-loathing film. Of the three male characters around whom the plot revolves one is a pretentious college professor, narcissistic, self-centred and untrustworthy, whose girlfriend leaves him for another woman. Another is a naïve married man unable to satisfy his wife sexually. The third is misogynistic and predatory, another version of the toxic male who pollutes *In the Company of Men*. Significantly here, as in the earlier film, these men are as vicious and uncaring towards each other as they are towards the women unfortunate enough to come within their reach. They are adrift in a world where women expect and demand more than their men can give. They are sexually inadequate, emotionally stunted, reduced to impotence, literally and meta-phorically. Men are the problem-makers and the failures. Women struggle to put up with them, and reserve the right to give up and walk out. The men in La Bute's world have no redeeming features.

Man (to his partner, as they lie together in bed):   I do everything that you ask, and you're still not satisfied.
Woman: I know.

In the pivotal steam room scene the myth of male camaraderie falls apart into backbiting and betrayal, as one man's confession of participation in homosexual rape – 'my best fuck' – is matched by the other's confession of adultery with his best friend's wife. He describes the gang rape, and the pleasure he took in it, in the following terms:

> I was the last one, so I don't know if he'd given over by this time or what. Nice. How can I explain this? It's never been like that with a woman. As many as I've fucked. Never. Not even close.

Labute's films exemplify the merciless deconstruction of certain styles of masculinity to be found in many indie movies of the 1990s. Todd Solonz's *Happiness* (1999) is also notable in this respect, with its cast of characters who 'lead secret lives as child-rapists, obscene phone-callers, murderers, thieves, wife-beaters'.[8] Not all examples of this ongoing auto-critique have been quite so full of self-loathing, however, seeking instead to present men coming to terms with the new world in ways which allow for humour and pragmatic acceptance. Less scabrous than the work of La Bute or Solonz, but equally reflective on the theme of the modern man's predica-ment is Doug Liman's *Swingers* (1996), where 'masculine repression and failure' are made to look like vulnerability and charm. In its account of a twenty-something man coming to terms with the loss of his girlfriend and the need to build a new life 'it accepts mediocrity as a condition afflicting all of us'.[9] Stephen Frears's *High*

Fidelity (2000), based on Nick Hornby's novel of the same name, occupies the same territory, if with a bigger budget, portraying a man's love-scarred journey from reckless post-adolescence to adult responsibility (and true love). *The Full Monty* (Peter Cattaneo, 1997) described with world-weary resignation the predicament of working-class men in post-industrial, post-Thatcher Britain, reduced to performing striptease at women's hen nights to make a living and support their families. For Rosalind Coward *The Full Monty* 'belongs to the new landscape of the disappearance of traditional male jobs and of gender reversal. In [it] the women even symbolically assume the male position, standing up to take a piss. And the film ends with the men economically powerless as women used to be, selling the only thing they have: their bodies' (1999, p. 62). As Chapter 5 noted, however, the men's striptease becomes a cause for celebration and humour, hinting at a way out of the crisis created by Coward's 'new landscape' – acceptance, followed by transcendence.

Mining the same vein of auto-critique as *Your Friends and Neighbours*, but holding out at least some hope of male redemption, P.T. Anderson's *Magnolia* (1998) (his follow-up to *Boogie Nights*) casts one of the most visible icons of late 1990s' masculinity, Tom Cruise, as a 'men's movement' therapist, T.J. Mackie. His breathtaking slogan – 'Tame the cunt, worship the cock' – recited with hypnotic intensity to an audience of drooling misogynists is the starting point for a movie which turns out to be about flawed fatherhood, and the damage men do to their children. T.J.'s progression from vicious woman-hater to a man-child crying over the death of a neglectful parent speaks to the processes men all over the western world are going through.

These films indicate that for many directors the priority is no longer to complain about feminism, or indeed to demonize it, but to explore new post-feminist models of heterosexual masculinity (and, of course, to understand what is wrong with currently dominant models). If David Fincher's *Fight Club* is an interesting exception to that trend, with its childish celebration of bare knuckle male violence as an antidote to alleged oppression by the system/parent (personified by IKEA, the phenomenon of group therapy, and the figure of Helena Bonham Carter), Ridley Scott's multi-Oscar winning *Gladiator* (2000) advocates a model of masculinity that is strong and sensitive, reluctantly heroic, and if still conforming to the conventions of the action hero genre, physically unassuming by comparison with the puffed-up bodies of Stallone and Schwarzenegger or the symmetrical perfection of Tom Cruise and Brad Pitt. In a cultural moment of pleasing irony, *What Women Want* (Nancy Meyers, 2000) puts the former action hero Mel Gibson in a position where he is forced to undergo a process of feminization which leads in the end to his redemption. The sex wars are over, that film suggests, and it is time to move on. Stephen Daldry's Oscar-winning *Billy Elliot* (2000), with its challenge to traditional models of working-class masculinity (of the kind favoured by Ken Loach, for example) and corresponding support for a generous, inclusive maleness represented by Billy's heterosexual dancer on the one hand, and his apparently gay friend on the other, also expanded the range.

New Men, new masculinities?

One of the trends attacked in *Fight Club* is the 'feminization' of men, by which is usually meant their increased dedication to style and grooming. Men have always been narcissistic, of course, as well as vain and self-obsessed. The upper-class male styles of eighteenth-century Europe, with their wigs and powder and fake beauty spots were hardly rugged, and wherever one looks in the world one finds evidence of male fascination with self-decoration and sexualized display. And there have always been ideals of male beauty in culture, varying from the lived-in imperfection of Humphrey Bogart to the symmetrical jaws of Tom Cruise. Men's magazines in the 1950s contained fashion shots of young male models every bit as posed and precious as those to be found in the pages of *The Face* or *i-D*. Now, however, forms of popular culture like advertising, cinema and fashion present what is generally recognized as a 'New Man', significantly modified from what must be, by implication, old man. So what has changed?

Sean Nixon describes the New Man persona as 'a more sexualised representation of the male body which draws on the codings traditionally associated with representations of femininity' (1996, p. 3). In advertising these include the passive, sexually receptive postures adopted by male models; the increased emphasis on their naked bodies; the signifiers of sexualized subordination identified by Goffman in his discussion of images of women (see Chapter 6). New Man, in short, invites the sexual objectification of the male body, and the linked commercial endorsement of voyeurism – in the sense both of men looking at themselves, and women looking at men.

For some observers this objectification is viewed as one of the negative effects of an oppressive 'consumer society' in which masculinity is realized through the consumption of style, and at the same time feminized. Barthel argues that 'advertising has encouraged a "feminisation" of culture, as it puts all potential consumers in the classic role of the female: manipulable, submissive, seeing themselves as objects' (1992, p. 148). One could of course put a more positive spin on that trend, by welcoming the transfer of certain qualities hitherto associated with femininity to the realm of acceptable male behaviour. Certainly, men's increased interest in style has been encouraged by the largely commercialized culture of leisure and recreation, but this need not dertact from the fact the heterosexual male is embracing, consciously or otherwise, an expanded range of masculinities.

New Man, moreover, is not just a feminized, but a *homo*sexualized vision of masculinity, in the sense that his studied narcissism and attention to self-grooming are traditionally associated with gayness. Indeed, the perception that contemporary models of straight masculinity have absorbed elements of *gay* as well as distinctively feminine style has been welcomed as a contribution to the mainstreaming of gayness discussed in the previous chapter. Mark Simpson observes that 'gay images no longer seem distinct from straight images. In advertising, the cinema and pop music, gay kinds of appearance, and gay kinds of invitation to look, challenge not only the idea that gay men should be invisible, but also the idea that they are deeply different from straight men' (1994, p. xi).

That the achievements of gay rights activists since the 1970s, and the general decline in homophobia which has been a feature of recent years, coincided with the 'queering' of heterosexual masculinity is self-evident. This trend has not been a product of political activism so much as the evolution of heterosexual style in an environment of increasing gay visibility. As already noted, male narcissism is not unusual, in a historical or cross-cultural context. That it should have taken the form of a homosexualized-feminized New Man in the 1980s and after was due largely to the influence of gay designers and fashion photographers like Ray Petrie, who filled *The Face* and other new-generation-style magazines with images of sexually ambiguous masculinity. Designers such as Jean Paul Gaultier, Gianni Versace and Giorgio Armani legitimised the concept of the 'sexy male', and targeted it at the increasingly style-conscious, affluent yuppie of the Thatcher-Reagan era, who was encouraged in advertisements and elsewhere to combine 'assertive masculinity' with 'softness and sensuality'. Heterosexual style leaders like film producer Don Simpson also incorporated many of these elements into their work. Frank Mort observes that in these ways 'the growing visibility of the homosexual marketplace began to exercise its own influence over mainstream versions of masculinity' (1996, p. 3).

The role of the heterosexually promiscuous, predatory Simpson in this process was noted in the previous chapter. Here it serves to remind us that while New Man's persona displayed some superficial resemblances to those associated with women and gay men, he was not necessarily a feminist, nor indeed a liberal in respect of homosexuality. An American scholar argued in 1992: 'the New Man lowers his resistance to formerly feminine products, but in service of a traditional masculine goal' (Barthel, p. 149) – that of sexual conquest. 1980s New Man was less the by-product of feminism or gay rights than an update of 1950s *Playboy* man. New Man, to an extent not qualitatively different from his *Playboy* predecessor, was allowed to be emotional, to admire himself, and still be a *real* man. There was a difference, however, in the cultural context within which New Man and his sophisticated 1950s *Playboy* predecessor existed. The latter shared his world with the aggressively heterosexual presences of Frank Sinatra, Dean Martin and Sean Connery. For New Man, the image of the male homosexual was an unavoidable feature of mainstream cultural life; challenging by his very presence, as Mark Simpson suggests, the traditional separation between hetero and homosexual masculinities. If that proximity to homosexuality did not actively promote the erosion of the western homophobic consensus, neither did it militate against that welcome movement.

From New Man to New Lad

There is a downside to this, some argue, in so far as the feminisation of masculinity has produced among men some of the 'feminine' concerns and anxieties discussed in Chapter 6. 'The heterosexual male's panic at his own cultural redundancy is translating into problems of body image that are just like those suffered by women', argues one style journalist.[10] The British Medical Association notes that 'if the media play a role in triggering eating disorder, then we would expect that as men become more preoccupied with their looks and are increasingly targeted by advertisers, they may develop a higher incidence of eating disorder'.[11] There is no evidence of that happening as yet, and even if there were, one might just as easily interpret it as a consequence of the male's increased vulnerability in a much more egalitarian sexual political environment, where women are more proactive and competitive in the mating game than ever before. Men, to put it simply, have to work harder to pull the birds, which may mean losing that beer gut and putting on a clean pair of pants.

That is too much for some, who have viewed the rise of New Man with the same alarm as feminists when confronted with impossibly narrow stereotypes of ideal female beauty. From this perspective New Man was an oppressive ideal to which real men could not possibly aspire. He was a poof and a pussy, or at least an effete wimp of the type played by Edward Norton's IKEA-idolizing yuppie in *Fight Club*. In response, New Lad was born.

The New Lad of the 1990s, as embodied in the editorial pages of British magazines like *FHM* and *Loaded* (and in the United States, *Maxim* and *Stuff*), presented a provocative, aggressively marketed alternative to New Man. In reaction to New Man's feminization of the modern male New Lad rediscovered the simple pleasures of football, beer, and birds; pleasures to be pursued henceforth without apology or guilt. 'Glamour' was reintroduced to these magazines in the shape of celebrity pin-ups who, if they were exercising their right of self-objectification in a post-feminist world,[12] were nonetheless being put to the service of pre-feminist attitudes. Magazines like *Loaded* 'correctly understood', argued one observer at the height of their success, 'that a large number of young men were fed up with or uninterested in the era of sexual politics'.[13] Shows like *Fantasy Football* in the UK and *The Guy Show* in America brought New Lad and 'the more assertive articulation of the post-permissive masculine heterosexual script' (Nixon, 1996, p. 203) into televisual culture. *Loaded, FHM, Maxim, Stuff* and the rest revived the top-shelf tradition of naked women posed in sexualized, subordinate positions. Though not explicit in the pornographic sense, and often contextualized with a nod and a wink to the feminist critique of sexism,[14] these images fuelled the argument that patriarchal society had entered a period of backlash and that, really, nothing much had changed in the average bloke's attitudes to women. Indeed, by using the dubious rationale of postmodern irony to disguise its misogyny the New Lad phenomenon was argued by some to be even more dangerous than the old-fashioned sexism of earlier generations. As one critic put it:

> Sexism, along with all those other Real Man things – football, porn, beer – has been re-appropriated to give it a veneer of laddish respectability.[15]

Whether or not he made sexism respectable, New Lad was undeniably popular, if popularity can be measured by the circulation figures of the men's magazines most identified with the trend. In Britain, *FHM* and *Loaded* far outsold the conventional men's magazines over the 1995–2000 period. This pattern was repeated in the United States where the new men's title *Maxim* achieved sales of 2 million in early 2001. Television manifestations of New Laddism such as the BBC's *Men Behaving Badly* were also successful in audience terms.

This was a reflection of the anxiety produced by the rise of feminism, certainly, and recognizable as a kind of backlash, but it was not one which seriously threatened to halt or reverse the process of sex-political change described in this book. On the contrary, as one male commentator observed, 'lad culture is an acceptance of the triumph of feminism. The lads know that their preoccupations are trivial and they wallow, like defiant children, in that triviality'.[16] *Viz* magazine – an adult comic launched in the 1980s – played this game in the most provocatively 'sexist' way. Enormously successful *Viz* cartoon strips like Sid the Sexist and the Fat Slags contained what one critic called 'all the most brutal words and clichés one can use about women', and acknowledging the postmodern context of such usage was not sufficient to justify it.

> By accepting the irony, we are also accepting the premise on which the Fat Slags is founded: that women who enjoy sex are slags, that 'slag' is an acceptable term to describe a woman, that women who are fat and enjoy sex are disgusting. No matter how much women are reclaiming our sexuality, we still don't want to be called slags.[17]

A reference *to* sexism for comic or other purposes is not the same thing as endorsement of it, of course. And it is clear from the cover of a publication like *The Joy of Sexism* (Figure 8.1) that, as in the Enfield sketch with which I began Chapter 6, *Viz* is not intended to be taken 'neat'. Which is not to say, of course, that some readers will not do precisely that, finding in its pages endorsement of their misogynistic attitudes. But if some of the lads celebrated a pre-feminist masculinity with provocative glee, they were more than matched by the legions of New Men to be found down the gym or the swimming pool, or purchasing millions of copies of self-improvement magazines like *Men's Health*. In this context, as Sharon Willis puts it, 'masculinity in crisis is really white heterosexual masculinity desperately seeking to reconstruct itself within a web of social differences, where its opposing terms include not only femininity, but black masculinity and male homosexuality' (1997, p. 31).

And not before time. Straight men are learning to be self-critical and reflective, just as gay audiences are learning to embrace negative as well as positive representations, and women to exploit and subvert the representational power of their sexuality. Self-reflection, self-criticism, and even a certain amount of self-loathing is for men a necessary coming to terms with the feminist critique of masculinity and the damage it has done to women and men both. It clears the way for a progression to something better.

Figure 8.1 Viz: The Joy of Sexism

Part 3

The aesthetics of sexual transgression

Introduction

Sex has been identified as 'the Big Theme of 20th century art, to be depicted, dissected and transgressed'.[1] Art addressing that big theme is part of striptease culture as I am defining it, in so far as it has focused on the exposed, sexualized body, often in contexts where the artist him- or herself is the subject. Some artists – and examples of this kind of work were discussed in the context of porno-chic (see Chapter 4) – have displayed their bodies 'pornographically'. Others have used the art of the body to expose and explore the sexual taboos and secrets of their societies.

Along the way there has been much controversy, of course, even where it was not deliberately sought out by the artist. As this book was nearing completion in March 2001 a wave of media-inspired outrage was being directed at the American photographer Tierney Gearon, whose nude images of her own children at play were accused of pandering to paedophiles. Police officers from the Obscene Publications Squad threatened to have the prints removed from their place in the Saatchi Gallery in London, and to ban the glossy book in which they were reproduced from sale in British shops. In the end, and after more media publicity for the work than either the artist or her supporters could have predicted in their most optimistic moments, censorship was averted. That it could even have been considered in the year 2001, in one of the world's acknowledged centres of liberal culture, shows how contentious such images continue to be. Like other forms of contemporary sexual representation examined in this book, the art of sexual transgression (or that which is perceived to be sexually transgressive) has been condemned as at worst obscene, at best a violation of decent morals and good taste. Since May 1989 when US Senator Alfonse D'Amato attacked the publicly funded National Endowment for the Arts for supporting Andre Serrano's *Piss Christ* America has been engaged in fierce debates around the status and legitimacy of those growing numbers of artists who deploy sexual imagery in their work. Organizations like the Christian Coalition have taken exception to the fact that American taxpayers 'were subsidising filth and obscenity foisted upon them by a distant (and rich) elite that did not share Christian values' (Jensen, 1996, p. 21).

In Britain the work of Gilbert & George, Tracy Emin, and the Chapman brothers[2] has provoked similar debates (though rarely conducted with the intensity and bitterness of the US 'culture wars'). Sexually explicit 'art house' films like *Crash* (David Cronenberg, 1996), *The Idiots* (Lars Von Trier, 1998) and *Romance* (Catherine Breillat, 1999) have periodically provoked moral anxiety in the United Kingdom, and in the case of Cronenberg's film at least one local authority (Westminster in London) sought a ban on the grounds that it would encourage sexually deviant behaviour among members of the audience (it was argued by one Tory councillor that the film would encourage dangerous driving). In March 1998 police raided the University of Central England and confiscated a book of photographs by Robert Mapplethorpe used in teaching. The institution was threatened with prosecution under the Obscene Publications Act (although, as in the Gearon case, no charges were ever brought).[3]

Some journalists and cultural commentators contributed to these panics in their writings. The tabloid *News of the World*'s shock-horror story which alerted the world to the existence of the Gearon photographs followed up on its widely criticized anti-paedophile campaign of summer 2000.[4] At the more cerebral level, around the time of the British cinema release of *Romance* broadsheet commentators were complaining that 'the crassest, crudest sexual acts are slipping into public currency with no more than a passing snigger',[5] and in 1997 the columnist Julie Burchill asserted that:

> These are the days of the politics of Why Not? These are the days in which the most obscenely oppressive images are not challenged, but actually celebrated as some sort of liberation. As censorship has retreated, only the society of the spectacle has advanced; only the society in which the atrocity can be made into art; and therefore stops being an atrocity because it is no longer 'real'.[6]

References to 'atrocity' and 'obscenity' in the public discussion of sexually explicit art are not unusual, if endowed with some irony in this case by the fact that they come from the author of the best-selling 'shopping and fucking' novel *Ambition* (1989), itself an aggressively marketed moment in the sexualization of culture of which she was complaining eight years later.[7] In her inimitable way, though (and provocative contrariness is her stock-in-trade, after all), Burchill expresses with useful clarity the view I want to contest in the next three chapters – that the art of sexual transgression is the art of obscenity and oppression, complicit in and symbolic of the moral degeneracy of our times. I wish to show that it can also be the art of liberation and self-interrogation, and that the aesthetics of transgression can be an important vehicle for the democratisation of desire.

9

MEN, SEX AND
TRANSGRESSION

The denunciation of sexually transgressive art as the culture of 'atrocity', at least when voiced by those like Burchill who would identify themselves as feminists, is founded on the fact that it has been most practised by men, in whose hands it has reflected what Camille Paglia calls the 'male-will-to-power' (1990). Sexually transgressive art has been an important weapon in the cultural armoury through which men have ruled over women in patriarchy. There is a certain inevitability about this, for Paglia, since it is a consequence not merely of man's emergence as the hunter-predator of the species, but of the penetrative, possessing nature of the male sexual anatomy itself, which provides for Paglia the model for artistic activity. As she puts it in *Sexual Personae* 'the male projection of erection and ejaculation is the paradigm for all cultural projection and conceptualisation – from art philosophy to fantasy, hallucination, and obsession' (ibid., p. 20). Men, she suggests, are anatomically and biologically driven to make symbols and conceptualize. Art is the cultural expression of male sexuality, and sexually transgressive art the expression of man's violatory impulse.[1] We might not like it, but there it is.

This theory is founded on the core idea of an active, domineering masculinity counterposed to a passive, submissive femininity, which is not so different in essence from that of her arch-enemies Dworkin and Mackinnon; a distinction which dates back to prehistory and 'the terrible duality of gender' (ibid., p. 27). Of course, neither Paglia nor anyone else can say with certainty that man's domination of art has biological rather than social roots. It is clear that in the case of the human species males have evolved to be, on average, bigger and stronger than females. But no one really knows why. Perhaps it is the product of a process of natural selection going back to the days of our non-human ancestors. Perhaps it is because men, in most societies, acquired the aggressive roles of hunters and predators, while their female mates bore and reared children. In any event, men were able to translate this division of labour into the system of male superiority we know as patriarchy. As human beings increased the sophistication of their social organisation and technology they learnt to produce more than they needed merely to survive. The concept of property which could be owned, stored and passed on emerged, and with it the need to transfer genes (biological) and property (social) from one generation to the next. This led to the evolution of the laws and customs which

167

reduced women to the subordinate social status they have occupied for most of human history. And regardless of how one chooses to explain patriarchy there is no dispute that men *have* monopolized wealth and political power throughout recorded history, and monopolized too the cultural resources of society, including the means of artistic production. Men have also controlled historical discourse, and the telling of historical narratives, so that the history of art has been the history of Male Art, and more precisely, until the late twentieth century at least, the history of *heterosexual* male art (though dividing the community of cultural producers into gay and straight, as already noted, can be problematic. Not all 'straight' artists have been heterosexual; not all 'gay' artists have an obviously gay focus in their work).

Because art (and thus art about sex) has been dominated by men it has reflected the conditions of existence of the male and his female mate, while promoting the value-system which supports their unequal relationship. It has expressed the full range of ambivalent emotions which men have for the women on whom they depend, but over whom they have been accustomed to rule. Art in patriarchy has largely been the articulation, in various styles and modes, of men's alternating feelings of love and hate, adoration and anger, lust and revulsion, for and towards women, expressed in whatever forms have been available to them at the time. From Delacroix's *Rape of Sardanapalus* to the Prodigy's 'Smack My Bitch Up' and Eminem's misogynistic rap; from the nudes of Titian and Velázquez to the hymns of loss and longing found on The Cure, Prefab Sprout, or Nick Cave records,[2] male art has reflected the tensions provoked by the demands of the sex drive on 'civilized' masculinity; by the contradictions between raw animality and socially proscribed 'humanity'.

But if, for those reasons, much of what men have said about sex in their art is infused with controlling, violatory impulses, a sociological rather than biological explanation for male dominance allows for the possibility that it need not always be so, always and everywhere in human society. On the contrary, if art is viewed as a social construction responsive to evolving environmental features such as the rise of feminism (and in this book it is) the *sexualized* art of men can be expressive of more than the 'male-will-to-power'. And thus one is led to ask, as Giles Neret does in his survey of erotic art: 'Has the male's relationship to the female, sexuality, and art edged forward over the course of the centuries?' (1998, p. 10).

From adoration to transgression

To which the obvious answer is yes. From the very beginnings of human society, archeological records suggest, men adored women and paid homage to them in culture. Ancient civilizations' worship of the female goddess figure can be traced back to the Paleolithic era, and prehistoric artefacts such as the Venus of Willendorf. The ancient temples to be found on the island of Malta, estimated at between five and seven thousand years old, are believed to represent the female genitalia and to have functioned as symbols of fertility. The prominence of the Madonna in Judaeo-

Christian art reflects the importance of the concepts of virginity, motherhood and the inviolability of women in western patriarchy. The reclining female nude in art (a tradition going back at least as far as the early 1500s[3]) is also a form of adoration, although the enduring power of the image has been read by feminist art historians as more than just a reflection of men's love and sexual need for women. For Lynda Nead the female nude 'is a metaphor for the value and significance of art generally' within patriarchy, and 'a means of containing femininity and female sexuality . . . [signifying] that the woman has come under the government of male style' (1992, p. 58). As censorship regimes changed over the centuries and representation became more graphic (assisted by new technologies like photography) the female nude was increasingly sexualized. Adoration of it came to have (especially in the era of feminism) the negative connotation of objectification and to stand for the oppressive, female-fetishizing qualities of patriarchal culture.

The centrality of idealized women in Judaeo-Christian art is regarded by many cultural historians as a possible explanation as to why her violation became a recurring motif of the anticlerical, iconoclastic movements of early modern Europe and after. From the seventeenth century, artistic discourses of sex contained an increasingly transgressive strand which deliberately and explicitly challenged the idealised, socially sanctioned imagery of the mainstream. Sexual transgression became a device employed by male artists to challenge the dominant cultural, philosophical, and even political norms of the societies within which they worked – a tool for subversion from within by artistic rebels who thus positioned themselves, through their use of sexual imagery, as *outsiders*. Neret argues that 'the false shame and prudish taboos sown by Judaeo-Christian civilisation gave rise to a compensating movement in art' (1998, p. 9), perhaps best personified by the archetypal figure of the Marquis de Sade.

Sade's work (though even more sexually explicit than that of Aretino, John Cleland or the other early producers of erotic literature) was not intended to arouse or titillate so much as to shock and subvert the moral codes and conventions of late-eighteenth-century France. As a rebellious member of the decadent French aristocracy he championed a philosophy of sexual libertinism, moral detachment, and philosophical idealism, in which only the sensual satisfaction of the self mattered. In his writings on sex this was reflected in his depictions of violent, abusive sexual acts carried out against men, women and children alike, without social boundaries and constraints of any kind.

Sade's literary cruelties gave rise, of course, to the concept of sadism, and have come to exemplify the 'atrocious' misogyny of sexually transgressive male art ever since. But while, as Georges Bataille once suggested, Sade believed in cruelty and violence as 'the foundation of sensuality', and does indeed appear to have been a rather nasty piece of work, there was more to his aesthetic than the gleeful subjection of the vulnerable to his peculiar fantasies. The reason for the durability of his work, and for the persistent efforts of 'respectable' artists and intellectuals to keep it alive in the western collective memory is not that it reads well, but that it launched, in so far as the aesthetic of sexual transgression is concerned, the modernist era. Sade espoused, at a time when the old feudal order of Europe was in terminal decay, a philosophy of extreme individualism which foreshadowed the economic liberalism of the next century. His decidedly unerotic writings – rightly characterized as an unreadable catalogue of perversions – were, whatever one thinks of them more than two centuries later, intended as an attack on the corrupt values of late feudal France; a savage critique of and commentary on aristocratic immorality and hypocrisy sufficiently subversive to cause him to be imprisoned and thus become a symbol of the artist's eternal battle with the censor. Philip Kaufman's *Quills*, released to critical acclaim and nominated for several Oscars in 2001, is the latest in a long line of art works which have been inspired by and explored this dimension of Sade's heritage.

Sade's work was not pornography, then, so much as a template for the kind of aesthetic revolt against established manners and rules which has driven many artists ever since. The sexually violent novels of Brett Easton Ellis (*American Psycho [1991]* and *Glamorama [1998]*), for example, can be read as a contemporary application of the Sadeian aesthetic in their combination of sexualized violence and social satire. When the feminist director Mary Harron chose to film the widely reviled (by feminists) *American Psycho* she acknowledged that Ellis's construction of sexual horror was more than mere misogyny.[4] Ellis's employment of sexual transgression, like Sade's, is too cold and surgical to be erotic, too exaggerated and absurd to work as pornography, even if the uncomfortable feelings of complicity evoked by reading it (and the later *Glamorama*, with its quasi-comic scenes of torture and terror, has a similar impact on the reader) are part of the work's aesthetic intentions.

The sexually explicit photography of Japanese artist Nobuyoshi Araki can also be seen as Sadeian in its exploration of taboo subjects. A former commercial photographer who repositioned himself as an artist after the death of his wife from cancer, Araki produces work that is an ongoing articulation of the idea that 'erotica and art . . . are equally and unquestionably products of the endless human quest for pleasure, with whatever "perversions" it may encompass' (Araki, 1997, p. 6). He believes that 'without obscenity, our cities are dreary places and life is bleak' (Ibid.), and documents that obscenity where he finds it. The *Tokyo Lucky Hole* collection portrays the women who work in the sex industry of Tokyo's Shinjuku district, and the men who pay for their services. The 'perversions' depicted are of the mildly sadomasochistic variety, linking sex and pain in the manner characteristic of much Japanese sexual culture. They are also full of humour.

Less playful are his portraits of women bound, gagged and otherwise constrained by the poses he bends and squeezes them into. Like the *eromanga* comics read by Japanese workers on the train ride home, or the *roman-porno* films made in Japan in the 1970s Araki's photographs can be characterized as 'often violent and brazenly sexy, steeped in fashionable nihilism and graphically sadistic'.[5] The fact that they are taken with the consent, and often at the instigation of the people who appear in them, makes them no less disturbing.[6]

Transgression and modernism

Long before Araki, and long before Brett Easton Ellis shocked Bush's America with his satire of a chainsaw-wielding, stock-broking serial killer who thinks that Genesis achieved their musical peak *after* the departure of Peter Gabriel from the group (such expressions of nerdish bad taste being important clues as to how the thought processes and actions of the book's central character are intended to be read), Sade's philosophical worldview had been a major influence on the modernist movement of the early twentieth century, and especially on the art produced by the surrealists. Surrealism was described by one of its founding figures as 'dictated by thought, in the absence of any control exercised by reason, exempt from any aesthetic or moral concerns'.[7] Coming out of the experience of the World War I, the surrealists were *apolitical* in a party sense, but radically anti-bourgeois, viewing their art as a means to wage war on mainstream society. One of André Breton's biographers notes that 'the enemy was literature and all its seductions. . . . The rage those young men felt, their bitterness against official notions of "culture", was fuelled in part by their fury at having seen the representatives of this culture embrace and promote a war they considered pointless and hateful' (Polizotti, 1995, p. 95).

In the articulation of that rage they developed Sade's subversive philosophy into a view of sexuality as something which should push at the limits of physical and emotional endurance; what Sontag describes as 'beyond good and evil, beyond love, beyond sanity; as a resource for ordeal and for breaking through the limits of consciousness' (1982, p. 104).[8] This notion was expressed in the concept of 'mad love' – *l'amour fou* (Breton wrote a novel of that title[9]), or 'a love that explodes the psyche', as the critic Waldemar Januszczak later expressed it.[10] Both phrases convey the idea that for the surrealists love was obsessive and irrational rather than romantic, leading to insanity rather than happiness; a disruptive social force to be celebrated, certainly, but also available for exploitation by avant-garde artists in their battle with established traditions.

The surrealists were also influenced by Freud and the theory of psychoanalysis, and in particular his suggestion that the human psyche could accommodate many selves, some of which were hidden or repressed by the rules and etiquette of polite bourgeois society. They sought to represent in art 'the return of the repressed' and to explore those many selves by highlighting the strangeness of everyday occurrences, transferring the ordinary into the realm of the *uncanny*; to create art in which 'repressed material returns in ways that disrupt unitary identity, aesthetic norms, and social order' (Foster, 1995, p. xv), and in which the unconscious mind, or dream state is made to seem real. This aesthetic was applied in its most transgressive form to surrealist representations of the sexualised body, which artists like Hans Bellmer and Salvador Dalí stretched, dismembered and deconstructed to weird effect. The surrealists thus sought to give form to 'a sexuality that is not grounded on an idea of human nature, or the natural, but instead, woven of fantasy and representation, fabricated' (Krauss, ed., 1985, p. 95).

These elements are nicely illustrated in the work of Emmanuel (Man) Ray, an American-born 'Dadaist' who moved to Paris in the 1920s and joined the surrealist project soon after. Sade was Man Ray's hero, inspiring his personal philosophy of 'absolute liberty'. As one critic records, 'Man Ray always stressed his admiration for the writings of the Marquis de Sade; Sade, though obsessed with sexual cruelty and using women as objects of pleasure, was the great ideal of freedom to Man Ray, as to all the surrealists' (Forestag, ed., 1988, p. 215). In some contrast to the accounts one reads of Sade's private life, however, Man Ray is reported by his friends and associates to have had a likeable, generous personality,[11] and the warmth of his sexual imagery (as opposed to Sade's straightforward cataloguing of transgressive fantasy) has been one of the reasons (apart from his technical and aesthetic skills as a photographer) for its enduring popularity.[12] In Man Ray's work the curves and shapes of women's bodies are refracted and highlighted through the use of special effects (many of them, such as solarization and the rayograph process, invented by the artist) and unexpected juxtapositions with objects such as tribal artefacts and machinery. In *Le Violon d'Ingres* (1924) the shapes of the sound holes of a violin are superimposed on the model's back (the famous Kiki of Montparnasse), as if she were an instrument to be played by the artist (or the spectator). Viewing the beautiful, luscious compositions of such as *Noire et blanche* (1926), *La Prière* (1930), *Érotique Voilée* (1935) and *Juliet* (1945) one is tempted to conclude that for all he idolised the Marquis, Man Ray's dreamlike, genuinely erotic treatment of sexuality was influenced by Freud more than Sade. It draws us into a luxurious world of dreams, rather than the horrors of Sade's sexual violence.

The writer Georges Bataille, on the other hand, steered closer to the aggressive sexual transgression of the Marquis, applying it to greatest aesthetic effect in his 1928 novella *The Story of the Eye*. For Bataille, as for Sade, writing should shock and provoke the reader while displaying what Michael Richardson characterizes as 'a visceral and direct relation with life' (Bataille, 1994, p. 16). His artistic project was 'erotic subversion', produced through depictions of sex which were out of the ordinary (to the point of being ridiculous or distressing), though arousing in a way that Sade's were not. In *The Story of the Eye* eroticism is produced from the interaction of human bodies, taboo sex acts, and everyday objects such as milk, eyes and eggs, as well as smatterings of casual, largely anti-clerical violence.

> The day was extremely hot. Simone put the saucer on a small bench, planted herself before me, and, with her eyes fixed on me, she sat down without my being able to see her burning buttocks under the skirt, dipping into the cool milk. The blood shot to my head, and I stood before her awhile, immobile and trembling, as she eyed my stiff cock bulging in my trousers. Then I lay down at her feet without stirring, and for the first time, I saw her 'pink and dark' flesh cooling in the white milk. We remained motionless, both of us equally overwhelmed.
>
> (p. 10)

Nead writes of Bataille's work that 'the erotic excess of pornography shatters the illusory unity of the viewing subject and thus forces a critical crack in the system of bourgeois values' (1992, p. 69).

The limits of modernist transgression

That at least was his aim, and the subversion of bourgeois values, given the minor crimes and major atrocities committed in their name down the centuries, is one with which many will readily sympathize, and which throughout the twentieth century has driven the work of artists as diverse as Joel-Peter Witkin and the Velvet Underground.[13] The power of transgressive, sexualised art (as of at least some forms of pornography) is particularly felt – and thus particularly valuable – in societies where political authoritarianism or religious fundamentalism (or both) have stunted human freedom and individuality. In such societies, indeed, it may become a form of oppositional political activity, and perhaps the only one possible. The South Korean director Jang Sun-Woo's *Lies* (1999), for example, has been applauded as 'a genuinely subversive film, not because it shows nudity, sado-masochist foreplay and sex but because of the wide-eyed curiosity and amusement with which Jang views these things'[14] in a society long used to suppressing sexual, as well as political freedom. In the west the end of Franco's dictatorship in Spain led to a flowering of sexually transgressive art, exemplified by the cinema of Pedro Almodovar and Bigas Lunas, which contributed much (although we will never know quite *how* much) to the construction of a cultural and political environment hostile to the return of fascism.

In the work of these and many other artists the progressive, *political* intention of sexual transgression is easily recognized, by all except the despotisms and tyrannies against which it is directed. Since Sade, nevertheless, the question has been asked – not least by feminist critics who note the frequency with which women are the sacrificial victims in such work – at what price have male artists pursued their aesthetic revolts? Kathy Myers, for example, doubts that the aesthetic of sexual transgression is really more than 'a dubious tradition of sexual libertarianism which invests that which is censored with the power to disrupt and liberate' (1987, p. 61).

The sexually transgressive artists of the post-Sadeian era (and of all eras before and after, for that matter) have for the most part been men, as already noted. Their art has been based on what one historian calls 'the reality of human desire', but it is male, heterosexual desire in which they have chiefly been interested, and the sexualisation of the female body on which they have expended the greatest part of their creative talents and energies. To that extent their transgressions have been limited to the critique of bourgeois rather than patriarchal values. Moreover, they have often been both misogynistic and homophobic.

André Breton, the self-styled 'pope of surrealism' did not, according to his biographer, 'tolerate the presence of homosexuals around him' (Polizotti, 1995). The surrealists' treatment of their female colleagues was less openly hostile, but still cavalier and exploitative. Neret observes that for the surrealists 'the female represented both idol and enemy' (1998, p. 145), while one critic writes of Man Ray – by no means the worst offender in this respect – not only that he 'made women into objects', but that many of his images refer to 'putting woman in her place, as a thing of pleasure. More than once he proudly commented on violently abusing women' (Forestag, ed., 1988, p. 215).[15]

Closely connected to these attitudes was a particular idea of what art is, and how it is made – 'the mythology of artistic genius', as Lynda Nead calls it (1992, p. 58). The focus on the female nude in art, from the Renaissance period through to surrealism and the twentieth-century modernists, expressed 'a particular ideal of artistic identity as male, virile and sexually uninhibited' (ibid., p. 44), exemplified in the work of Pablo Picasso, 'the prime painter-penetrator, the man who put the *trop* into heterosexual, harnessing his powers of invention to his libido and, when his libido began to flag, punctuating his work with ever-more audacious couplings and visual-genital puns'.[16] Picasso articulated the purpose of his transgressive aesthetic thus:

> We must wake people up. Upset their ways of identifying things. It is necessary to create unacceptable images. Make people foam at the mouth. Force them to understand that they live in a mad world. A disquieting world, not reassuring. A world which is not as they see it.[17]

Whatever kind of genius he was (and *Guernica* is probably the most important work of visual art to have emerged from the era of Nazism) Picasso was at the same time (and like many great artists before and since) a vicious, controlling misogynist who seduced and discarded women with monotonous regularity throughout his life.

The rehabilitation of sexual transgression

The art of Sade, Bataille, Man Ray, Picasso, and the modernist movement in general, for all that it reflects the conditions of its production – in particular, a pre-feminist, pre-gay liberation political culture – and thus excludes from its subversive reach the inequalities and hypocrisies of sexual stratification and gender relations, *did* have the power to disrupt and unsettle the repressive, controlling structures of bourgeois society in ways which had value beyond their political limitations. Recognizing that fact, contemporary artists informed by a more progressive sexual politics have sought to appropriate the subversive spirit of modernism in less masculinist, less heterocentric ways. These artists, working in a range of media, employ the aesthetics of sexual transgression to subvert, not merely bourgeois society (whatever that term means anymore) but the hierarchies, inequalities and injustices associated with patriarchy.

The Danish film-maker Lars von Trier, for example, through his championing of the Dogma movement, represents a new generation inspired by, and aspiring to, the unsettling impact of the modernists. His work frequently uses sex to shock, as in the famous scene from *The Idiots* where the 'spazzers' (young Danes playing the roles of mentally handicapped people) embark on a group sex session, or when one of the 'spazzing' women removes the top of her bathing suit in a crowded public baths. In *Breaking the Waves* (1995) von Trier explores the impact of oppressive religious and social (patriarchal) expectations on the development of a young woman's sexuality. Cast at the beginning of the film as the victim of a deeply sexist church, she ends up sacrificing herself to brutal misogynists in the effort to please her man. These works are conscious of their location in patriarchal society, and embrace the evils and hypocrisies of that society as a subject. Thus, while von Trier has compared the *The Idiots* with Sade's *Justine* in its violation of social and cultural conventions, his film avoids the violence and the cruelty of the latter to present instead a poignant study of dominant attitudes to disability and disabled sexuality, not dissimilar in style and effect to the UK-produced social realist dramas of such as Mike Leigh and G.F. Newman. Thomas Vinterberg's Dogma film *The Celebration* (1998), about child abuse and family dysfunction, has been compared in its style and emotional impact with Buñuel's classic anti-bourgeois satires, but applies its transgressive tools to patriarchal rather than bourgeois structures.

Not all critics are convinced of the worth of these strategies. I have already quoted Kathy Myers' suspicions of what she terms a 'dubious tradition'. One critic refers to Dogma as 'a movement of nostalgic transgression',[18] complaining that von Trier and his followers 'hark back to the naive belief held by audiences and film-makers in the past that pushing the boundaries of notional good taste, liberating sexual representation or declaring a modernist disdain of bourgeois hypocrisy could rock the status quo'. The Dogma directors are said to 'mimic a revolutionary stance that pretends to want to revive a modernist transgressive cinema within a sceptical post-modern climate'. Evaluating the success of these films in achieving the stated aims of their directors is a matter of opinion, of course, as von Trier's *Dancer In the Dark* (2000) showed when it produced wildly varying responses amongst professional critics and audiences. But the difference between the searing anti-patriarchal content of *Breaking the Waves* or *The Celebration* and the frequently misogynistic products of Great Man modernism is clear.[19]

In France, the 1990s saw an upsurge of sexually transgressive films containing what were routinely described by reviewers as 'pornographic' imagery, such as Gaspar Noe's *Seul Contre Tous* (1998) and Catherine Breillat's *Romance* (1998). These were taboo-breaking in their calculated use, in an ostensibly non-pornographic context, of pornographic staples such as 'come shots' and scenes of penile erection and penetration – scenes which, as Chapter 3 discussed, contributed in their explicitness to the crisis of censorship faced by the UK authorities in the late 1990s. In contrast to the work of the Dogma movement, however, several of these films were criticized as 'backlash' texts, nostalgic not only for the modernist aesthetic of transgression but for the misogyny which frequently went with it. Philippe Harel's *Whatever* (2000), based on the novel by the iconoclastic novelist Michelle Houellebecq, was described by one reviewer as 'a grand pessimistic narrative . . . a wicked satire of the corporate world',[20] but one with a 'wholly male perspective, in which women are described verbally and visually in terms of their genitalia'. Why France should have been the site of such a movement is beyond the scope of this book. In any case, the provocative misogyny of French directors like Harel is not typical of the way in which male film-makers elsewhere used sex to shock in the late twentieth century. One thinks, in this respect, of the Canadians Atom Egoyan and David Cronenberg, both of whom have been making sexually transgressive cinema since long before the emergence of the late 1990s modernists. Egoyan's films address such themes as sexual abuse, homophobia and the frequently oppressive nature of masculinity in ways which, though challenging and disturbing, never endorse them. *Exotica* (1996), like many of Egoyan's films, is *about* voyeurism, rather than simply representing it uncritically. Its images of striptease are unquestionably sexy to the heterosexual male eye, but are only the door through which we pass into a world of politically-charged mystery – why does the man attend the strip club? What is the nature of his obsessive desire? Why does the woman strip? *Felicia's Journey* (1999) stars Bob Hoskins as an obsessed serial killer who appears to be loosely modelled on the case of Fred West. *The Adjustor* (1992) is about censorship and pornography, and the lingering impact of child abuse on adulthood, a theme also at the centre of *The Sweet Hereafter* (1997).

The films of Egoyan's Canadian peer David Cronenberg have explored the themes of sexual epidemic, pornographic desire and paraphilia. The much-criticized *Crash*, for example, is a satire about the iconic status of cars in contemporary capitalist societies, which the director addresses through the metaphor of their sexual appeal to both men and women. It is also a film about bi- and homosexuality, 'perversion' in general, sexual inadequacy, and the possibilities of redemption through sexual experimentation and the transcending of taboos. Whether *Crash* succeeds as a work of art is for the viewer to decide (and like the output of the Dogma directors, critics dispute its aesthetic worth), but there can be little doubt that its attempt to 'democratize desire' by subverting dominant stereotypes of disability and masculinity is sincere. Barbara Creed argues that, despite its good intentions, *Crash* 'speaks male, not female desire; its visual style is brilliant, its subject matter is confrontational but its sexual politics are phallocentric' (1998, p. 179). This is true, but only in so far as the work is by a male director, adapting a male-authored novel about male sexuality. The same 'criticism' could be made of Egoyan or the Dogma directors, but efforts to impose the critical framework of the male gaze on their work rather miss the point that in most of these films male auteurs question and subvert maleness and phallocentrism, rather than endorse or celebrate it. These films articulate male desires, certainly, but they are desires which are uncertain, confused, and guilt-ridden.

Postmodernity and the art of striptease

Parallelling this revival of what many of the artists referred to above would themselves characterize as a form of modernism (let's call it *late modernism*), has been the movement toward a *post*modern aesthetic of transgression. By this I mean, on one level, art which reflects 'a growing awareness that not only do the meanings of the sexual change as the sociohistorical context within which it is experienced changes, but also that the very nature of the sexual changes as well' (Simon, 1996, p. 27). In the work associated with this trend yesterday's sexism is today's sexually charged play. The objectification once seen as an instrument of patriarchal oppression comes to be viewed as a tool in the critique of patriarchy, as well as the celebration of voyeurism.

At the level of aesthetics postmodern sexualised art involves the incorporation by artists into their work of popular cultural forms such as pornography and advertising and, associated with that, the purposeful and often provocative blurring of the taste distinctions separating those cultural categories from art. In work of this kind the taboo nature of pornography becomes a resource for the creation of aesthetic effects which may or may not be 'erotic' but are almost always controversial. Araki, for example, 'may take porn pictures, but he is not a porn photographer'[21] (although he employs pornographic conventions with such integrity that his work was found to be obscene by the Japanese censor in 1988). British artist Rankin's *Raw Nudes* series of images (1999) uses unpaid volunteers 'to undermine the connection between nakedness and pornography'.[22]

Jeff Koons's *Made in Heaven*, as Chapter 4 described, borrows from the conventions of pornography to make the viewer think about the art/porn distinction, and about the ways in which sexual culture is policed. The images display his then wife and porn star Cicciolina in classic pornographic poses, in homage to the institution of marriage and the ideal of romantic love. As Giles Neret puts it, he 'makes monuments out of his conjugal, vaginal penetrations, taking them as society's most widely recognised signifier' (1998, p. 44). In the same way that Gilbert & George package sexually transgressive content in symmetrical shapes and translucent colours which rob them of much of their shock value (see Chapter 10) Koons's photographs, though not flinching from the uncensored depiction of the sex act, are saturated in gorgeous colour, and composed with elaborate scenic backdrops. They are genuinely beautiful artefacts. In semiological terms they denote porn, while connoting art.

In all these ways Koons's aesthetics are rooted in the work of Andy Warhol, who frequently played with the conventions of pornography in his experimental films of the 1960s and 1970s. They documented the sexual revolution, or at least a significant moment in it, in an unashamedly voyeuristic manner. Unlike the modernists, however, from whom he distanced himself, Warhol's voyeurism was not expressive of the domination of the straight male artist over his subject. Warhol was gay, and his images fetishized the male body as much as the female. He did not discriminate between men and women in his cultivation of a modish bohemia which he then committed to film. In this respect his work was founded on an 'equality of exploitation', anticipating the late-twentieth-century movement in art beyond what Horne and Lewis call 'the critique of objectification to a belief in the pleasures and potentials of looking and voyeurism' (1996, p. 8). These pleasures are clearly evident in the art of Jeff Koons, and *Made In Heaven* in particular, where his voyeurism is accompanied by the representation of his own sexualized body. In these images Koons reveals and exhibits *himself* as much as Cicciolina. As Koons has said of *Made in Heaven*, 'I had to go to the depths of my own sexuality, my own morality, to be able to remove fear, guilt and shame from myself. All of this has been removed for the viewer' (1992, p. 130).

In a later variation of a technique which had by the late 1990s become routine Japanese performance artist Hiroshi Sumari 'offers himself up on a plate: the artist as model as object of desire as porn star, spread out for the pleasure of others, trying to suck his penis, squeezing his balls'.[23] In the words of the artist: 'I look at them while they look at me. In doing this, I am also a voyeur. The fact that I can make art in the pornographic context is interesting to me'.[24]

In the work of these *post*modern artists pornographic iconography is used not only in the service of disruption but to signify beauty. They objectify their subjects, but their subjects are often themselves, changing the nature of the contract between artist and viewer. Where modernist art routinely expressed misogynistic attitudes, much of the sexually transgressive male art of the late twentieth century (late modern and postmodern) has been concerned with reflection on, and criticism of, patriarchy and its cultural conventions. If modernism has traditionally been associated with the rapacious, amoral genius and the cult of the (male) individual exemplified by Pablo Picasso; and if it can be seen as the quintessential aesthetic expression of unreconstructed heterosexist masculinity, the contemporary male art of sexual transgression expresses an awareness of the limitations and even absurdity of that cult,[25] and a readiness to subject it to the voyeuristic gaze of the viewer.

10

QUEER CULTURE

Men have ruled the art of sexual transgression, then, for better or worse. But not all men are heterosexual, and the perception that there are more homosexual men (and indeed women) working in the production of art and culture than in some other spheres of life is probably true, if only because the creative industries provide more scope than most others for professional and personal nonconformity. Even in the art world, however, homosexuals of both sexes had to hide or disguise their sexual orientation from public view for most of the twentieth century. With very few exceptions, only after the change in the political climate symbolized by Stonewall did it become possible for them to come out through their work, and to find acceptance for and appreciation of it in mainstream culture. When they did so, the increased visibility of gay art became an index of the late twentieth century's democratization of desire, not least because it often employed strategies of aesthetic transgression similar to those discussed in the previous chapter. What counts as 'transgression' in the representation of homsexuality, artistic or otherwise, must of course be contextualized by the fact that the zone of the societally unacceptable is much more extensive for gay artists than that encountered by heterosexuals. Soap operatic same-sex kisses of the type famously undertaken by Beth Jordache in Channel 4's *Brookside*, or Colin in the BBC's *EastEnders* (no tongues, please!) have been received on both sides of the Atlantic as taboo-breaking cultural moments (see Chapter 7), whereas a film like Adrian Lyne's *Lolita* (1998) can achieve mass cinematic distribution while depicting heterosexual penetration and oral sex (albeit simulated) between a man in his fifties and a 14-year-old girl. Homosexualized art may be transgressive, then, merely in making the figure of the homosexual visible, or in showing sexual activity which in a heterosexual context would hardly register with an audience. That said, this chapter explores the ways in which gay artists *have* made gayness visible and, in doing so, fuelled a cultural revolution to parallel the sexual revolution described in Chapter 2.

Gay art before Stonewall – from aesthetes to Andy

Gay men and women have been making art throughout history, if in conditions where the public existence of homosexuality was not tolerated (and the concept of

179

homosexuality unknown). Leonardo da Vinci, Michelangelo, Christopher Marlowe and Sergei Eisenstein are among those great artists of the past believed to have been actively homosexual. The fact that their sexual orientation remained unknown for so long (and there is frequent dispute, of course, as to whether this or that figure was gay or not) is a consequence of the pressing reality that until the liberalization of sexual culture in the 1960s gay artists were suppressed, marginalized, persecuted, and thus underground of necessity.[1] When active on the public stage they were required to work in heavily coded forms. Oscar Wilde, for example, unable to be 'out' in Victorian England adopted a style euphemistically known as aestheticism – 'the earliest important gay discourse' (La Valley, 1995, p. 61) – which permeates his novel *The Picture of Dorian Gray*.[2]

Wilde's aestheticism formed the template for a certain type of homosexual (or possibly homosexual) dandy in the late twentieth century. David Bowie in his glam rock heyday drew extensively on it (see Chapter 7), as film director Todd Haynes acknowledged by juxtaposing the Ziggy Stardust/Brian Slade character with snapshots from an imaginary life of Wilde in *Velvet Goldmine* (1998). In the first half of the twentieth century, though, with the lesson of Wilde's prosecution and imprisonment still fresh and institutionalized homophobia near universal, gay artists had no opportunity or desire to be so brazen. Even the avant-garde artists of the surrealist movement, as we have seen, for all their anti-bourgeois, anti-clerical posturing displayed an ugly intolerance of their gay colleagues. Emmanuel Cooper records that 'Jean Cocteau was hated and despised by his one-time associate André Breton precisely because he was homosexual. Breton's dislike and distrust of homosexuals extended to other artists, most notably the writer René Crevel, the only self-proclaimed homosexual in the surrealist group, who was given a mock trial for his sexual tastes' (Cooper, 1994, p. 139).

Homophobia continued to dominate the art world, and the art audience, until the 1960s. Artists who were 'out' before this period – the significantly pseudonymous Tom of Finland, for example[3] – were working within and for a specifically gay audience. Those few who tried to explore sexual subjects felt compelled, as Patricia Morrisroe notes in her biography of Robert Mapplethorpe, 'to tone down their work to make it less threatening to the status quo, and an elaborate code developed to help them express homoerotic feelings. The male nude was placed within an acceptable context, such as a gymnasium, boxing ring, or swimming hole, or else it was elevated beyond contemporary morality by the use of classical and religious themes' (1995, p. 78).

Only with the onset of the sexual revolution did the art establishment grow more tolerant of homosexuality, if still far from understanding or accepting of it. Most artists who were openly gay in their private circles, such as Andy Warhol, avoided public self-identification. Warhol, now recognized as one of the most important artists of the twentieth century, was not widely perceived in the 1960s as a 'gay' artist. In his carefully manufactured public persona he occupied an uneasy space between gay and straight, hiding his private homosexuality behind the public permissiveness licensed by the sexual revolution. In his displays of camp flamboyance and sardonic wit he was, indeed, a kind of Oscar Wilde of his era (Wilde obscured or hedged around his homosexuality for much of his life, presenting a public front of happily married domesticity and fatherhood until the Marquis of Queensberry provoked him into a very public, and personally disastrous court case).

Warhol *chose* not to identify himself as a 'gay artist', not least because he was a Catholic who felt, by the accounts of many of his associates and biographers, shame and self-disgust at the knowledge of his 'perverse' sexuality.[4] His explicit homo-erotic drawings and polaroids (the latter inspired by his encounters with Robert Mapplethorpe in the 1970s) were kept hidden from his public until after his death. For all his coyness and obfuscation, however, Warhol was one of the first artists – and certainly the first major artist – to make homosexuality visible in his work. Warhol's associates and 'superstars', as the young wannabes who gathered around him in the Factory and formed the cast of his art became known, were a mix of the decadently heterosexual (Edie Sedgwick), the flamboyantly homosexual (Paul Morrissey) and the unhappily transvestite (Candy Darling). Many of the experimental films he directed or produced (*Blow Job*, *Lonesome Cowboys*, *My Hustler*) represented homosexuality with unprecedented directness,[5] and were by any standards transgressive. His mass-produced screen prints of Marilyn Monroe, Elizabeth Taylor, Elvis Presley and Marlon Brando pastiched the work of those 'downtown macho' modernists whom he despised.[6] Horne and Lewis observe that in Warhol 'the gay artist's opposition to what was experienced as the masculinist forms of the dominant aesthetic of Abstract Expressionism found an alternative visual resource in the camp appreciation of popular culture' (1996, eds., p. 5). Warhol's was exemplary of the gay art which dared not speak its name in clear and direct language, although the accessibility and inclusiveness of his imagery, as much as the way in which it resonated with the intensifying consumer culture of late-twentieth-century capitalism made it immensely popular and influential, then and since. It is ironic, as well as poignant, that this gay man's reluctance to concede his gayness to a homophobic public should have contributed to his status as one of the truly visionary artists of the twentieth century (as opposed to merely one of the great gay artists of the twentieth century).

After Stonewall

Warhol achieved fame in the pre-Stonewall 1960s, though it was only after 1969, as a consequence of the politicization of the homosexual community which the Stonewall events set in motion, and the development of a commercialized gay sub-culture which that encouraged in the big cities of the United States and Europe, that an overt, unapologetic, homosexualized art could emerge into public view, led by such as Robert Mapplethorpe.

Mapplethorpe was born to middle-class Catholic parents in 1946, in Queens, New York. He discovered his homosexuality in his early teens and, like Warhol, appears to have developed something of a guilt complex, though he was more successful than Warhol in overcoming it, and then integrating it into his work.

Like most young men he became interested in pornography, and its illicit seductions stayed with him throughout his career. He went to art school in 1963, still hiding his homosexuality (and indeed unsure if he was gay or straight), where Warhol (also a sexually repressed gay Catholic) came to his attention. Mapplethorpe admired both Warhol's art and his glamorous New York lifestyle (although several sources record his disappointment with Warhol when they finally met in the early 1970s, and with the Factory scene in general[7]). Warhol's influence drew him to New York, where he met the poet and musician Patti Smith in 1967. They lived together for a year in the Chelsea Hotel while he grappled with his sexuality, and though the gay sub-culture eventually won the battle for his sexual affections Smith inspired and supported him throughout his formative years as a working artist. He took the photographs which adorn two of her records, including the classic *Horses* (1975), famous almost as much for his black-and-white cover shot as for the music within.[8] Mapplethorpe remained on good terms with Smith until his death from AIDS in 1989.

His first important artworks were Warhol-inspired collages using explicit images cut from the pages of gay porn magazines. He was, indeed, one of the first artists, gay or straight, to use pornography as a source of aesthetic inspiration. He was also steeped in the self-imposed guilt and repressed eroticism of the Catholic Church, an eroticism heightened by and refracted through his own 'perverted' sexual desires. When he emerged as a self-taught photographer in the 1970s these influences combined to shape work which has many references to religious symbolism as well as to the sadomasochism and homoeroticism for which Mapplethorpe is best known.

Mapplethorpe is important to the democratization of desire for three reasons. He was the first artist (gay or straight) of the sexually explicit (and the explicitly deviant) to become a household name. His NEA[9]-supported *Perfect Moment* exhibition, which toured the United States in 1988–90, became a symbol of the 'culture wars' and made him famous.[10] Second, he was the first *homoerotic* photographer to break through into the mainstream art world. And third, he was the first photographer of *black* male nudes to do so.[11] For all of these reasons he has become not only a key figure in the history of gay art, but a pivotal figure in the debates around sexually transgressive art in general – a symbol of its radical potential, or its degenerative effects, depending on your viewpoint.

Mapplethorpe used his considerable technical and creative abilities to produce photographs of a type never before seen in a public space. He presented sexually graphic, sometimes bloodily sadomasochistic content in expertly executed mono- chrome and colour prints. Mapplethorpe's affinity with colour, contrast and composition were employed in the development of a disciplined, studio-bound style strongly evocative of classical aesthetics and the formalized, posed photog- raphy of Man Ray.[12] Like Man Ray he photographed flowers and objects, often with a strongly religious flavour (Christ on the cross, for example), endowing them with genitalic sexuality. Like Man Ray, too, he placed the human body in dramatic juxtaposition to geometric shapes and organic nature, as in the photographs of his lover Milton Moore, and the *Lady: Lisa Lyon* series (dedicated, incidentally, to Patti Smith). The bodybuilder-cum-performance artist Lyons had developed herself into 'a sculptor of her own body'[13] whose taut, muscular frame wilfully blurred the masculine/feminine divide. Mapplethorpe's photographs highlighted both elements of her persona, combining the referents of feminity (white lace and skimpy bikinis, for example) with suggestions of masculine strength (bulging veins, clenched fists). Viewed as a book-length photographic essay in what would become known in the popular vernacular as gender-bending, *Lady* was a pioneering work.

Mapplethorpe the pornographer

Mapplethorpe was not political, but he and his transgressive art were the by-product of gay liberation and that period in the 1970s and early 1980s before HIV/AIDS when the gay sexual lifestyle 'came out of the closet' and acquired visibility as a personal and political statement. He lived the life he photographed, and his images serve as a macabre accompaniment to the emergence of the HIV virus.[14] Arthur Danto observes that

> Mapplethorpe was not an activist. His interests in sex were somehow more aesthetic and in a sense metaphysical. . . . Even so, the politics of liberation made it possible for him to build a body of artistic work on what would largely have been forbidden themes as little as a decade earlier. If S&M devotees had been photographed at an earlier time, they would have been exposed to blackmail. Now they sought out Mapplethorpe as a photographer because their activities were ennobled as well as licensed.
>
> (1994)

It is, of course, his homosexually explicit photographs for which Mapplethorpe is best known. Many artists – and especially gay artists, to whom opportunities for public exhibition were long denied – have created sexually explicit images for private consumption, including Pablo Picasso[15] and Andy Warhol. Mapplethorpe did so for the world to see (although even he made images which he considered too shocking to show, and which have never been seen in public), leading to the familiar criticism that he was not an artist but a pornographer. Danto believes that Mapplethorpe *was* a pornographer, in so far as he recognized the erotic, taboo-breaking content of his work, and saw nothing immoral about the production or consumption of porn, if by that is meant sexually explicit images which are intentionally arousing. He was a pornographer, though, 'with high art aims' (Danto, 1994, p. 78) (as opposed to Jeff Koons, an artist who occasionally utilizes the pornographic repertoire). For Edmund White, Mapplethorpe's aesthetic goal was 'to raise gay male pornography to the level of high art'.[16] Mapplethorpe's work from the beginning anticipates the deliberate blurring of the pornographic and the artistic characteristic of so much of the sexualized art of the late twentieth century.

Where Koons's *Made In Heaven* aestheticizes the sexual relationship between the artist and his porno-wife Mapplethorpe's photographs document in explicit detail the promiscuous gay lifestyle of 1970s New York, making them art, porn and documentary all at the same time. The historian John Pultz suggests that 'Mapplethorpe's photography functions as erotica for gay men while making male homosexuality visible' (1995, p. 157). Mapplethorpe's images were transgressive not only in showing sex, but in showing gay sex, and sadomasochistic gay sex at that, at a time when it was still a hidden zone to all but those involved in it.

It is not necessary to decide whether Mapplethorpe was a pornographer or an artist, then, since he was, by reputation and intention, both. Where Koons and Madonna distance themselves from the realm of the pornographic (at the same time as seeking to appropriate its taboo qualities), Mapplethorpe embraces the label. His transgressive images, pre-dating theirs by more than a decade, celebrate the pornographic in a way which reflects its distinctive role in gay culture. They are less confused as to their status and thus, one might argue, more honest – which is one reason for the intensely polarised responses they provoked when they came to the attention of straight critics. For Lisa Duggan:

> Mapplethorpe's work exposes the contradictions and hypocrisy at the heart of the postwar [moral] consensus. His images cross the designated boundaries, appropriating images from the stigmatized zone of 'pornography' and carting them across the lines into the free zone of 'art'. Mapplethorpe's strategy was radically to disrupt the belief that images of some bodies and practices are fit only for squalid, hidden or persecuted surroundings.
>
> (Duggan and Hunter, 1995, p. 77)

For Camille Paglia the value of his work lies precisely in this refusal to deny his status as a maker of dirty pictures.

> I accept Mapplethorpe as a pornographer. . . . Degradation is at the heart of his eroticism. To deny the degradation in the photos of one man urinating into the mouth of another is to remove all their erotic charge. Such acts have never been sanctioned in any culture. That is why they are now and will remain radical.
>
> (1992, p. 43)

Radical, perhaps. Lethal, in the HIV-infected fast lane of the New York city gay scene, most probably, and the biologically dangerous activities depicted in many of Mapplethorpe's photographs underpin one of the main criticisms made of him – that he was irresponsible, amoral, and exploitative in his relations with his models and subjects. Edmund White points out, however, that 'his portraits were almost always shot in the studio under controlled conditions and with the full cooperation and even complicity of the sitter'.[17] Susan Sontag agrees that he was not 'in a predatory relation to his subjects'.[18] He *did* fuck many of them, before or after a shoot, but would probably have done so whether he was an artist or not, given the circles in which he moved.

And if Mapplethorpe was a voyeur he was also an auto-voyeur. A notorious 1978 self-portrait shows him with a leather bull whip inserted in his anus. Transgressive self-objectification is a crucial element in his aesthetic, as it was later to be of Koons's and Madonna's work, though it is less obviously manufactured than that of either. When Mapplethorpe photographs himself in a sexually explicit or sadomasochistic pose it's real rather than staged fantasy.[19]

Mapplethorpe the racist

More serious than the question of whether Mapplethorpe exploited his subjects in the manner that a male pornographer might be argued to exploit his female 'object', is the question of whether he was a racist. This issue arose, paradoxically, because Mapplethorpe was the first photographer of nude black men to gain wide public attention. He was sexually attracted to black men, and had many black male lovers, some of whom are immortalized in his best-known works. He clearly found black men inspirational, and his representations of them are dignified and statuesque, as well as highly sexualized. Their large penises are often accentuated in the frame, as in the famous portrait of Milton Moore, *Man in a Polyester Suit* (1981). These features of his work led to criticisms such as the following:

> Some Western photographers have shown that they can desire Black males (albeit rather neurotically). But [Mapplethorpe's] exploitative mythologising of Black virility on behalf of the homosexual bourgeoisie is ultimately no different from the vulgar objectification of Africa which we know at one extreme from the work of Leni Riefenstahl and, at the other, from the 'victim' images which appear constantly in the media.
> (Reid, 1998, p. 220)

> Mapplethorpe appropriates the conventions of porn's racialised codes of representation and by abstracting its stereotypes into 'art' he makes racism's phantasms of desire respectable. . . . In pictures like *Man In a Polyester Suit*, the dialectics of fear and fascination in colonial fantasy are reinscribed by the centrality of the black man's 'monstrous' phallus. The black subject is objectified into Otherness as the size of his penis symbolises a threat to the secure identity of the white male ego.
> (film director Isaac Julien, quoted in Reid, 1998, p. 225)

Mapplethorpe was not sensitive to gay or black liberation, and he was hardly politically correct in his attitudes to ethnicity (or anything else, for that matter). He shared the stereotypes and casual racisms of his white middle-class parent culture, and often articulated them in private, but his photographs are increasingly

185

acknowledged by black and white critics alike to be positive representations, and at the very least an advance on the relative invisibility and stereotyping of the black male nude which characterized photographic art before him. Edmund White points out that 'Mapplethorpe was virtually the only photographer [of his time or before] who was giving them [black men] exciting and beautiful images of their race'.[20] Comparing Mapplethorpe's work with the likes of Riefenstahl, or presenting him as a latter-day Colonel Kurtz on the grounds that the photographs contain sexualised images of black men, ignores their intended meaning – that black men are, to Mapplethorpe, aesthetically beautiful and sexually desirable to *him*, not least because they (or the ones in some of these photographs) have big cocks.

These are images, moreover, which extend the range of representations of the black American male beyond those exemplified by the familiar machismo of the sports star or the rapper.[21] In homoeroticizing black men (as opposed to merely eroticising them) Mapplethorpe helped, as the curator of the 1994 *Black Male* exhibition mounted at the Whitney Museum of Contemporary Art put it, to 'detach compulsive heterosexuality from black masculinity' (Golden, 1994, p. 33) and to undermine, if only marginally, the aggressive misogyny and homophobia which permeates much black male culture. Mapplethorpe's black nudes are an antidote to the big-dick nigga-speak of 'hos' and 'bitches' lionised by Snoop Doggy Dogg, Tupac Shakur and the like. In his wake black visual artists like Lyle Ashton Harris and Christian Walker have developed his themes and given them new resonances. Whatever other functions they have performed for those who view them, Mapplethorpe's black nudes have inspired black photographers such as Renee Cox, Ajamu and Lyle Ashton Harris.

On the broader stage, the impact of Mapplethorpe's work on mainstream society's awareness and understanding of male homosexuality has been profound, not least because of its catalysing effect on the 'culture wars' of the 1990s. In 1989, as a result of pressure from the American Family Coalition and other conservative lobby groups, Congress passed a law preventing the National Endowment for the Arts (NEA) from funding obscene or homoerotic work. The law was ruled unconstitutional in 1990, and as so often happens with works of art attacked in this way the publicity given Mapplethorpe and other sexual transgressors as a result (Andre Serrano's *Piss Christ* was similarly elevated) provides a large part of the explanation as to why they became global celebrities and saw their images disseminated to a mass audience. Frank Pierson's drama documentary on the Mapplethorpe controversy (*Dirty Pictures*, 2000) stars James Wood as the liberal art curator faced with threats, harassment, dismissal and family breakdown when he successfully defends the right of his institution (the Cincinnati Contemporary Arts museum) to show *The Perfect Moment* photographs, including the image of a naked young boy pronounced during the culture wars as paedophiliac.[22]

Today sexually explicit collections like *Altars* can be found in high street book shops and university libraries,[23] while Mapplethorpe's portraits, flowers and still lives sell thousands of wall calendars and desk diaries throughout the world. In doing so Mapplethorpe's life and work have added an important gay dimension to the broader sexualisation of western culture which took place in the 1980s and 1990s, and have inspired many others to follow his example.

The queering of gay art

Despite his political importance Mapplethorpe was not 'political'. Like Warhol he was, if anything, politically conservative, becoming towards the end of his life a celebrity portrait artist for the rich and famous of New York society. He resisted identification with 'gay liberation', preferring just to live the life and make it into art. But his lifestyle and his aesthetic were unsustainable after the discovery of HIV in the early 1980s. As the homosexual population emerged into public view and sexual citizenship, on the one hand, and witnessed its members being decimated by AIDS on the other, a different kind of 'queer culture' accompanied the progress of HIV, more politicized and more public than anything Mapplethorpe would have been comfortable with.

At the forefront of this new movement was Keith Haring. Born in 1957 (he too died of AIDS, a year after Mapplethorpe, in February 1990), Haring emerged in the early 1980s as a multimedia artist with a distinctive visual style characterized by the use of bold colours, organic shapes and clear flowing lines intentionally reminiscent of aboriginal painting. His work engaged with controversial sex-political issues – HIV and homophobia in particular – and he used it as 'a means of raising political issues around gay identity and the AIDS epidemic' (Cooper, 1996, p. 17). He was an artist of the left, when that term still meant something. As he put it before his death:

> I am sure that in time mine will be understood to have been a very clear, selective, hopefully intelligent, politically sound, humanistic and imaginative approach to the 'role' of Contemporary Artists.
>
> (Haring, 1996, p. 103)

He was also influenced by Brion Gysin, William Burroughs, and above all Andy Warhol, of whom he wrote in his diaries:

> Andy's life and work made my work possible. Andy set the precedent for the possibility of my art to exist. He was the first real public artist in a holistic sense, and his art and life changed the concept we have of 'art and life' in the 20th century. He was the first real 'modern artist'.
>
> (ibid., p. 117)

His work had a strong sexual dimension, although it was not shocking in the way Mapplethorpe's photographs often are. From Warhol, with whom he worked on several collaborations, he took the idea that art – even the art of sexual transgression – should be accessible and inclusive, and should aspire to be part of popular culture. Where Mapplethorpe's most graphic work invites the viewer to look furtively into a darkened, exclusive world of deviant sexuality directly descended from the fantasies of the Marquis de Sade, Haring's work connotes humanity, generosity and warmth. His images are calls for tolerance and understanding in the age of HIV, reaching out to each of us whether we define ourselves as gay, straight or queer. He is optimistic (despite his own status as HIV-positive), where Mapplethorpe's work cannot be viewed without knowledge of the fate awaiting the lifestyle, the community and many of the individuals he photographs (including himself). In his introduction to Haring's diaries Robert Farris Thompson makes an observation which nicely sumarizes the distinction between his sexual aesthetic and that of Mapplethorpe.

> Sex lights up, directly or in code, his intermeshing forms. Call this dimension to his work erography, as opposed to pornography. Erography transforms sex into a script of liberation, so that many can benefit, partaking of the freedom and the energy, whereas porn plays for single consumers.
>
> (Haring, 1996)

Haring was confident in his sexuality,[24] and it featured prominently in his work throughout his life, but like Warhol he sought to avoid ghettoization as a gay artist. Haring in this sense was one of the first 'queer' artists, in that he sought to break free not just of heterosexist, homophobic stereotypes but from the constraints and roles imposed on its own members by the gay community. His art was informed by a homosexual identity, but not targeted at or intended just for a gay audience. It was politicized but not propagandistic, aware of its status within mainstream culture; quintessentially *queer* in its 'transgressive difference from what are perceived as heterosexist norms', but also self-consciously distinct from '"politically correct" forms of gay and lesbian identity' (Horne and Lewis, eds., 1996, p. 1). Haring exemplified queer culture's rejection of the idea of 'gayness' as a label for non-heterosexuals to be forced into.[25] Queer, in Haring's hands, was:

> A celebratory banner for a new breed of gay men and women; irreverent, unapologetic, defiantly unworried about 'positive' images. Queer combines an aesthetic, a way of being in the world, and a subversive way of knowing.[26]

His art embodied that celebratory approach, and indeed became one of the most recognized visual symbols of it throughout the world.

English and queer

If Haring is emblematic of the assertive queerness of the 1980s and 1990s (see too the music of Bronski Beat and Jimmy Somerville, discussed in Chapter 7) a quieter, distinctively English aesthetic of subversion is evident in the evermore transgressive work of Gilbert & George. They too resist definition as 'gay' artists. When asked about their sexual orientation they avoid the question, and their work eschews politics as such. As they put it:

> We never campaign for homosexual art. Asked 'are you homosexuals?', we don't accept that; it's too limited a term, a quasi-medical term from Denmark in the nineteenth century.
>
> (quoted in Farson, 1999, p. 76)

Their work, however, is unmistakeably homoerotic, typically depicting male figures (usually themselves, or young men of the type one imagines they might fancy). Theirs is a world devoid of women, their lives an ongoing art work about what it is to be English and queer (while not declaring one's homosexuality) at the millennial turn.

Gilbert & George began their careers as conceptual artists. Their early works juxtaposed taboo language with images of the familiar and the banal – a 1969 self-portrait of the artists was titled *George the Cunt and Gilbert the Shit*; a collage of otherwise unshocking scenes from inner-city British life was grouped together under the title of *Cunt Scum* (1977). By the onset of sexual epidemic in the 1980s they had become interested in more overtly sexual themes, choosing to make visible aspects of homosexuality never before depicted in public art (such as *Coming* and *Sperm Eaters* from *The Sexual Pictures*). These included transgressive representations of uroglania and coprophilia (*Shit, Friendship Pissing*) presented in a Day-Glo pop art style reminiscent of Warhol and Haring. By the late 1990s they were declaring that 'the subject of sex is one of the most important ones in art'.[27]

As their work broke more taboos in its treatment of sexuality it also became more confessional and self-revelatory. 'We believe in doing it through our pictures',[28] they explained as explicit photographic images of the artists themselves began to appear in their collages, often with trousers at their knees, bent over and buttocks bared to the viewer. The aim of this work, in their own words, was 'sexual confession'; to demystify sex; to remove the guilt from it and normalize its taboos. The transgressive effect of the pictures was intensified by the artists' demure public persona – politely spoken, middle-aged English gentlemen, clad always in identical uniforms of expensive tailor-made suits, innocent and yet capable of breaking such taboos as were depicted in *The Naked Shit Pictures* (1994). In these, as the title of the series suggests, Gilbert & George were naked, and they were taking a shit. Their biographer and friend Daniel Farson defended the work thus:

> At the moment when we begin to ask ourselves why the human body and its functions should so appal us, we begin to understand what Gilbert & George are all about. Far from being gratuitously offensive, these pictures are the contemporary equivalent of medieval representations of corpses in the process of decomposition. And when we ask ourselves 'to what end?' the answer is that these pictures proclaim

a messianic, visionary message; nothing human is disgusting. We are all the same.

(1999)

Readers will have their own views on the worth of Gilbert & George and the other artists discussed here. I hope, however, to have shown that whatever one thinks of their aesthetic qualities these artefacts have a value and a role worth defending. They have provided erotic pleasure for a group traditionally denied public articulation of their sexual desires (the taboo status of homosexuality has meant, indeed, that gay art and porn have been even more closely connected than in straight art). They have provided a means of documenting homosexual life and culture, and thus of articulating identity (regardless of how it fares with the critics of the future, Mapplethorpe's work will stand forever as a historical record of a sub-culture now gone). They have been put to the service of gay liberation and identity politics. For those reasons if for no other they deserve protection from the censors.

11

BAD GIRLS

Sexual transgression as feminist strategy

If homosexuality has historically been marginalized in the art world, then so to an even greater extent has femininity. Germaine Greer asks in *The Obstacle Race* why it is that there are 'no great women artists'? To which, as we saw in Chapter 9, Camille Paglia provides the answer that cultural production is a male prerogative; the symbolic expression of man's aggressive, penetrative sexuality. If most porn is the representation of heterosexual male fantasy, art about sex is his 'Appollonian response toward and away from woman' (1981, p. 31). The argument has a certain logic to it, if little empirical foundation (the pre-historic roots of contemporary social behaviour are and will probably remain irrecoverable beyond the level of informed speculation). Nor is the biological determinism of Paglia's thesis easily reconcilable with a feminist programme of sex-political progress. If men are, by nature and nurture, always and everywhere, the transgressors and the predators, in art as elsewhere in life, those who envision a more egalitarian and humane system of sexual stratification and culture might as well give up.

There is, fortunately, another explanation as to why there are no 'great' women artists, and it is simply that women have been written out of art history by men. Greer's book shows beyond doubt that if indeed there *have* been no great women artists this is not because of biology but because 'greatness' is a construction of patriarchal art history from which women have been excluded, or at the very least marginalised. Women have, historically, been 'underachievers' in art because they have lacked not talent so much as the social, economic and cultural power to *be* artists in a male-dominated world. Where they have, against the odds, made art, they have lacked the discursive power – the cultural capital – to have their contributions remembered down through the ages.

This is illustrated by the exceptions which prove the rule. In the field of literature, there are many acknowledged female 'greats' (in English one thinks of Jane Austen, George Eliot, the Brontë sisters, Mary Wollstonecraft and Elizabeth Barrett Browning). How could so many women in those pre-feminist times be great writers, where there were no painters, sculptors, architects or composers acknowledged as 'great'? Because, perhaps, the private act of sitting at home in a bedroom or study, writing a novel or a poem, was not in those times the affront to prevailing notions of how women should behave that would be presented by, say, a female painter working with live nude models (especially male), or an architect commanding an army of workers and financiers. If the public act of going out and rehearsing a group of young men for a stage play or a concert would not have been acceptable behaviour for respectable women in centuries and even decades past the private act of writing a book was less likely to attract censure. Poems and novels were written by women with at least as much facility and genius as men (although some, like George Eliot, still felt it necessary to take men's names). And having been written, the expanding reach of public education and cultural capitalism ensured their distribution to large audiences. The works of Jane Austen have stood the test of time as well as those of Fielding or Dickens, consequently, where there is barely a single female painter or composer of British origin (active before World War II, at least) whose name would be familiar to any but specialists and art historians.

Women's creative energies have traditionally been invested in domestically located crafts (generally denied the status of art) like weaving and quilt-making. But even in these female-dominated realms the social division of labour characteristic of patriarchy has determined the awarding of 'greatness'. Cooking is sometimes acknowledged to be an art form as well as a domestic chore. And yet, in a field where women have always been expected to bear the heaviest workload it is men who have spearheaded the public exercise of that skill. Great chefs and restaurateurs, like great artists, have usually been men because the attainment of that elevated status is related in large part to the greater cultural and financial resources which men have wielded.

In 1962, a textbook called *The History of Art* could be published in America without a single reference to a woman artist. Nearly forty years later Judy Chicago could still write of:

> An art system that privileges male artists, as evidenced by the centuries of discrimination against women artists; the omission of their achievements from the canon of art history; and the fact that even today, only five per cent of the art found in the collections of American museums consists of work by female artists.
>
> (Chicago and Lucie-Smith, 1999, p. 10)

Now, however, we live in the twenty-first century, and with the hindsight enabled by the feminist historiography of the late twentieth we can see that there have indeed been many women artists who should be considered, by any reasonable criteria of evaluation, 'great': women like Artemisia Gentileschi (1593–1653), identified by Judy Chicago as 'one of the first women to make a living from her art' (ibid., p. 46), and one of a handful of female painters active in Renaissance Italy to have her works exhibited alongside the acknowledged male greats in the show of 'masters' which toured Europe in 2001. Rediscovered by Germaine Greer and others in their efforts to undermine the Great Man theory of art, Gentileschi's remarkable life was the subject of a biopic by Agnes Merlet (*Artemisia*, 1997), and she has become something of an icon for the contemporary generation of 'Bad Girls' artists (see below).

192

There have been many successors to Gentileschi, of course: women who have struggled, without access to the support provided by a feminist politics, to find space and recognition as artists within a male-dominated culture.[1] Tina Modotti, for example (1896–1942), the Italian-born actress turned photographer, has gradually won recognition as an artist of long-standing importance, and her works now command large sums at auction. Typically for women artists in this pre-feminist era, during her life and for some time after her death, she was seen as an inferior practitioner of the emerging art of photography, better known for her romantic and professional associations (often scandalous) with Edward Weston and others than for the quality of her own work. Her public notoriety peaked in 1929 when she was present at, and implicated (erroneously) in the political assassination of her then-lover Cuban revolutionary Julio Antonio Mella in Mexico City.[2] She is today best known for her photographic still lives, and for her studies of working women and peasants taken in Mexico (where she lived for many years). These were informed by a socialist sensibility rather than a feminist one, though they convey what some critics have identified as a woman's viewpoint. Her female subjects, as Laura Mulvey and Peter Wollen put it, are 'represented in the process of activity and work, rather than isolated in a pose for the camera' (1987, p. 214).

Modotti's contemporary and friend Frieda Kahlo experienced a comparable professional marginalization in the context of her relationship with the muralist Diego Rivera, in whose shadow she spent most of her artistic life. Rediscovered by feminist art historians and now eagerly sought out by contemporary female artists such as Madonna, the enduring value of Kahlo's paintings was overlooked during her own lifetime. Meanwhile, back in Europe the surrealists were offering only a limited artistic space to women like Meret Oppenheim, and that largely for selfish reasons (the surrealist equivalent of 'coffee and cunt', one imagines – see Chapter 2). Broude and Garrard's essay on feminism and art in the twentieth century observes that

> the concept of the *Femme-Child*, the 'Woman-Child', was extolled as
> ideal and muse by the men of Surrealism, who regarded woman as the
> incarnation of spontaneity and innocence, untrammelled by reason or
> logic, and therefore naturally in touch with intuitive knowledge and the
> world of dreams and the imagination. Surrealism exalted the female,
> but the female imprisoned within a world of childhood and immaturity.
>
> (1994, p. 12)

In conforming to this exalted status Oppenheim appeared frequently as a model in the work of Man Ray and others (see for example *Érotique Voilée* [1936]) but she was a committed artist in her own right. Only at the end of the twentieth century, however, did she begin to be written of in the same awed terms as Man Ray, Breton and the rest of the surrealist establishment, or her works such as *Lunch in Fur* (1932) and *Ma Gouvernante* (1930) achieve recognition as significant products of the surrealist movement. Though she was not a feminist in the modern sense of the term, Oppenheim's art often contained critical commentaries on the sexist attitudes of the men who, as we have seen, combined their anti-bourgeois modernism with conspicuous misogyny and homophobia. Marcia Tanner writes of *Lunch in Fur* that it

> comically condenses the domestic, erotic and inspirational functions of the male Surrealist artist's female consort into one convenient, simultaneously seductive and repellent household object. Properly used, it could render his need for an actual woman obsolete, thus freeing her to pursue her own projects, artistic or otherwise. At the same time, it also gives three-dimensional form – perhaps for the first time – to a specifically female experience of erotic pleasure: the fur-lined vessel awaiting the lips, the tongue, the stirring of the spoon.
>
> (1994, p. 58)

Bad girls

Although the names of Gentileschi, Oppenheim, Modotti and Kahlo can now be found in glossy art books, increasing numbers of which are written by women,[3] contemporaneous critical and public recognition of their achievements was constrained by the sexual politics of the times in which they lived and the assumption that women, by definition, could not be 'great' artists. In the latter half of the twentieth century, however, and taking advantage of the expanded cultural possibilities won by feminism, women increasingly won recognition of their artistic achievements. This process accompanied and became part of the broader sexual-ization of capitalist culture, and many of these women employed the aesthetics of sexual transgression to create a femin*ist*, as well as a femin*ized* body of art. In doing so they were embroiled in debates about the appropriateness of women adopting aesthetic strategies and motifs hitherto associated with patriarchal culture. The art of many of these women – the 'bad girls' as they have come to be known (although the phrase does not describe a coherent or unified movement, so much as a spirit of transgression running through the work of a very diverse group of women) – has often been included in the culture of 'atrocity' (to recall Burchill's term), its makers dismissed either as collaborationist traitors to the feminist cause or as media sluts and pop tarts kowtowing to the tyranny of the male gaze in return for wealth and fame.

Who are the bad girls, then? As Marcia Tucker puts it in her essay introducing the 1994 exhibition of that name mounted at the New Museum of Contemporary Art in New York, bad girls are those 'increasing numbers of women artists, photographers, cartoonists, performers, video and filmmakers [who] are defying the conventions and proprieties of traditional femininity to define themselves according to their own terms, their own pleasures, their own interests' (1994, p. 5). The term came into widespread usage only in the 1990s, parallelling the adoption of 'queer' as a badge of pride by some homosexuals, and the earlier reappropriation of 'nigger' as a positive term of self-identification by American blacks. For self-proclaimed 'bad girls' their use of the label was an intentional subversion of its original patriarchal connotations; a rejection of the notion that women had to be good (where goodness is defined by the moral and gender codes of patriarchy), and a countervailing assertion of their 'badness' as a statement of intellectual, political and sexual empowerment. 'Bad' is good, in other words, and the term has become a collective label for many of those female artists who, as Tucker puts it, 'challenge audiences to see women as they have been, as they are, and as they want to be' (ibid., p. 5). Tucker's *Bad Girls* provides an excellent illustrated introduction to the work of some of these artists, as does the Institute of Contemporary Art's 1993 volume of the same name, published to accompany a touring exibition in the United Kingdom.

Bad before bad

But if the label is relatively new, the aesthetic of nonconformity with and resistance to patriarchy which characterizes the work of the modern bad girls is centuries old, going back at least as far as Artemisia Gentileschi. Not only was Gentileschi one of the first working women artists, as already noted, she has become something of a heroine for the bad girls. She was, on the one hand, a female artist operating in a male-dominated culture, and one of the first 'to twist mainstream art practice to include her own perspective as a woman, not only by focusing upon and honouring biblical heroines, but also by interceding in traditional narratives to present a female viewpoint' (Chicago and Lucie-smith, 1999, p. 46). Her *Judith Beheading Holofernes* shares its subject matter with Caravaggio's earlier and more famous painting of the same Old Testament episode. But Gentileschi's Judith, to this observer's eye at least, gives the impression of strength and determination, where the male artist's representation seems softer and less threatening in her demeanour.

Meret Oppenheim and the other artists mentioned above can also be described as prototypical bad girls, working as they did within male-dominated environments to produce art that was recognisably feminist in its take on the world, even if its makers would not have defined themselves as feminists (many of them, indeed, were explicitly hostile to the notion of women's liberation).

In the sphere of popular music artists such as Bessie Smith, Billie Holiday, Judy Garland and Patsy Cline, singing as they did so often about the problems faced by women in a man's world, may be regarded as pioneers of 'bad'. Archer and Simmonds's *A Star Is Torn* (1986) tells the stories of how so many of these talented women succumbed to alcohol, drugs and domestic subjugation as they sought to reconcile their creative abilities with the expectations placed upon them by patriarchal society. These were 'bad' women in so far as they 'deliberately created personae which dared to live on the wild side' (ibid., p. 181). Even although they were in the end defeated by the pressures to conform, their rebellions against conventional stereotypes of femininity have inspired women artists ever since.

As has the example of another pioneering bad girl – musician and poet Patti Smith. Smith's best work was done in the 1970s, long before the phrase 'bad girls' was adopted by feminists. Indeed, she herself had little time for feminist politics (declaring to an interviewer in 1972, for example, that 'most women writers don't interest me because they're hung up with being a woman'[quoted in Bockris, 1998, p. 58]). There is irony in that, since her lover and friend in the late 1960s, Robert Mapplethorpe, was just as clearly queer, twenty years before the term was adopted by artists like Todd Haynes. He too rejected the preferred labels and roles of politicized gay liberation, as Smith rejected feminism.

Having left Robert Mapplethorpe at the end of the 1960s to pursue a career as a poet and singer-songwriter she emerged into the limelight in 1975 with the innovative and still-influential album *Horses*. Its black-and-white portrait of the artist (shot by Mapplethorpe) and its iconoclastic songs celebrating hedonism, decadence and rebellion – 'Jesus died for somebody's sins, but not mine' – introduced a powerful new image of assertive femininity to the male-dominated music industry. Where the 1960s star Janis Joplin exemplified the archetype of abused (and self-abusive), exploited victim, and Joni Mitchell the wistful hippy chick, Smith avoided both stereotypes to present a model of feminine independence and aesthetic originality which effortlessly overcame the deep-rooted sexism of the music industry. Bockris writes that she presented 'a new image of a rock-and-roll woman, ambiguous, androgynous but strong and in control' (1998, p. 100). Her anticipation (unintended, of course) of the bad girls' aesthetic can be seen in the title and lyrics of an irreverential song like 'Rock 'n' Roll Nigger' (1978). Her use of the N-word, incidentally, pre-dates its positive redefinition by American blacks, and in the sleeve notes to the *Easter* album on which it appears she declares that 'the word must be reinvented'.[4]

It may be overstating the case to argue, as Bockris does, that '*Horses* freed millions of women all over the world, by saying they could do anything they wanted to, that men no longer dominated the field', but Smith's achievement undoubtedly advanced the status of women in the industry and inspired future generations of musical 'bad girls' like p. j. harvey and Chrissie Hynde. These in turn inspired the 'girrl power' and 'Riot Grrrls' movements of the mid- to late 1990s, and the angry, iconoclastic, sexually transgressive performances of such as L7, Courtney Love and Hole. These in turn fed through into the emergence of a more mainstream generation of sexually assertive, creatively involved girl groups such as the Spice Girls, All Saints and, in America, Destiny's Child (who in 2000, of course, provided the theme song – 'Independent Woman' – for the ultimate girrl power movie, the remake of *Charlie's Angels*).

Feminism and the anti-modernists

While Patti Smith was making waves in the masculinist circles of the 1970s music industry more overtly feminist women were producing what Rebecca Schneider

(1997) calls 'explicit body art'. Coming out of the 1960s sexual revolution feminist artists applied their ideological critique of male culture (crucial, as we have seen, in defining feminism's initial hostility to pornography and advertising) to make what they hoped was a distinctively female art using such elements as the abstract representation of female genitals and other symbols of femininity and female sexuality (as in Judy Chicago's 1979 installation *The Dinner Party*). Performance artists such as Carole Schneeman and Yoko Ono exposed their bodies and reappropriated oppressor words like 'cunt' and 'bitch' in aid of a consciously articulated culture war. They pursued an aesthetics of cultural separatism which paralleled the broader political strategies of feminism at this time, aiming for what Marcia Tanner calls 'a specifically female art deliberately distinct from mainstream modernism and its perceived misogyny, patriarchal history and arcane inaccessability' (1994). Judy Chicago – one of the most influential practitioners of this art – recalls that in both subject matter and method it was made in pointed opposition to the Great Man theory of modernism. This was art produced by an 'empowering, co-operative method rather than in a competitive, individualistic mode' (Chicago and Lucie-Smith, 1999).

This work, though often sexually transgressive, was defiantly unerotic to the heterosexual male gaze. If it used the visual and verbal language of patriarchal culture it did so chiefly in order to dissect and expose its deep structural misogyny, and to draw attention to the contempt for women which its unreflective use embodied. Schneeman's *Interior Scroll* – a stage performance involving nudity, body paint, and the extraction of a written scroll from the artist's vagina – *may* have been arousing for some who saw it, but that was not its intention. Here, as in most examples of early feminist-inspired body art, the aim was to alienate the viewer and, in a feminist adaptation of modernism's strategy of liberation through disruption, to encourage the viewer's shocked reflection on the nature of patriarchy and its use (or abuse) of the female body. Explicit sexuality in these works was a distancing mechanism, rather than a seductive instrument.

Of course, much of the feminist art of this period was neither explicitly sexual nor transgressive. Alongside Judy Chicago's *Cock and Cunt Play* (1970), or the Fresno State College Feminist Art Programme production of *Cunt Cheerleaders* (1970) there was work simply celebrating the emotional, physical and intellectual qualities of the female, stressing her essential difference from the male, who was at this time implicated in the Vietnam war and all things violent and rapacious. Much of this art, inspired by the call for female separation from the world of men, proposed a view of women which verged on the sacred, as reflected in the extensive use of the ancient iconography of the goddess by artists like Louise Bourgeois and Romare Bearden. Schneider notes that 'cultural feminist performance art in the 1960s and 1970s carried a reverence for the female body and often a nostalgia for a lost matriarchal heritage' (1997, p. 131). Like the militant anti-pornography stance of many feminists in the 1970s the emergence of this aesthetic was an important stage in the struggle to create a zone of female autonomy and power within a male-dominated cultural sphere.

As is appropriate for a movement that was in large part a female reaction to the casual misogyny of modernism this art anticipated the postmodern aesthetic of engagement with popular culture and the manipulation of mass cultural artefacts. Marcia Tucker comments that 'authentic' art had traditionally 'been configured as masculine, its priests and acolytes all too happy to be saved from the contaminating effects of the inferior, grossly sexual, kitschy blight of mass and popular culture, configured as feminine' (1994, p. 38). Feminist art of the 1960s and 1970s sought to elevate the marginalised elements of feminine culture (including mediated forms of popular culture) to the status of art, and in the process pioneered many of what Broude and Garrard consider 'the most basic tenets of postmodernism', including:

> The understanding that gender is socially and not naturally constructed; the widespread validation of non-'high art' forms such as craft, video, and performance art; the questioning of the cult of 'genius' and 'greatness' in Western art history; the awareness that behind the claim of 'universality' lies an aggregate of particular standpoints and biases, leading in turn to an emphasis upon pluralist variety rather than totalising unity.
>
> (1994, p. 10)

Work made in the 1970s by such as the Guerrilla Girls, Lynda Benglis and Barbara Kruger, all of whom borrowed extensively from the image banks of advertising and commercial art, pioneered the intertextualization and cross-referencing strategies typical of the contemporary multimedia era. Less playful, but also pioneering in its manipulation of pop cultural imagery, was the photography of Cindy Sherman (hugely influential in the later emergence of a distinctive 'bad girls' aesthetic). Her *Film Stills*, produced between 1975 and 1980, comprised a series of eight-by-ten monochrome photographs in the style of film studio promo-shots. Not self-portraits as such (although Sherman is the photographed object in each), they were 'portraits of an identity she shares with every woman who conceives the narratives of her life in the idiom of the cheap movie' (Danto, 1990, p. 10) – imaginary quotations from films that were never made, but whose female characters as performed by Sherman we somehow 'recognize' from our memories of popular Hollywood cinema. These photographs, like the bulk of her subsequent output up to the present, are the documents of Sherman's performance art; a body of work moulded, as one critic puts it, 'by an interest in the image of woman, a critical examination of the recurrent stereotype of the female body in the media' (Brehm, 1996, p. 108).

After *Film Stills* Sherman made *Centre Folds* and *Fashion*, which further developed this interest in sexual representation, followed in the 1990s by *Sex Pictures*. The latter comprised her most sexually transgressive images to date, depicting grotesquely distorted mannequins and dummies in explicit sexual tableaus. They repel and disgust in their depiction of 'perverted' scenes constructed from Sherman's imagination of what we might reasonably assume to be abusive male fantasy.

Sherman is an important link between the anti-modernist aesthetic of the generation of Chicago and Schneeman, and the postmodernism of the bad girls proper. The latter share her interest in sexual representation, and the sexualisation of the female body in particular, but apply this in an era where the ambivalence and polysemic nature of images is more widely recognized within the feminist movement. A 1970s feminist politics, with its notion of the essential oppressiveness of the male gaze, informs Sherman's work, even where her use of popular cultural iconography looks ahead to the post-feminist 1980s and 1990s. In her work we see two of what would become characteristic features of the bad girls' output (features also present in the art of staight and gay men discussed earlier) – a self-objectifying focus on the artist's own body, often represented in a sexualized manner (though not necessarily erotic); and the referencing of, and commenting on, the iconography of patriarchal culture such as Hollywood movies, fashion shoots and pornographic magazines. Rosa Olivares writes of Sherman: 'there is no doubt that we are dealing with a bad girl . . . a perverse woman who is telling us a fairy story in which the prince is not going to get there in time, and in which the leading role is played out by the beast' (Sherman, 1996, p. 13). But for all that she has inspired the bad girls of the 1990s, Sherman's work is firmly founded on the critique of patriarchy and the position of women within it developed by cultural feminism in the 1970s. She has little room for relativism, at least on questions of sexual politics, and the preferred readings (intended meanings) in her work are clear.

The bad girls who came after Sherman differ from her in so far as they frequently disrupt the smooth functioning of the male gaze at both ends of the artistic process. The bad girls share Sherman's aesthetic, but combine it with a characteristically postmodern recognition of the multiplicity of meanings to be conjured from all manner of texts, even those, such as pornography and advertising, which have been most implicated in the maintenance of patriarchy. They also use iconoclastic humour and pastiche in the tradition of the Guerrilla Girls. In Tracy Emin's *My Bed*, or Sarah Lucas's *Chicken Knickers* we see the application by bad girls of what Jo Anna Isaak calls 'the revolutionary power of women's laughter' (1996). In doing so they challenge – as queer culture challenges not only homophobia but some models of gay liberation – not just patriarchal but proscriptive feminist notions of 'what women are'. In this sense the bad girls express in art the fragmentation of a once-unified feminist orthodoxy and its replacement by a multiplicity of feminisms, differing in their approaches to sexuality and sexual representation. Bad girls' art is the cultural expression of 'post-feminism'.

Bad girls and the pornographication of feminist art

Like the feminist artists of the 1960s and 1970s, many of the bad girls practise an explicit art of the body. Unlike their predecessors, however, the bad girls often produce provocatively sexualised images of themselves and other women. Through their manipulations of these images they seek to transform the conditions of their reception and consumption, opening up possibilities for alternative readings of the sexualized female body to occur. Where Sherman appears to be unambiguously critical of the objectification of women inherent to pornography, for example, the bad girls embrace porn as a tool for exploring the meaning of sexual representation and of female sexuality itself. One critic observes that 'all these artists are united by a sense of freedom when depicting the body. They play with the idea of fiction or performance as a liberation from the stricter codes of feminism or gay rights – the body has become a strategy in its own right'.[5] The goal of this 'liberation' is to create cultural space for women's articulation and interrogation of their sexualities, so long constrained by the demands of patriarchy. Bad girls' art, like porn for women, is embraced by its advocates as a sexually subversive tool – a means of overcoming stereotypical notions of femininity, from whichever source they spring. It only exists *because* feminism has produced the conditions which make it possible, but in its content and subject matter advances beyond that kind of feminism which defines itself in relation to a particular notion of male sexuality as inherently predatory and violent. In bad girls' art women are often represented as sexually aggressive, domineering, predatory, in precisely the ways that men can be.

Nowhere is this more true than in the work of bad girls who are also queer. Lesbian artists frequently utilize 'politically incorrect' motifs, including those drawn from the worlds of sadomasochism and dyke bars, as in Nicole Eisenman's *Betty Gets It* (a carnivalesque subversion of the Flintstones' cartoon, with Wilma and Betty recast as s&m dykes),[6] or in the homoerotic photography of Della Grace, an example of which graces the cover of Grosz and Probyn's *Sexy Bodies* (1995). Her work has attracted criticism from some feminists for its non-judgemental depiction of lesbian sub/dom sex play (in the same way that Mapplethorpe's work was criticized).

Grace's work is a photographic application of the idea that sadomasochistic imagery, whether deployed in artistic or pornographic contexts, can provide lesbians with 'the most powerful strategy with which to confront a culture still enmeshed in prescriptive images of women as mothers, nurturers, and sexual satisfiers of male desire' (Fernandez, 1991, p. 35). The homoerotic photographer Phyliss Christopher concedes that 'some people could look at my images and say they're pornographic, meaning obscene', but defends her focus on the sexualised lesbian body by recalling that 'ten years ago [the late 1980s] there was virtually nothing of lesbian sexual images published. I enjoy contributing to what I felt was a real sexual revolution happening'.[7] Her models, she insisted, 'don't do it for money. They do it because they want to have beautiful images of themselves, and they want to have them out there in the world'.

The photographer Bettina Rheims, though not herself a lesbian, also specialises in sexualized images of women, and she too has been condemned by some feminist critics. Though reminiscent in style and subject matter to the fashion and advertising work of Helmut Newton, Rheims strongly rejects any straightforward comparison between her work and that produced by the unreflective fixing of the male gaze on the objectified female. 'If you look at *Chambres Closes* [Rheims's 1998 collection]', she has argued, 'a lot of [the models] are really smiling in front of the camera, and that's what probably bothered people most. It's not that they were showing parts of their bodies or opening their legs up. It was that they were doing it smiling. Sex and pleasure and art are three notions that are not supposed to go together'.[8]

Among the best known of all the bad girls (not least because of her much-publicized relationship with the briefly bisexual Madonna, captured for posterity in 1991's *In Bed with Madonna*) is the performance artist, stand-up comic and sometime movie actress Sandra Bernhard. The film of her late 1980s stage show (*Without You I'm Nothing [Boskovich, 1990]*) illustrates several elements of bad girl art, especially its frequent use of humour to subvert conventional stereotypes of masculinity and femininity. The targets of Bernhard's sophisticated pastiches include Karen Carpenter, Barbra Streisand, Diana Ross, Madonna, Warren Beatty (romantically involved with Madonna around the same time as Bernhard), and male sex symbols in general. Her version of Prince's 'Little Red Corvette' (performed in a giant cloak of stars and stripes, and backed by an arrangement of pan pipes and acoustic guitars which contrasts vividly with Prince's more muscular approach to the song) pokes gentle fun at the oversexed star, while paying homage to his status as a key figure in the sexualisation of late twentieth-century American culture. Prince, as Chapter 2 noted, has in the course of his career combined a vigorous public sexuality with gender-bending and ambivalent sexual orientation (see, for example, 'If I Was Your Girlfriend'). Not gay, of course, and not even queer, his celebration of the healing power of sexuality and his own flirtation with sexually ambivalent styles and practices is celebrated in Bernhard's pastiche. Then, when her arrangement of the song is concluded, the original record begins to play, and she removes the cloak to reveal herself dressed in nothing but a sequinned G-string. The dance with which she plays out the movie is a classic bad girls moment (and also a good example of striptease culture), inviting the viewer to watch her sexualized body while at the same time drawing attention to our complicity in doing so. The editor of *The Advocate* has defined the purpose of her sexually transgressive performances thus:

> Sandra wants to talk about sex, she wants to talk about political issues, she wants to talk about things that are on her mind. She goes out there and becomes a spokesmodel for the movement. By bridging a gap between entertainment, sexuality and politics, she's definitely got her finger on the pulse of what's going on in America.[9]

Bad girls like Bernhard employ the sexualized female body with the added twist that it is often the artist herself who is objectified in the image. Rebecca Schneider observes of this work that 'it is the pornographicised object, the woman in front of the camera, who is reincarnated as an artist' (1997, p. 11). Bad girls reject the once orthodox feminist notion that there is such a thing as an 'authentic' female art defined by its rejection of and distance from male images and symbols. They 'take the [patriarchal] heritage and work with it – attack it, reverse it, expose it and use it for their own purpose' (Tickner, 1987, p. 239).

201

The strategy has had its most direct application in the work of Annie Sprinkle, the American ex-porn star and 'post-porn performance artist' whose stage shows such as *Hardcore from the Heart* deconstruct the pornographic experience in ways which are hardly less explicit and transgressive than the real thing. Cicciolina has also transformed her low cultural status as porn star into something else – high art in her collaboration with Jeff Koons, and 'porno-politics' in her advocacy of sexual libertarianism in Italy (culminating in her 1987 election as a 'sex radical' member of the Italian parliament).

This approach to the art of the female body was popularized in Madonna's late 1980s and early 1990s performances, discussed earlier in the context of porno-chic. And because of her popularity Madonna's role in crystallizing debates inside and out of the feminist movement about the legitimacy of female artists employing strategies and symbols traditionally associated with 'the male gaze' was pivotal.[10] After Madonna's *Sex* feminine self-portraiture – much of it overtly sexualized – became what Waldemar Januszczak calls 'one of the obsessions' of 1990s art.[11] And the trend was internationals. Japan, for example, saw the emergence of the 'girl photographer' movement spearheaded by Hiromix Tashigawa, and artists specializing in 'self-nudes' such as Yurie Nagashima.

2000 saw a new phase in this artistic auto-voyeurism, with the publication of the American photographer Natasha Merritt's *Digital Diaries* – a volume of digital self-portraits taken by a 21-year-old woman depicting her hotel room sexual encounters with various male and female partners. These combined the techniques of self-objectification and sexual confession to produce images which blurred the art/porn distinction in a manner by now routine among female artists, but in an even more provocative manner. *Digital Diaries* depicted fellatio and bondage, among other exotic acts (without attracting the attentions of the Obscene Publications Squad, interestingly). These were transferred from the realm of the pornographic to that of art in the volume editor's insistence that they were 'a means for self-exploration, self-realisation . . . for the new millennium'.[12] Merritt's work, packaged in a glossy Taschen edition, carried an erotic charge but, wrote one reviewer, 'there is beauty here as well as pornography, and a distinct female voice that takes candid self-revelation to new heights of wonderful indecency'.[13] The fact that her 'unposed photographs of herself and sexual partners in repose and at play' invited the viewer's voyeuristic gaze was not seen by this reviewer as incompatible with their status as art.

Others, however, were less at ease, putting the question which has accompanied the critical response to all such work, especially in the period after Madonna's *Sex* thrust it into the commercial mainstream – does a male reviewer's perception of the artist's 'wonderful indecency' signal that she has actually entered into a kind of collaboration with the predatory male gaze, producing porn dressed up as art for a male-oriented audience? There are, we know, a variety of possible responses to images of the type contained in Madonna's and Merritt's books – sexual arousal, quite easily; curiosity at the motivation underlying such self-revelation; admiration for the courage (or brazenness, perhaps) of the artist; anger at her apparent complicity with the iconography and sexual language of patriarchal culture. In the late 1980s, even before the emergence of the *Sex*-ed up Madonna or the digitized Natasha, Lisa Tickner argued that

> The depiction of women by women (sometimes themselves) in this quasi-sexist manner as a political statement grows potentially more powerful as it approaches actual exploitation but then, within an ace of it, collapses into ambiguity and confusion. The more attractive the women, the higher the risk, since the more closely they approach conventional stereotypes in the first place.
>
> (1987, p. 248)

Self-objectification is a risky aesthetic strategy, then. For Rebecca Schneider, however, it is also arguable that 'this work, rather than positioning itself against the sexualisation of the female body, attempts to wield the master's tools against the master's house, to force a second look at the terms and terrain of that sexualisation' (1997, p. 105). To put it another way, if the female nude has traditionally been the symbolic expression of the containment of the female in patriarchy, its deployment by women artists (including the production of nude images of themselves) can subvert that symbolism, and encourage a reassessment and redefinition of women's sexual identity in terms consistent with feminism's broader political project.

Context and power are all here. The images of Natasha Merritt and her friends in *Digital Diaries*, or the photographs of Rheims and Christopher referred to earlier, are clearly capable of being used as masturbatory aids by men (thus fulfilling at least one characteristic of pornography). Indeed, they might also be used that way by women. More important than their status as art, erotica or porn, however, is the fact that they are all the product of the considered reflection of a *woman*'s gaze – that of the empowered artist herself, who reserves control over what is shown and how, and exercises her power to represent her sexuality in the manner that *she* chooses. The same is true of the less overtly sexualized work of such as Hiromix and the Japanese 'girl photographers'. In the context of a culture which until recently has forbidden the representation of pubic hair while endorsing a pornography of extreme sadomasochism the girl photographer movement is a significant manifestation of the liberation of Japanese women from the subservience of tradition.

The challenge, or disruption, offered by the sexual transgressions of the bad girls is their daring us to accept that in a post-feminist world (by which I mean a still-patriarchal world coming to terms with, and adapting to, the demands of feminism) there can be no doctrinal policing of what images mean; no top-down dictation of what kinds of images can and should be produced by women. The art of sexual transgression traditionally monopolized by men is now part of the artistic repertoire of women, even if not all women (nor all men) are comfortable with the work which results from that fact. Not least because of the campaigning achivements of feminism, women now share with men the power to articulate their sexual desires and identities through all the media of art and culture, mainstream and marginal, popular and avant garde. These, it turns out, include desires and identities which contradict not only traditional patriarchal stereotypes of femininity (hardly surprising), but also once-orthodox feminist notions of what women are and what they want from sex.

12

CONCLUSIONS

Let me end this journey through the varied, often challenging terrain of sex-confessional, 'striptease' culture with three main conclusions.

First, it is clear that our media system can no longer be characterized as an oppressive ideological apparatus relentlessly supportive of patriarchal and hetero-sexist values; that it is, on the contrary, responsive to changes in capitalist social and sexual relations (such as the changing role of women, or the gradual erosion of homophobic and other types of sexual discrimination). I have argued further that it is contributing to those processes. Part I showed that the process of the sexualization of culture, from the pornosphere to the public sphere, has included within it a democratization and diversification of sexual discourse. Part III showed how, despite the accusations of obscenity and atrocity often directed at it by critics of every ideological hue, and notwithstanding its origins in the patriarchal 'will to power', the aesthetic of transgression in art has often been applied by men and women, gay and straight, to subversive, socially transformative explorations of sexuality and the articulation of sexual identity. Part II showed that there have been significant and positive changes in the way that the media represent sex, sexuality and gender. The 'relentless parade of insults', the 'invisibility and demeaning stereotypes' to which women and gays have traditionally been subjected has been replaced, I argued there, by an altogether more complex and satisfying representational diversity. The structure of sexual representation has become more pluralistic than all but a few critics would have thought possible even a decade ago.

One honourable exception is Linda Nochlin, who predicted in 1973 that 'the growing power of women in the politics of both sex and art is bound to revo-lutionise the realm of erotic representation' (quoted in Betterton, 1987, p. 235). A few years later an American scholar detected a growing diversity in the content of sexual representation in the popular media, 'sketching the contours for a changed society that is less patriarchal, open to a wider range of emotions, more playful and fun loving, and less sexist' (La Valley, 1995, p. 70). The evidence presented above suggests that these optimistic visions have been borne out. The various categories of sexual representation discussed there have been the vehicle for a widening of popular access to sexual discourse. At the same time they have facilitated the increased public visibility of once-marginal sexualities and sexual communities. And, in response to that trend, they have provided an arena for the expression of 'straight' male unease caused by the shifting patterns of sexual stratification. Sometimes, it is true, this anxiety has taken the unwelcome, if intelligible form of 'backlash' directed at the perceived agents of male emasculation. At others it has involved self-criticism and exploration of alternatives to traditional models of masculinity.

In all of these ways striptease culture has had important, and progressive, sociological and political meanings.

Which is not to deny that it has also had crassly commercial motivations, based on the familiar principle that sex sells (even if that is only because people in general want information about, discussion of, and exposure to, all aspects of the sexual). But as I have also argued – and this is my second broad conclusion – the pressures imposed by the cultural marketplace have worked for rather than against these progressive trends. Though the critics of 'chic' sexual commercialisation are reluctant to recognise it, it has been cultural capitalism, driven by the competitive pressures of a newly constituted marketplace of sexually defined niches, built in turn on decades of political activism and lobbying by both feminist and gay liberation organizations, which has propelled the styles and signifiers of what were once marginal, oppositional movements and sub-cultures into the mainstream of popular consciousness. Fuelled by the introduction of new communication technologies, the late twentieth century witnessed the expansion of commercialized modes of sexual representation which, through their relationship of economic interdependence with emerging sexual communities, were required to break with many of the most restrictive and patronising stereotypes of the past.

Richard Dyer has argued that 'capitalism can just as well make a profit from something that is ideologically opposed to bourgeois society as something that supports it' (1995, p. 409). I would go further than that, and assert that the cultural and political trends described in this book have only been possible because there is nothing fundamentally anti-bourgeois or anti-capitalist about either homosexuality or feminism. On the contrary, in an era when reproductive technology erodes the age-old link between heterosexism, the patriarchal family and social stability, capitalism is stronger if women are stronger, and if gays have more equality. In these conditions, seen from the broader systemic perspective, misogyny and homophobia are of no obvious benefit to the maintenance of social order. For this reason, and in combination with the persuasive economics of sexual citizenship, the commodified cultures of advanced capitalist societies have come to function as spaces for the articulation and dissemination of diverse sexual identities and radical sexual politics. From pornography to pop music, from advertising to art, and from talk shows to reality television, I have argued that our media are making a significant contribution – as both barometers and catalysts – to the processes whereby traditionally patriarchal societies are learning to live with, if not necessarily love, a sexual economy and politics in which not only women and gays, but straight men are occupying different social positions than those to which they have been used.

We are, for all that, still far from the 'end' of patriarchy, and if the contemporary media *are* receptive to the tastes and demands of emerging sexual communities, they will also continue to reflect the presence of conservative values and beliefs in the population, and to act as vehicles for *their* dissemination and reproduction. The pornosphere continues to be a space where the likes of Max Hardcore can find an audience. 'Backlash' rears its ugly head from time to time, here and there, as the conservative and the progressive compete in the sexual arena. There are moments when the forces of sexual reaction gain confidence and visibility, such as the debate around the repeal of Section 28 in Britain, or in the debates around the status of gays in the US military. But the relatively level terrain on which that ideological competition is played out, and the apparent openness of the media to arguments, opinions, tastes and styles other than those once favoured by the moral guardians of patriarchy, mean that there are now unprecedented opportunities for effective intervention and participation in sexual culture, whether avant garde or mainstream, popular or elite, by those willing and able to do so. The institutional sexism and homophobia of the culture industries continue to act as structural constraints in this respect, but they are constraints in measurable decline. As that decline continues (and it shows every sign of doing so), the media's contribution to the process of sexual democratization is likely to be consolidated and enhanced.

One final point, and a third conclusion. The consequences of sexual democratisation – and their expression in sexual culture – cannot be restricted to dogmatically predetermined assertions of what *should* happen when women and homosexuals are free from patriarchal oppression, and when straight men are conscious of their responsibilities to adapt to the new environment in which they find themselves. That road leads straight to the 'policing of desire', as Simon Watney's important book once called it (1987), and such policing is no less authoritarian when it comes from a right-on 'radical' source as from a Catholic cardinal, a Muslim mullah, or a reactionary rabbi. The whole point of a sexual politics worthy of the adjective 'democratic' is that we gain and exercise the right to find, articulate and celebrate our own sexualities, while showing due respect for the tastes, desires and sensitivities of others. That is the real challenge posed by striptease culture.

NOTES

1 SEX MATTERS

1 Timothy Taylor's *Prehistory of Sex* suggests that the development of human sexuality was a product of the expansion of hominid brain size and intellectual capacity which appears to have occurred between 1 and 2 million years ago. As brain size increased, language and fantasy became possible. These opened up the possibility that sex could become 'an act of potentially ecstatic mutual contemplation' (1996, p. 51).

2 'When love breaks down' by Paddy McAloon, from the album *Steve McQueen* (Kitchenware Records, 1985).

3 See for example the influential work of Judith Butler, and her social constructionist position that 'the category of women is a variable cultural accomplishment, a set of meanings taken on or taken up within a cultural field, and that no one is born with a gender – gender is always acquired' (1990, p. 111).

4 There are also culturally-determined behavioural characteristics conventionally associated with particular forms of sexuality. Some male homosexuals are 'queens', for example; others choose to adopt the butch mannerisms of jeans and leather-clad hyper-masculinity. Some lesbians play the role of dominant 'dykes'; others submissive 'femmes'.

5 See Reay Tannahill's *Sex In History* (1992) for a broad overview of the many theories and explanations commonly deployed in the history of human sexuality.

6 In this sense I share Andrew Sullivan's description of the homosexual experience that it 'may be deemed an illness, a disorder, a privilege, or a curse: it may be deemed worthy of a "cure", rectified, embraced, or endured. But it exists' (1995, p. 17).

7 There are exceptions to the patriarchal norm, including some of the societies described in Ann Oakley's seminal *Sex, Gender and Society* (1972) such as the Mbuti tribe of Africa, 'in which the role of biological sex as a determinant of social role and status seems to be negligible' (p. 149). These *are* exceptions, however, important in proving that if patriarchy is the most common form of human socio-sexual organization, it is not necessarily the only one.

8 For a study of the British government's response to the AIDS crisis in the 1980s see Miller *et al.*, 1999.

9 More remarkable still, for many, was the fact that these exposures enhanced rather than diminished the president's popularity.

10 Phillips, M., 'Brainwashed by the sexual activists', *Sunday Times*, 24 January 1999.

11 Appleyard, B., 'Between you, me and the bed post', *Sunday Times*, 23 November 1997.

12 Wolfe, T., 'Daydream believers', *Guardian*, 11 November 2000.

13 Kimball, R., 'Taboo, or not taboo, that is the question', *Guardian*, 27 April 1996.

14 Satirical journalist Hunter Thompson noted with wry satisfaction when the Meese

report was published that 'it will apparently be a voluminous guide to everything ever written or photographed in all aspects of the sex business – hundreds of colour photos, thousands of films and massive lists, discussions and descriptions of every kink, crime and subhuman perversion since Nero and prehistoric Japan. The book is already a guaranteed best-seller' (1988, p. 129).

15 For a detailed history of 'the culture wars' of the post-1960s period in the United States see Jensen, 1996.

16 Quoted in Hickman, 1999, p. 248.

17 Anderson, D. and Mosbacher, M., 'Sex-mad, silly and selfish', *Guardian*, 24 November 1997. The report from which this article was taken is published as *The British Woman Today – A Qualitative Survey of Images in Women's Magazines*, London, Social Affairs Unit, 1997.

18 Even cars and washing machines have meanings, of course, in so far as they connote in their design, branding and price qualities beyond the merely functional. But cultural commodities of the type I am discussing here contain explicit messages about love, hate, loss and the whole range of emotions which surround sexuality and sexual politics.

19 It is a necessary presumption of all media studies that the content of media images tell us much about the individuals and the societies which produce them. Through the analysis and evaluation of sexual imagery in the media, and the critical responses which journalists, politicians and other commentators have made to those images, we can also make legitimate inferences and judgements about the state of a given society's sexual politics and culture.

2 FROM WILDE TO WILD

1 'Wild', by the artist formerly (and now once again) known as Prince, is a good example of the extent to which western culture had, a century after Wilde's death, become quite used to the most sexually explicit texts circulating in the most popular media. Prince, with his ambiguous, hyperactive sexuality (best expressed in his song 'If I Was Your Girlfriend', included in 1987's *Sign O' the Times*), is an important figure in the sexual-ization of late twentieth-century popular music. The lyrics of 1998's 'Wild', with their reference to 'jockstraps full of jizz' and the like, are not his most explicit, but 'Sexy Motherfucker' would not have fitted so neatly into the title of this chapter.

2 Figures released by the Higher Education Statistics Agency show that in 2000, 11,000 women were awarded first class honours by British universities, as compared to 10,800 males.

3 *The Cheaper Sex: How Women Lose Out in Journalism*, Women In Journalism, July 1998.

4 Observations of this kind, when produced in the United States, formed an important part of the evidence for Susan Faludi's 'backlash' thesis (1991).

5 Also published in Sontag, S., 'Women', *Guardian*, 16 October 1999.

6 Sontag's optimistic analysis is not shared by all feminists, of course. Marilyn French, for example, while acknowledging that 'American and European feminists have altered their own societies profoundly and reached out to women in other continents and cultures, creating a real global network', qualifies this by asserting that:

> Media controlled by a few men censor discussion of feminism and allow only slanted, hate-driven and mocking mention of it.
> (French, M., 'How was it for them?', *Guardian*, 8 November 1999)

No examples of this tendency are cited by French, it has to be said, and her comments are at best a rather distorted caricature of how the contemporary media report feminist ideas.

7 There were female campaigners for women's rights before the 1800s. Sheila Rowbotham's *Hidden from History* (1977) gives an account of women's struggles for greater rights from the Puritan revolution of the 1500s.

8 Karl Marx and Friedrich Engels called the political philosophy which they founded 'historical materialism' to express their belief that history was driven not by ideas such as God (as Hegel and others argued) but by real (i.e. material) processes.

9 For a biography of Stopes see Rose, 1992.

10 Exemplified, perhaps, in the work of such as Pat Califia (1994).

11 In this respect, of course, history *is* repeating. The 'sex hysteria' and 'startling frankness' complained of by this author in 1913 anticipates much of the critical discourse around late-twentieth-century sexual culture.

12 The 1982 Merchant Ivory film adaptation of *The Bostonians*, starring Christopher Reeve, accurately captures the 'backlash' flavour of the work.

13 In her seminal 1975 essay 'Visual pleasure and narrative cinema' Mulvey argued that all visual culture in patriarchy was structured by the 'male gaze', which tended to objectify the female body, and to render her as a passive subject.

14 For a useful collection of essays which document the progress of the intra-feminist 'sex wars', and analyse the debates, see Duggan and Hunter, eds., 1995. A specifically American take on the issues is contained in Adele M. Stan's edited collection (1995).

15 For Faludi, 'pseudo-scientific' research suggesting that women could not or should not attempt to combine paid work with child rearing was part of a patriarchal reaction to the expansion of women in the workforce, to be resisted by feminists. It is now acknowledged by feminists that in the absence of workplace flexibility geared to parents, and women in particular, feminism has indeed put many women in the position of bearing an even greater workload than they faced when a serious career and motherhood were regarded as mutually exclusive.

16 Dworkin's credibility was seriously undermined in 2000 by several developments. In an article published in the *New Statesman* magazine she claimed to have been raped by an unnamed hotel waiter in an unnamed hotel (Dworkin, A., 'The day I was drugged and raped', *New Statesman*, 5 June 2000). A few days later *Guardian* journalist Catherine Bennett accused Dworkin of devaluing the issue of rape, and noted the deafening silence which had accompanied the *New Statesman* piece as evidence of the feminist community's embarrassment at its contents. On BBC radio on 16 August 2000, as mobs in several English towns were driving suspected paedophiles (many of whom were entirely innocent) from their homes and (in at least one case) to suicide, Dworkin advocated their castration and defended the mob behaviour with the odd claim that in Britain 'women and children are not protected by the law'.

17 From a profile of Segal in Hill, D., 'The truth about men and women', *Guardian*, 11 December 2000.

18 St Thomas Aquinas argued, as Reay Tannahill explains, that 'homosexuality was a deviation from the natural order laid down by God' (1992, p. 160).

19 Queer theorist Deborah Bright explains that 'the older terms, gay and lesbian, embody two polarities: one between the biological sexes of men and women; the other between hetero- and homosexuality as mutually exclusive modes of erotic object choice. The term "queer", on the other hand, connotes a radical assault on both of these naturalised sex-gender binaries' (1998, p. 3).

20 Quoted in James, N., 'American Voyeur', *Sight and Sound*, vol. 8, no. 7, 1998. Haynes's collaborator Michael Stipe, lead singer of one of the world's most successful rock bands, when asked if he was gay in *Q* magazine after years of is-he-or-isn't-he speculation illustrated the queer ethos well when he replied: 'Gay? I don't like that term. The very concept of gay puts people in categories. Queer to me is much broader, the idea that sexuality is extremely fluid and not capable of being reduced

to a category. Am I queer? Absolutely. I have enjoyed sex with men and women throughout my life' (Interview with Andy Pemberton in *Q*, May 1999, pp. 11–14).

21 Freedland, J., 'Goodbye to all this', *Guardian*, 9 February 2000.
22 Men's movement guru Mackie's motivational catchphrase, 'Worship the cock, tame the cunt', and the name of his movement – 'Seduce and Destroy' – are shocking in their bluntness, and at the same time, thanks to Cruise's actorly skills in the role, mercilessly debunking of backlash ideology.
23 'Such men', she added, 'are aware of the extent to which women have been discriminated against, and are the victims of violence and sexual aggression. They have become sensitised to the way conventional expectations of sexual behaviour have treated women as sex objects and fantasy figures.'

3 THE AMAZING EXPANDING PORNOSPHERE

1 Schlosser, E., 'The business of pornography', *US News and World Report*, August 1997.
2 Hamilton, W., 'The mainstream flirts with pornography chic', *New York Times*, 21 March 1999.
3 Sharkey, A., 'The land of the free', *Guardian*, 22 November 1997.
4 Definitions of hard and soft core vary from country to country, and change over time. A member of the Video Appeals Committee, which acts in the UK as a court of appeal for film-makers who feel that their works have been wrongly classified by the British Board of Film Classification, argues that 'the customary division of porn into two, "soft" and "hard", is now too crude. There needs to be a third, "medium" category to reflect the increasing sexual tolerance of the young' (Weldon, F., 'There's hard porn, and porn the public wants', *Sunday Times*, 6 August 2000). By 'hard core' in this book I mean images of unsimulated penetrative sex (vaginal, oral and anal). These were permitted in Britain in top shelf magazines and legally sold videos for the first time in 2000.
5 Figures quoted in 'Porn wars' (BBC *Panorama*, 1999).
6 The historian John Pultz concludes that 'photography and the increase during the nineteenth century in visual pornography are dual products of the mass culture born at the same time' (1995, p. 38). William Ewing agrees that 'photographic erotica became a mass-market phenomenon only in the 1850s with the introduction of the positive/negative process, which allowed unlimited numbers of copies of any image' (1994, p. 208).
7 Schlosser, E., 'The business of pornography', *US News and World Report*, August 1997.
8 Sprenger, P., 'The porn pioneers', *Guardian*, 30 September 1999.
9 *Guardian*, 16 January 2001.
10 Figures by Forester Research, reported in Haynes, M., 'Risqué business', *Guardian*, op. cit.
11 Davies, G., Wonke, A., 'We want porn', *Guardian*, 13 November 2000.
12 There are almost as many definitions of pornography as there are writers on the subject, and I will not rehearse them all here. Three basic categories can be identified, however: i) those which, like the one I use above, refer only to the content and function of the material (sexual explicitness and sexual arousal respectively); ii) those which refer to its obscene and offensive qualities, usually as defined by a religious perspective; iii) those which stress its exploitative and degradatory qualities, usually against women and children (though some critics of gay porn have not exempted the latter).
13 Linda Williams notes that 'pornography aims frankly at arousal; it addresses the bodies of its observers in their sexual desires and pleasures. It boldly sells this sexual address to

viewers as a commodity and it does not let aesthetic concerns or cultural prohibitions limit what it shows' (1994, p. 3).

14 On the release of *Romance* in the UK Breillat stated her view that 'pornography doesn't exist. What exists is censorship, which defines pornography and separates it from the rest of film. Pornography is the sexual act taken out of context, and made into a product for consumption' (quoted in Felperin, L., 'The edge of the razor', *Sight & Sound*, vol. 9, no. 10, October 1999.

15 Tanya Krzywinska puts it well in her essay on 'Cicciolina and the dynamics of trans-gression and abjection in explicit sex films' (1999). 'The aim of the genre of Explicit Sex Films is to elicit sexual desire by presenting the film's users with sexual images which are deemed exotic or sinful because they foreground sexual acts other than heterosexual coitus' (p. 192).

16 In Japan, for example, the representation of pubic hair has traditionally been forbidden in even the most extreme forms of hard core pornography, while paedophiliac and rape fantasies are routine features of the erotic manga comics widely read by Japanese men and women as they travel home from work on the train (Allison, 1996). This, to the western eye alien structure of obscenity and taboo is the product of a distinctive cultural history.

17 Bailey, F., 'Let it all hang out', *Guardian*, 8 October 1999.

18 Although the women who perform in these movies are consenting adults, often attracted by the relatively good money on offer (up to $1,000 for a day's work at 2000 prices).

19 Pelling, R., 'Generation sex', *Guardian*, 25 February 1999.

20 From the documentary *Erotica: A Journey into Female Sexuality* broadcast by Channel 4 television in 1999.

21 A definition embraced by the Dworkin–Mackinnon school of anti-porn feminism.

22 Sharkey, A., 'The land of the free', *Guardian*, 22 November 1997.

23 This observation was tinged with regret. 'The falling sales of porn mags', Lawson warned, 'may lead women to feel that men have finally, as they say, got it. The sad truth is that they are simply getting it somewhere else – and with knobs on' (Lawson, M., 'Lifting the net curtain on a hardcore world', *Guardian*, 15 February 1997).

24 Jones, D., 'Being sexy', *Guardian*, 12 July 1999.

25 Anne-Marie Crawford of *Marketing* magazine, quoted in Chaudhary, V., 'Backlash against lads' mags', *Guardian*, 27 August 1997.

26 For an account of the place of *Playboy* in American and western sexual culture see Dines, 1995.

27 O'Rourke, I., 'Kind of blue', *Guardian*, 28 July 1997.

28 *Penthouse*, September 1997.

29 Reported in O'Rourke, I., 'Kind of blue', *Guardian*, 28 July 1997.

30 See for example the cover story of *Time* magazine, 3 July 1995 (Elmer-Dewitt, P., 'On a screen near you: cyberporn'), reporting on the explosion of cyberporn. See also Holt, M., 'For adults only', *New Scientist*, 22 July 1995, for an explanation of the technical difficulties associated with censorship of the internet.

31 Elmer-Dewitt, P., 'On a screen near you: cyberporn', *Time*, 3 July 1995.

32 See *Pornography: a secret history of civilisation*, broadcast on Channel 4 television in 1999, and Isobel Tang's book of the series for examples (1999).

33 There is an interesting parallel between pornography and journalism here. Just as the radical journalism of the early nineteenth century was supplanted by a commercialized popular journalism in the late 1800s, so the anti-establishment subversiveness of early and pre-pornographic sexual representation was gradually diluted into forms of erotic entertainment which eschewed anti-establishment politics, while embodying patri-archal assumptions about sexuality and how it should be represented. As the publishing industry was revolutionized in the mid- to late nineteenth century, so new methods of

printing allowed for the commercial mass production of pornographic texts. Commercialization deradicalized them, as it destroyed the radical journalism of the early nineteenth century in Britain, stripping away the political ideas and challenges to authority which had informed the work of de Sade, John Cleland and others.

34 Fenton Bailey argues that 'the story of pornography is no less than the story of the evolution of mediating technologies. Interwoven with this is the story of the struggle to control them. From the printing press, through photography, film and video, to the computer age, each of these media is a democratising force, giving increasing numbers of people the power of representation. At the same time, each has largely been demonised as an agent of chaos' (Bailey, F., 'Let it all hang out', *Guardian*, 8 October 1999).

35 The word has its roots in the Greek for 'writing about harlots' and appears in various, usually critical contexts (sexual and non-sexual) from the 17th century onwards. Though Nathaniel Butter is reported to have used the term in the 1500s to describe the new journalism of sexual sensationalism (Boston, 1990). Its English-language contemporary was established in the 1850s with the first appearance of 'pornography ' in dictionaries to refer to 'lewd' and 'sexually licentious' texts. Inspired by the excavation of sexually explicit artifacts in Pompeii, and the establishment of 'secret museums' for hiding them away from the delicate eyes of women, children, and the poorly educated (Kendrick, 1987), the discovery of a dangerous type of sexually explicit image called 'pornography'was part of the nineteenth century's rationalization of sexuality; one manifestation of the intensified pathologizing of all its forms which the attempt to understand sex scientifically brought with it.

36 For a book-length study of the history of pornography and erotica in Russia see Barker, ed., 1999.

37 See John Carey's *The Intellectuals and the Masses* (1992) for a devastating critique of intellectual elitism since the late nineteenth century.

38 Appleyard, B., 'Pornography all dolled up as literature', *Sunday Times*, 2 November 1997.

39 Richard Dyer observes, 'the fact that porn, like weepies, thrillers and low comedy, is realised in/through the body has given it low status in our culture' (1992, p. 122).

40 John Huntley notes that

> Pornography is a historically specific as well as a class-based category. The distinctions made between pornography and erotica vary across time periods and cultures. Debates about censorship are inevitably about this boundary between art and smut, reality and fantasy, legitimate and illegitimate culture.
>
> (1998, p. 69)

41 Hill, D., 'The invisible men', *Guardian*, 11 November 1998.

42 Hitchens, P., 'Oh brother, what a time', *Sunday Times*, 1 March 1998.

43 Raven, C., 'Postporn', *Guardian*, 13 August 1998.

44 For a useful selection of feminist essays for and against pornography see *Debating Sexual Correctness* (Stan, ed., 1995), especially Part I, 'Passionate polemics'.

45 Quoted in Heins, 'Sworn in the USA', *Guardian*, 20 June 1996.

46 This book went to press just as the Taliban were being forcibly removed from power by the post-11 September coalition.

47 Set up in 1984 by the British Board of Film Classification to act as a court of appeal for the producers of video releases who felt that they had been treated unfairly by the BBFC.

48 A risqué magazine show broadcast by Channel 4.

49 Weldon, F., 'There's hard porn, and porn the public wants', *Sunday Times*, 6 August 2000.

50 In 1996, foreign companies like Rendez-Vous, Eurotica and SX TV were transmitting hard core pornography into the UK on the crest of what one journalist called an 'unstoppable tide' (Gaskell, J., 'The unstoppable tide', *Sunday Telegraph*, 13 October 1996). While the 1990 Broadcasting Act allowed the UK government to proscribe any satellite service 'which might seriously impair the physical or moral development of minors', enforcement was difficult in the context of organizations operating outwith UK territory.

51 Quoted in Heins, M., 'Sworn in the USA', *Guardian*, 20 June 1996.

52 Jones, C., 'Flesh-eating bug', *Sight and Sound*, July 1997.

53 See John Naughton's *Brief History of the Future* for a readable account of the history of the internet (1999).

54 Though these are flawed at best. One observer remarks that software packages like Net Nanny and Image Censor 'can't necessarily distinguish between a bikini-clad Spice Girl, your grandma sunbathing, a hardcore centrefold or a pile of uncooked sausages'. Jones, C., 'Flesh-eating bug', *Sight and Sound*, July 1997.

55 Whittam-Smith, A., 'Worried about porn? You too can be an Internet policeman', *Independent*, 10 March 1998.

56 In Britain, following the election of the Labour government in May 1997, home secretary Jack Straw resisted growing pressure to allow some limited, and licensed consumption of material which would be defined in Britain at that time as 'hard core', but was soft core for the rest of the European continent.

57 Quoted in *The Last Days of the Board*, Channel 4, 20 February 1999.

58 Falcon, R., 'How far can we go?', *Sight and Sound*, January 2001.

59 Ibid.

60 Matthews, T.D., 'Sex: the final frontier', *Guardian*, 13 November 1998.

61 From the statement by BSC chairwoman Lady Howe, January 1999.

62 Phillips, M.: 'Brainwashed by the sexual activists', *Sunday Times*, 24 January 1999.

63 The Independent Television Commission, which regulates commercial television in Britain.

64 Cox, B., 'Say goodbye to nanny', *Guardian*, 20 November 2000.

65 Healey, M., 'Hardcore!', *The Face*, November 2000.

66 *Scotland On Sunday*, 11 June 2000.

4 PORNO-CHIC

1 Kupfermann, J., 'The sexual sickness at the heart of our society', *Mail On Sunday*, 13 October 1996.

2 Hamilton, W.L., 'The mainstream flirts with pornography chic', *New York Times*, 21 March 1999.

3 Appleyard, B., 'Between you, me and the bed post', *Sunday Times*, 23 November 1997.

4 In *Pornography and so on* (London, Faber and Faber, 1936) Lawrence opined that 'you can recognise it [pornography] by the insult it offers, invariably, to sex, and to the human spirit' (p. 23).

5 Freedland, J., 'Getting it all off', *Guardian*, 10 May 2000.

6 Though commercially successful, *Emmanuelle* and the other 'sexploitation' films of the 1970s are viewed by contemporary critics as being of historical interest only. For Linda Ruth Williams, *Emmanuelle* was 'exploitation tosh dressed up as a pretentious Euro-meditation on the limits of desire' ('The oldest swinger in town', *Sight and Sound*, vol. 10. no. 8, pp. 24–7).

7 Leon Hunt's *British Low Culture* observes that 'the early part of the [1970s] saw a "mainstreaming" of pornography, indeed, a shift in what might be characterised as pornography' (1998, p. 24). In Japan the 1970s saw the emergence of a popular

cinematic sub-genre known as porno-roman which combined social radicalism and sadomasochistic sexual explicitness. Porno-roman films have now acquired cult status of the kind enjoyed by the 1970s British sex comedies, and a number of established Japanese film directors began their careers in this version of porno-chic (such as Tatsumi Kumashiro, Noboru Tanaka and Kiji Wakamutsa).

8 Appleyard, B., 'Between you, me and the bed post', *Sunday Times*, 23 November 1997.

9 Amis returned to the subject in an essay published by the *Guardian* newspaper on 17 March 2001 ('A rough trade'). Despite the changed status of the pornographic described in Chapter 3, the piece was heavy with the smell of porno-fear, focusing on the violent, sadomasochistic sectors of the industry, and describing their activities in detail. Ironically, these very details – clearly intended by the author to shock and horrify rather than arouse – led to him being accused of peddling 'gratuitous filth' by several readers. According to the readers' editor, charged with responding to controversies stirred up by published articles, twenty letters expressed strong objections to the piece, while ten welcomed it or made 'interested comment'.

10 Kendrick's *The Secret Museum* (1987), a pioneering study of the roots of pornography's demonization in Victorian-era patriarchy, is one.

11 Allen-Mills, T., 'Sadists take whip hand in America', *Sunday Times*, 7 December 1997.

12 Appleyard, B., 'Between you, me and the bed post', *Sunday Times*, 23 November 1997.

13 Newton's best-known photographs, the subject of a retrospective exhibition at London's Barbican Gallery in 2001, depicted women in positions and apparel hitherto associated with the worlds of sadomasochism, bondage and fetishism. Newton's aesthetic vision, according to one critic, was 'fuelled by sex, status, power and, above all, voyeurism' (Frankel, S., 'The Master', *The Independent*, 9 May 2001). In his work for the fashion and advertising industries he made this vision part of mainstream style culture in the 1980s. Newton's work, however, unlike that of the photographic and other artists associated with porno-chic in the 1990s, was generally read within what was then the dominant interpretive framework of anti-porn feminism, criticized for its alleged misogyny and objectification/exploitation of the female body.

14 That time in the evening (after 9 p.m.) when programmes of an adult nature can be shown.

15 The debate about Madonna's contribution to the feminist struggle has been a long and somewhat circular one, mirroring the pornography debate itself. Those feminists who oppose pornography also tend to find Madonna, whom they view as a deluded exploiter of her own good looks, objectionable. Anti-censorship feminists, on the other hand, celebrate her place as a pioneer of a new kind of female sexuality.

16 Quoted in Smith, A., 'Material girl to earth mother', *Sunday Times*, 1 March 1998.

17 See for example *The Madonna Connection* (Schwichtenberg, ed., 1993); *Madonnarama* (Frank and Smith, eds., 1993); and *Deconstructing Madonna* (Lloyd, ed., 1993).

18 Williams, L.R. 'Nothing to find', *Sight and Sound*, January 1996, pp. 28–30.

19 Writers have also played with the conventions of porn. Chapter 14 of Nicholson Baker's *The Fermata* (1994), for example, depicts a scatological *ménage à trois* sex scene of the type usually to be found only in the hardest of hard core pornography. The chapter – or the section within it which is clearly intended to be read as pornographic – works as pornography, and perhaps as art, in so far as the author wishes to problematize the art/porn distinction by saying 'I, the literary novelist Nicholson Baker, have written *this*.'

20 Bailey, A., 'Tokyo porn warning', *The Face*, November 2000, pp. 139–42.

21 Bruzzi, S., *Sight and Sound*, vol. 7, no. 3, p. 59.

22 In the years following *The People vs. . . .* the real Larry Flynt achieved further acceptance as a 'chic' cultural figure, his new respectability illustrated by his opening of a chain of

Hustler Hollywood latte bars in various American cities in 1999. In 2000 he was interviewed at length on BBC News 24, in a series which also featured Nelson Mandela. Around the same time newspaper articles were observing the revived fortunes of Hugh Hefner's *Playboy* empire, and the fact that both Flynt and Hefner were highly visible supporters of, and contributors to, the Democratic Party's 2000 presidential campaign.

23 Quoted in Smith, G., 'Night Fever', *Sight and Sound*, vol. 8, no. 1, January 1998, pp. 7–10.
24 From the Twin Palms website.
25 Hamilton, W.L., 'The mainstream flirts with pornography chic', *New York Times*, 21 March 1999.
26 Shave, C., 'Constant stiffies', *I-D*, May 1999, pp. 113–15.
27 *Sight and Sound*, vol. 9, no. 5, p. 45.
28 As long ago as 1987 one cultural commentator could observe that 'notions of hard-core pornography as mediated through auteuristic eroticism affect the form and presentation of certain up-market fashion images' (Myers, 1987, p. 64).
29 Around the same time, porno-chic featured in the spring–summer issue of *Vogue*.
30 For an introduction to the magazine go to www.richardsonmag.com
31 For a practitioner's selection of some of the bext sex-inflected advertisements of recent years, see Saunders, 1996.
32 Amis, M., 'A rough trade', *Guardian*, 17 March 2001.
33 'Strip Programming', *Journal of the Royal Television Society*, May 1999, pp. 12–14.
34 From Mark Kermode's introduction to *Censored*, Channel 4, 20 February 1999.
35 Compton, E., 'Suburban sex scandal', *Company*, January 1995.
36 Raven, C., 'The opposite of sexy', *Guardian*, 13 June 2000.
37 *Porn Wars*, BBC1, 1999.
38 The same conclusion was made more explicit in Channel 4's *The Last Days of the Board*, which dissected the problems faced by the British Board of Film Classification in policing the boundaries of sex and violence on screen (*The Last Days of the Board*, Channel 4, 20 February 1999).

5 STRIPTEASE CULTURE

1 Notwithstanding the argument of writers such as D. Kirk Davidson that 'pornography is encroaching on mainstream television' through the treatment in sitcoms, dramas and daytime talk shows of previously taboo topics like rape, prostitution and child abuse (1996, p. 92). This encroachment constitutes part of the sexualization of popular culture, to be sure, but not 'pornographication' as I decribed it in the previous chapter.
2 Mark Ford, head of development at Rapido, quoted in 'Strip programming', *Journal of the Royal Television Society*, May 1999, pp. 12–14.
3 Consistent with this cultural reappraisal of striptease is the fact that the second series of the UK version of *Big Brother*, which began in May 2001, featured among its ten 'house mates' a 23-year-old 'table dancer' or 'stripper', as she described herself. Far from being ashamed of or defensive about her occupation, Amma championed it aggressively, describing in one conversation to a housemate how she particularly enjoyed stripping before customers she didn't like, because she perceived it as her opportunity to exert power over him. 'I want to see the rise in your trousers. I want to see you sweat.'
4 Quoted in Chrisafis, A., 'Body of work', *Guardian*, 16 March 2001.
5 For an account of this period in British politics, and its treatment by the press and broadcast media, see McNair, 2000.
6 See Neal Gabler's excellent biography of Winchell and the heyday of celebrity journalism in the United States (1994).

7 I refer here to the experience of *Coronation Street* star Rachel Starr who, though happy to pose semi-naked for *GQ* in pursuit of her career, felt that tabloid press coverage of her father's affairs and subsequent divorce was an indefensible intrusion on her, and their, privacy.

8 See my essay on 'Journalism, politics and public relations' (McNair, 1998) for a fuller discussion of journalistic ethics in this area.

9 In 2000, for example, Channel 5 had a programme budget of £150 million, compared to the approximately £600 million available to Channel 4.

10 Ford, A., 'Sex objection', *Guardian*, 19 December 1998. In its 1999 *Sex and Sensibility* report the Broadcasting Standards Commission found 72 per cent of those questioned believing that sex is used by the broadcasters to boost viewing figures. That figure was read by the BSC as a criticism of TV's sexualization, although there is no obvious reason why satisfying viewers' interests in sex should be deemed a less than sufficient reason for transmitting such material (unless, of course, one has moral or political reasons for objecting to the inclusion of sex on the legitimate agenda of the public sphere).

11 Garside, J., 'Channel 4 hires Black ID', *Sunday Herald*, 8 October 2000. This article reported on Channel 4's plans to launch a website linked to its adult programming called Forbidden4.com.

12 Contained in his *Mythologies* (1973).

13 *Fantasy Club* was a one-off documentary shot by a single director with a digital video camera. There have also been series devoted to striptease, and many 'docu-soaps' which fit my definition of striptease culture. *Ibiza Uncovered*, for example, focused on the 'sun, sea, sand and sex' lifestyles of young Britons on holiday in the Balearics. Tapping into late-night British television's desire to reflect and be part of an increasingly sexualized club culture, wet t-shirt and mud-wrestling contests featured prominently in *Ibiza Uncovered*.

14 Brockes, M., 'Welcome to Me TV', *Guardian*, 10 December 1999.

15 www.bravo.co.uk/dolls/ invites visitors to

> Meet the Dolls – three amazing babes living in a London house with five live cams. Watch their every move, chat with them live, send them email . . .

16 Walker, S., 'Weblife:webcams', *Guardian*, 10 February 2000.

17 www.cam-station.com/top100/girlcams

18 Brockes, M., 'Welcome to Me TV', *Guardian*, 10 December 1999.

19 See Hibberd, M. *et al.*, *Consenting Adults?*, London, Broadcasting Standards Commission, 2000.

20 Quoted in *Naked London*, broadcast by Channel 5 in December 1999.

21 *Panorama*, BBC1, January 2001.

22 *So You Want To Be On TV?*, Channel 4, 20 March 2001.

23 Woods, R., Wroe, M., 'Beyond laddism', *Sunday Times*, 17 October 1999.

24 Ford, A., 'Sex objection', *Guardian*, 19 December 1998.

25 Ibid.

26 From *The Last Days of the Board*, Channel 4, 20 February 1999.

27 Willis, J., 'Turning on the TV', *Guardian*, 13 September 1999. For a US perspective on talk show treatment of homosexuality, see Gamson, 1998.

Notes

INTRODUCTION TO PART II

1 Quoted in Golden, ed., 1994, p. 24.

6 'WOMEN, KNOW YOUR LIMITS!'

1 Brooks, L., 'Anatomy of desire', *Guardian*, 12 December 2000.
2 Freedland, J., 'Wash the dishes and stand by your man', *Guardian*, 20 August 1997.
3 Bell, E., 'Brylcreem's naked ambition', *Observer*, 14 July 1991.
4 Reported in Mackay, N., 'Media blamed for increase in underage sex', *Sunday Herald*, 28 November 1999. For the full report see Kitzinger, J., *The Representation of Teenage Sexuality in the Media*, Edinburgh, Health Education Board for Scotland, 1999.
5 The murder of a young girl, Sarah Payne, prompted the newspaper to launch a ratings-led 'name and shame' campaign against suspected paedophiles, leading to mob rule in the streets of several English cities, and the death by suicide of at least one man wrongly targeted.
6 Dr Michelle Elliot, speaking on the *Today* programme, Radio 4, 5 February 2001.
7 For some feminists, of course, it is precisely the adoption of 'promiscuous' sexual lifestyles traditionally monopolized by men which can be counted as one of the benefits of feminist struggle.
8 Also of importance are believed to be such factors as sexual abuse, mental illness and genetics. The BMA acknowledges the important point that:

> All research on 'media effects' needs to consider the contextual complexities involved in receiving media messages: the media do not 'brainwash' people, but receive different levels of attention and interpretation by individuals with different motivations, personalities, immediate situations and sociocultural contexts, who bring different information processing strategies to the task. The media are not monolithic, and do not affect everybody in the same way.
>
> (BMA Board of Science and Education, May 2000)

9 Sontag, S., 'Women', *Guardian*, 16 October 1999.
10 Grant, L., 'Le Sex', *Guardian*, 9 October 1999.
11 *Showgirls* was confused and ill-judged by comparison (though even its messy mix of porno-chic and mainstream musical can be read as at least in part a tale of one woman's fight against patriarchy, represented, in this case, by the owners of the club where its female protagonist finds work).
12 Lane argues that 'while there is no need to label Bigelow's films "feminist" per se, they certainly move within a "feminist orbit" and engage political issues. Her films encourage spectators to ask questions about gender, genre and power' (2000, p. 123). *The Weight of Water*, released in 2000, has however been described by one critic as 'a radical departure' from Bigelow's previous films in so far as it was 'a contemporary woman's picture' (review by Monica Dargis in *Sight and Sound*, vol. 10, no. 2, November 2000). Significantly, perhaps, the film was the least commercially successful of her films to date.
13 Seidelman directed Madonna in the successful indie crossover *Desperately Seeking Susan* (1987) before flopping with *She-Devil*.
14 Helford's essay on Xena notes that

> The series effectively challenges problematic aspects of gender essentialism, such as linking women with passivity, emotionalism, and weakness. It shows friendship between women as positive influences and central to women's lives. And it escapes the static notion of sexuality and representations of homosexuality on television by

218

offering characters who can be read as lesbian or bisexual and nonmonogamous without critique of their lifestyles within the narrative.

(2000, p. 158)

15 'In spite of the dominance of patriarchal culture', argues Lynda Nead, 'more spaces are being made by feminism, both in high and popular culture, for representations of the female body that express women's identities, desires and needs' (1992, p. 4).

7 THE MAINSTREAMING OF GAYNESS

1 Beckett, A., 'On the gay and narrow', *Guardian*, 3 July 1997.
2 Medhurst, A., *The Face*, January 1999, pp. 50–5.
3 Perretti, J., 'Ooh, you are awful', *Guardian*, 19 November 1999.
4 To the extent that the film and television industries have been and remain businesses run mainly by men (though that domination is in decline), lesbians have been relatively invisible, and where visible represented in largely stereotypical terms (gay men are not necessarily pro-lesbian). British television led the way towards a richer representational field with *Oranges Are Not the Only Fruit* in the 1980s. In cinema there had been, as of writing, no mainstream feature films (I restrict this remark to English-language films) about lesbians written or directed by women (the exceptions being *Boys Don't Cry* and *I Shot Andy Warhol*, both of which found crossover success), and only a handful made by men. Paul Verhoeven's *Basic Instinct* featured two, of course, in a film which was only in the most flexible sense of the term 'about' lesbianism.
5 Though certainly not all. For Tom Waugh it embodied 'an anachronistic defeatism, a morbid, self-directed hatred that reinforced homophobia within [its] straight audience' (2000, p. 19).
6 With reference to the qualifiying remarks made at the beginning of the chapter, it is interesting that the director of *Midnight Cowboy*, John Schlesinger, is gay, whereas Friedkin is not.
7 Quoted in Kermode, M., 'Cruise control', *Sight and Sound*, vol. 9, no. 11, 1998.
8 'Go West' was covered by the Pet Shop Boys in 1993, and was again a huge international hit.
9 One thinks of the suicide of Brian Epstein, for example, and his reported 'love affair' with John Lennon in the 1960s, as detailed in Albert Goldman's 1988 biography, *The Lives of John Lennon*. Whether the affair happened or not, it is clear that Epstein, despite his success and influence, was just as emotionally disabled by his homosexuality and the need to hide it from the public as other gay men of the time.
10 David Buckley records that the cover was promptly withdrawn in the United States, where 'having a rock star so graphically feminised was anathema. This was Bowie's first taboo-breaking album, and a sign that a young generation was about to bring all the hippy-era certainties crashing down' (1999, p. 89).
11 See Barney Hoskyns's *Glam* (1998) for a lively account of the period.
12 Bowie's gay phase anticipated the flirtation with bi- and homosexuality pursued by Madonna nearly twenty years later. Combining her feminist politics (the 1970s glam stars had little understanding of, or sympathy with, feminism) with a camp aesthetic in performances such as *Vogue* and the *Sex* book, she feminized the glam aesthetic.
13 James, N., 'American voyeur', *Sight and Sound*, vol. 8, no. 7, 1998
14 Quoted in James, N., op. cit.
15 The first 'gay soap' to be broadcast on British television.
16 Brown, A., 'Jimmy's back on track', *Sunday Times*, 13 June 1999.
17 Tarantino fans will be familiar with his *Top Gun*-is-a-gay-movie speech in the otherwise unmemorable 1994 production *Sleep with Me*.

18 Also worthy of mention in this respect is *As Good As It Gets* (Mike Nichols, 1999), in which Jack Nicholson plays a homophobic sociopath who learns to love his gay neighbour.

19 Trying to explain the attraction which someone like Madonna (or indeed Bowie in the early 1970s) might have for gay culture one observer suggested that 'overt homosexuality is so compatible with celebrity these days because it dramatises the masculine/feminine, active/passive gender quandary. . . . The homosexual is also a contemporary cultural hero battling against the oppressive "inauthenticity" of convention' (Simpson, M., 'He only wants to be loved', *Guardian*, 27 April 1996). Madonna herself suggested a more prosaic explanation in the article referred to above. 'We're both minorities, and we both love to shop' (Zeman, N., 'Just great friends', *Vanity Fair*, March 2000.

20 Review by Andy Medhurst, *Sight and Sound*, vol. 8, no. 11, 1998.

21 Although even the mainstreaming of gayness could not save Barrymore from a course of self-destruction. When a dead body was found floating in his swimming pool after a drinking and sex session in April 2001 media references to the plot of *Sunset Boulevard* seemed entirely reasonable.

22 Launched on BBC Choice in April 2001.

23 *USA Today*, February 22 1999. For a detailed history of the representation of homosexuality in American television see Capsuto, 2000.

24 Steven Capsuto observes of the United States that 'gay-themed scripts have been approved most frequently during periods when gay issues were receiving heavy news coverage' (2000, p. 2).

25 Greenslade, R., 'Surprising my sun', *Guardian*, 21 June 1999.

26 Review by Peter Matthews, *Sight and Sound*, vol. 7, no. 3, 1996.

27 A prime example, for one observer, of Hollywood's flirtation with lesbian plots around this time (Letts, Q., 'Girl-meets-girl comes out of the closet', *Times*, 25 November 1996).

28 A growing number of queer critics are prepared to adopt the latter interpretation. Of *Bound*, Ellis Hanson observes 'a welcome alternative to the spate of clunky and vacuous lesbian romances and comedies' which, though amateurish in their production, had been canonized as examples of the 'correct' approach to female homosexual representation (1999, ed., p. 1).

29 Smith, J., 'Why is it in for lesbians to be out?', *Independent on Sunday*, 25 June 1995.

30 Medhurst, A., 'Licensed to cheek', *Sight and Sound*, vol. 7, no. 10, 1997.

31 Review by Andy Medhurst, *Sight and Sound*, vol. 8, no. 2, 1997.

32 Rich, B. Ruby, 'Queer and present danger', *Sight and Sound*, March 2000, pp. 22–5.

33 'What primarily differentiates New Queer cinema from other types of post-modern movie is its recognition of the transformative impact of AIDS – which mobilized a community and caused an epistemic shift in gay culture – on attitudes towards society, bodies, relationships, history, culture, sexuality, time and mortality' (Gloss, H., 'Queer', *Sight and Sound*, vol. 7, no. 10, 1997).

34 Rich, B. Ruby, op. cit.

35 This trend was further boosted by the introduction from 2000 of TIVO technology – a digital recorder which allows viewers to cut 'n' mix their own schedules from the proliferating jungle of cable, satellite and digital channels. As one media analyst put it 'the TIVO is really just a fantastically powerful accelerator of the fragmentation of markets caused by non-terrestrial TV and the internet' (Lewis, M., 'Box of tricks', *Guardian*, 28 August 2000). Technologies of this kind will increase the representational opportunities for all minorities in the twenty-first century.

36 As reported in *USA Today*, 22 February 1999.

37 Willis, J., 'Turning on the TV', *Guardian*, 13 September 1999.

8 MEN BEHAVING SADLY

1 Gill, A.A. and Hellen, N., 'Men portrayed badly', *Sunday Times*, 1 March 1998.
2 Appleyard, B., 'Why is modern man so girlie?', *Sunday Times*, 28 June 1998.
3 Mark Simpson argues that 'the phasing out of traditional masculinity by capitalism, its redundancy in many modern families and its undesirability in the social sphere has resulted in what has been termed a 'crisis of masculinity' (1996, p. 244).
4 Quoted in Mahoney, E., 'Prophet of loss', *Sunday Herald*, 14 November 1999.
5 A British television screening in 2001 was advertised to readers of one newspaper in the following terms: 'It's very naughty 90s, but it's the same old message: bad women get their come-uppance' (*Guardian*, 15 February 2001).
6 In a British television documentary about the actor Camille Paglia expressed her approval of his contribution in this respect.

> We've had all kinds of parodies of masculinity in cinema of the last twenty five years. We have the Schwarzenegger style, the Stallone style which is impressive in its own way but verges on the cartoonish. The world of action-adventure is really a kind of fantasy. And then we have also the young actor, the brat pack style, who wants to be a punk, and who's really in the shadow of Marlon Brando and James Dean. And that also doesn't work. These are middle class guys trying to be working class. And there is just no intelligent version of masculinity, as far as I'm concerned, on the screen in the last twenty years, except for Michael Douglas.
> (*The South Bank Show*'s profile of Douglas, broadcast on ITV, February 2000)

7 Review in *Sight and Sound*, vol. 8, no. 2, 1998.
8 Taylor, C., 'Welcome to the Nerdhouse', *Sight and Sound*, vol. 9, no. 3 1999.
9 Review by Peter Matthews in *Sight and Sound*, vol. 7, no. 7, 1997.
10 Marcus, T., 'Let there be flesh', *i-D*, no. 186, May 1999.
11 BMA Board of Science and Education, May 2000.
12 'I felt I was kind of de-sexed. I'd done all these movies and all of a sudden I was like someone's wife and that image had gone completely. I'm 32, I'm a woman now and I feel it's right, I feel it's empowering. I don't feel vulnerable or like I'm being exploited in any way. I feel that I'm actually very in control of it' (actress Patsy Kensit discussing her nude photographs in *Arena* magazine, quoted in the *Guardian*, 15 February 2001).
13 Aaronovitch, D., 'Outrageous!', *Independent*, 21 November 1995.
14 *FHM*'s February 1997 issue led an article about the relative toughness of being 'a bloke or a bird' with a quote from Andrea Dworkin, 'the leading feminist'. What followed was a jokey, but still serious investigation of how men and women would cope were their social and sexual roles reversed.
15 Viner, K., 'Who are you calling a slag?', *Guardian*, 28 August 1997.
16 Appleyard, B., 'Why is modern man so girlie?', *Sunday Times*, 28 June 1998.
17 Viner, K., op. cit.

INTRODUCTION TO PART III

1 Buck, L., 'Not in front of the British', *Independent*, 21 November 1995. Sex has been a big theme not just of twentieth-century art, of course. Frank Whitford observes that 'from ancient Greek vase painting to the athletic couplings depicted on the Indian temple sculptures at Khajurasho, from the frescoes of Pompeii to the often staggeringly explicit paintings and prints of feudal Japan, the history of Art pulsates with full-blooded descriptions of sexual activity' ('The shock of the nude', *Sunday Times*, 20 December 1993.

2 Jake and Dinos Chapman have used sexually explicit models to explore the subjects of child abuse and, in their work first shown in 2000, the Holocaust ('Hell').

3 A student had taken photographs of some of the images in her preparation of a course assignment, and submitted them for processing to a commercial developer, who had alerted the police.

4 Criticized because it led to mob rule in the streets of some English towns, and to the harassment of individuals wrongly identified by the paper as paedophile. In one celebrated case, which demonstrated the ignorance surrounding this particular moral panic, an angry mob chased a paediatrician from her home in the sincere belief that she had something to do with child molestation. In another, the harassment was alleged to have provoked a suicide.

5 Allen-Mills, T. and Wavell, S., 'No holds barred', *Sunday Times*, 18 April 1999.

6 Burchill, J., 'Death of innocence', *Guardian*, 12 November 1997.

7 Fans of the book may recall the following passage:

> The crowd moved as one. She was pushed down on to her back and someone sat on her face, though whether for kicks or to obscure her view of the participants she couldn't decide. She couldn't see or speak or hear; her senses were all in her body as mouths sucked at her breasts, different mouths taking turns and being wrenched urgently away to be replaced by other, rougher mouths. Talk about fast food. When it seemed the whole bar had had their *hors d'oeuvres*, they went for the main attraction, taking her with their hands and mouths till she lost count. Then she was ridden by half a dozen women wearing the longest, hardest dildoes imaginable; two seemed filed to a point, and one spurted something warm and thick into her.
>
> (*Ambition*, p. 259)

This depiction of 'rough' lesbian sex, culminating with penetration by sharpened dildoes does not, apparently, qualify as obscenity or atrocity in Burchill's critical schema, though others might beg to differ (and indeed did when *Ambition* was published).

9 MEN, SEX AND TRANSGRESSION

1 In a later essay Paglia argues that 'aggression and eroticism are deeply intertwined. Hunt, pursuit and capture are biologically programmed into male sexuality' (1995, p. 23).

2 To accompany his 2001 album *And No More Shall We Part* (Mute), Cave published the text of a lecture he had given on the nature of his melancholic, love-struck writing. The love song, he writes, 'must be borne into the realm of the irrational, the absurd, the distracted, the melancholic, the obsessive and the insane, for it is the clamour of love itself, and love is, of course, a form of madness' (Cave, N., 'Love is the drug', *Guardian*, 21 April 2001).

3 Deirdre Robson's *The Art of the Nude* (1995) notes that the first modern example of a reclining female nude was painted by Giorgione around 1505.

4 *American Psycho* catalogues with Sadeian detail the excesses of a serial killer in late 1980s New York: crimes which which may or may not be fantasy. The extreme sexualized violence is a device for satirizing the elitist, consumerist values of 1980s America.

5 Bornoff, N., 'Finest filth', *Guardian*, 10 June 1997. In addition to his staged images of constrained and dominated women, Araki has documented the distinctive trajectory of Japan's cultural sexualization. In his photographs of the Tokyo-Shinjuku sex industry he has constructed 'a historical record of sex and morals in the early 1980s' (from Akihito Yasumi's introductory essay to Araki, *Tokyo Lucky Hole*, 1997).

6 The curious idolization extended to Araki in Japan was captured in the documentary *Fake Love*, broadcast by Channel 4 in 1995 as part of its Red Light Zone series. The film shows Araki being stopped in a Tokyo street by young women, who beg for his autograph and the opportunity to pose for him in sexually explicit photographs.

7 From André Breton's *First Manifesto of Surrealism*, published in 1924.

8 Giles Neret writes that

> the Surrealists are of one mind with Charles Fourier, the theoretician whom they admire for his evaluation of eroticism as a dynamic power capable of cutting through the tyrannical web of taboos which society spins in order to safeguard its own survival. Fourier also contends that it is by virtue of eroticism that humankind first discovers the fullness of its nature, that eroticism restores the integrity of identity by allowing people to live out their lusts.
>
> (1998, p. 127)

9 An English language translation is available as *Mad Love* (Breton, 1987).

10 Writing in the *Guardian* in the late 1980s.

11 See *Man Ray* by Roland Penrose (1989) for an authoritative and accessible biography by someone who knew the artist intimately.

12 Man Ray was one of those early-twentieth-century artists who secured the status of photography as a legitimate art form, to be treated with the respect traditionally accorded painting and sculpture. He himself worked in all three media, but it was as a photographer that he achieved his greatest artistic successes.

13 Whose song 'Femme Fatale' is implicated in the general atrociousness of sexually transgressive art for its celebration 'of the perversity and excesses of pornography for their own sake' (Appleyard, B., 'Way beyond the erogenous zone', *Times*, 12 September 1992).

14 Though an international hit, the film was refused a distribution licence by the country's Ethics Committee.

15 Man Ray, like many men of his era, regarded domestic violence as a legitimate means of controlling his female partners.

16 Buck, L., 'Not in front of the British', *Independent*, 21 November 1995.

17 Op. cit.

18 Falcon, R., 'Reality is too shocking', *Sight and Sound*, vol.9, no.1.

19 Inspired by Von Trier and the Dogma example, the US-based Good Machine production company (responsible for decidedly non-sexual titles like *The Butterfly's Tongue* [Cuerda, 1998]) established a division called Uncensored Films in 1999, which would 'explore the subject of sexuality, without limitation, while granting the director full creative expression' (Farrow, B., 'Porn again', *Sight and Sound*, vol. 10, no. 8, 2000, pp. 24–7).

20 Review by Ginette Vincendeau, *Sight and Sound*, vol. 10, no. 9.

21 Brittain, D., 'Indecent exposure', *Dazed and Confused*, August 1997.

22 Aidin, R., 'Invasion of the body snappers', *Sunday Times*, 5 September 1999.

23 Brittain, D., 'Indecent exposure', *Dazed and Confused*, August 1997.

24 Ibid.

25 The patently absurd persona of Nobuyoshi Araki, for example, has been viewed by some western feminists as an expression of his misogyny. But what are we to make of the fact that many Japanese women go along with his 'violations' enthusiastically, and precisely at a time when that country's patriarchal structures are under unprecedented strain? Allison Assiter notes that in Japan 'male recreative sexuality' has long been socially sanctioned (1996, p. 48) while women have been subject to oppressive rules of etiquette and decorum as embodied in the rituals of geisha and genko. This is now changing as Japanese women follow their western sisters into an era of more assertive

and visible feminine sexuality. Araki's iconic status in Japan, and the willing participation of Japanese women in his work appear to be one manifestation of that movement. In Japan, as in western societies, progress in women's rights has been accompanied by their greater participation in sexual culture, including their 'submission' to the simulated violations of Araki. Submission to Araki also became fashionable in the west, as indicated when the Icelandic pop star Björk employed his services in the making of the cover for her album *Postcard*.

10 QUEER CULTURE

1 This chapter addresses the art of gay men. Gay, or queer women, are discussed in Chapter 11 on 'Bad Girls'. I will note here that artistic lesbians like actress Sarah Bernhardt, painter Romaine Brooks and writer Radclyffe Hall, though not actually criminalized, were also required to obscure their sexualities from the glare of public scrutiny (Bernhardt is said to have constructed a coded lesbian identity from 'a bricolage of cultural sources, including theatrical images, utopian fiction, Greek and Roman literature, medieval texts, male pornographic and semi-pornographic literature, the flourishing male homosexual culture of the times, and the inventiveness of confident women claiming a new public sexual identity' (Vicinus, 1996, p. 190)

2 In aestheticism

> Art functions as a utopian second world opposed to the middle-class boredom and dullness of the 'real' world. By espousing art, the artist also endorses an indulgence in individualistic and dandyish behaviour, a dedication to beauty, sensuality, style, wit, and the exotic – and by implication homosexual behaviour.
>
> (La Valley, 1995, p. 61)

3 Tom of Finland, who died in 1992, produced homoerotic drawings from the late 1950s. Cooper records that his work 'has come to exemplify a particular American style. His icons of masculinity include truck drivers, leather-clad motor bike riders, denim-clad cowboys, soldiers and policemen' (1994, p. 236). See Blake, 1995, for an appreciation of the artist.

4 Good insights into Warhol's life and the nature of his work are contained in *The Andy Warhol Diaries* (1989), Jean Stein and George Plimpton's biography of Warhol 'superstar' Edie Sedgwick (1982), and Bob Colacello's insider's account of Warhol's post-1960s life (1990).

5 For a book-length review of Warhol's film work see O'Pray, ed., 1989.

6 As John Cale credits him with saying in the album he and Lou Reed produced as a tribute to Warhol, 'those downtown macho painters are all just alcoholics' (*Songs For Drella*).

7 The feeling was mutual, it seems, with Warhol perceiving Mapplethorpe to be a potential rival for his place in the New York art world.

8 For Camille Paglia the *Horses* cover was, when she encountered it as a young university lecturer, 'the most electrifying image I had ever seen of a woman of my generation. Now, two decades later, I think it ranks in art history among a half-dozen supreme images of modern woman since the French Revolution' ('What's in a picture?', *Civilization*, December–January 1996/7).

9 National Endowment for the Arts, the official US body for channelling public money into the arts.

10 Frank Pierson's feature-length drama documentary *Dirty Pictures* (2000) tells the story of one episode in the 'culture wars', and art curator Dennis Barry's prosecution for obscenity after exhibiting *The Perfect Moment* in Cincinnati.

11 Some critics reject the 'canonical' status which Mapplethorpe's work has acquired since his death, asserting that others were doing similar things before and alongside

him. Why Mapplethorpe, they ask, and not the black photographer Carl Van Vechten, making images of black, and black with white male nudes from the 1930s until the 1960s (Smalls, 1998)? Or F. Holland Day, whose 1897 portrait of an 'African chief' is reproduced in Tom Waugh's history of homoerotic photography (1996)? Or Lyle Ashton Harris, the contemporary black artist (see Bright, ed., 1998), or Renée Cox (see Golden, ed., 1994)? For Van Vechten and Holland Day, active before Stonewall, mainstream acceptance was simply not on the agenda. Mapplethorpe was fortuituous enough to capture the post-Stonewall moment, and thus to be received in the context of the broader sexualization of American art and culture which characterized the 1970s and 1980s. As for Harris and Cox, they come after Mapplethorpe, and are clearly influenced by him in their compositions and subject matter. Mapplethorpe can thus lay some claim to aesthetic originality.

12 This 'classical symmetry of form', for Schneider, is precisely what

> beckons a viewer to place his photograph alongside other 'formally correct' canonical entries across the history of Western art. And yet it is their very placing that becomes confrontative because Mapplethorpe's content, rife with contemporary taboos of class, race and subcultural references, can be seen to comment on social and political histories eclipsed from formalist approaches to art.
>
> (1997, p. 15)

13 The phrase is Bruce Chatwin's, from his introductory essay to *Lady* (Mapplethorpe, 1983).

14 Although Robert Hughes believes that

> Mapplethorpe's more sexually extreme images are in some sense didactic; dionysian in themselves, they have the character of a moral spectacle, stripping away the veils of prudery and ignorance and thus promoting gay rights by confronting us with the outer limits of human sexual behaviour, beyond which only death is possible.
>
> (1995, p. 156)

15 An erotic Picasso exhibition containing works never seen before in public opened in Paris in March 2001.

16 From his postface essay in *Altars* (Mapplethorpe, 1995).

17 Op. cit.

18 From her introductory essay to Mapplethorpe's *Certain People* (1985).

19 Emmanuel Cooper writes that

> Mapplethorpe called directly on his own experience, presenting it in a form which was able not only to reflect that experience, but to communicate his desire effectively to others. The autobiographical aspects of his s/m images, his love of and desire for black men, and his own participation in s/m rituals, were crucial to a contemporary concern with attempting to speak for yourself while also seeking to indicate that involvement to others. In reflecting his personal involvement and translating it into something wider and more general, Mapplethorpe broke for ever the unspoken vows of silence which had restricted images of gay life to boys by the pool, or endless images of youthful, muscular young men.
>
> (1996, p. 18)

20 From his essay in Mapplethorpe's *Altars* (1995).

21 Apart from those contexts in which it arises directly from the work under discussion, as in the case of Mapplethorpe's photography, I have not addressed the sexualization of ethnicity in this book. Limitations of space would have prevented any more than a

tokenistic passage or two, and the subject requires much more than that to be dealt with adequately. Apart from Thelma Golden's *Black Male* collection of essays (1994), cited in the introduction to Part II, readers interested in the sexual representation of ethnicity will find discussion of the subject in Sharon Willis's *High Contrast* (1997), and Lisa Young's *Fear of the Dark* (1996). Both books focus on cinema, the latter arguing that 'many cinematic images of black women and men obsessively repeat well-worn stereotypes of black femininity and masculinity' (p. 37). Moreover, 'when it comes to the cinematic aestheticisation of the feminine, white women's faces and bodies are privileged signifiers of female beauty and desire' (p. 17).

This may well have been the case when Young's book was written. My feeling, however (and it is acquired, I concede, only on the basis of my personal experience as a cultural consumer) is that many of the processes I have argued to be affecting the representation of sexual communities are also relevant to communities defined by their ethnic origin. The content, and the mainstream success of a British film such as *East Is East*, for example (Damian O'Donnell, 1999), would have been inconceivable just a few years ago. Racism, like sexism and homophobia, is far from exhausted as an ideology, but as ethnic minorities in Britain, the United States and other countries have made advances in their socio-economic status, media representations have begun to convey a much more pluralistic, diverse, realistic image of ethnicity, and of the often difficult relations between ethnic groupings, than has hitherto been the case.

22 *Dirty Pictures* includes an interview with the subject of this photograph, the child of one of Mapplethorpe's friends, who states for the record that the image was made in 1974 with the full consent of him and his parents, and had never been regarded by them as anything other than an asexual portrait.

23 Though not without occasional efforts to censor them, as the introduction to this section noted.

24 Although, like Mapplethorpe, it took him some to recognize precisely what it was. According to his biographer Haring had a girlfriend in the late 1970s, and did not have sex with a man until 1977/8 (Gruen, 1991).

25 'Queer' is broader than gay. The influential queer film-maker Matthew Barney – director of the *Cremaster* cycle – is not known to be gay, though his work often explores what might be regarded as 'gay' themes. One critic writes, 'Barney represents a crystallisation of the techniques, themes and obsessions of the last decade or so . . . and he shares with his contemporaries a passionate interest in sexual politics, sexual identity, and gross primary sexual morphology' (Hodge, R.D., 'Onan the magnificent: the triumph of the testicle in contemporary art', *Harper's*, March 2000, pp. 77–80.

26 Gloss, H., 'Queer', *Sight and Sound*, vol. 7, no. 10, 1997.

27 From Shere Hite's interview with Gilbert & George, published in 'The bother boys', *Guardian*, 25 October 1997.

28 Quoted in Farson, 1999.

11 BAD GIRLS

1 For examples see Germaine Greer's *The Obstacle Race* (1981).
2 For an account of Modotti's life see Margaret Hooks's 1995 biography, *Tina Modotti*.
3 See for example Broude and Garrard's *The Power of Feminist Art* (1994), Chicago and Lucie-Smith's *Women and Art* (1999) and, published just as this book went to press, Reckitt and Phelan's *Art and Feminism* (2001).
4 The success of *Horses* (which also assisted cover photographer Mapplethorpe's emergence as an artistic star) propelled her to make three further albums of varying quality. In 1980 she abandoned her career in favour of looking after her husband and fellow musician Fred Smith. Never having seen herself as a feminist (if up until that point living and working as one) she was frank about where her priorities as a woman

lay – 'I've found the man I love, all I've been looking for all my life.' She retreated to domesticity in Detroit, and despite several attempted comebacks in the 1980s and 1990s her career never recovered.

5 Shave, C., 'Constant stiffies', *I-D*, May 1999, pp. 113–15.

6 See too her *Minotaur Hunt* (1991) which, with its Picasso-like depiction of male castration by a group of female warriors, subverts a common theme of male art through the ages (the rape and sexual violation of women by men).

7 Quoted in *Erotica: A Journey into Female Sexuality*, Channel 4 documentary, February 1999.

8 Quoted in *Erotica: A Journey into Female Sexuality*.

9 Quoted in the *Arena* documentary on Bernhard broadcast by BBC2 in 1996.

10 After the controversies of *Erotica* and *Sex*, and the relative commercial failure of 1994's *Bedtime Stories*, she abandoned the aesthetic of sexual transgression. In 1996 she played the title role in Alan Parker's *Evita*, remaking herself as Mother (of the Argentine nation, in the film, and by extension of her audience). She had a baby, and then bounced back into the pop charts with the *Ray of Light* album and the theme tune for Mike Myers's second Austin Powers movie, following that with the Grammy award-winning *Music* in 2000. Her transition from awakening virgin to let's-pretend-pornostar to gender-defying fag hag to maternal maturity emerges as an ongoing masterpiece of feminist art.

11 Januszczak, W., 'A mini mirror', *Sunday Times*, 28 November 1999.

12 From Eric Kroll's introduction.

13 *Guardian*, 29 April 2000.

BIBLIOGRAPHY

Aaron, M., ed., 1999. *The Body's Perilous Pleasures: Dangerous Desires and Contemporary Culture*, Edinburgh, Edinburgh University Press, 1999.

—— 1999. 'Till death do us part: cinema's queer couples who kill', in Aaron, ed., pp. 76–84.

Abramson, P.R. and Pinkerton, S.D. 1995. *With Pleasure: Thoughts on the Nature of Human Sexuality*, Oxford, Oxford University Press.

Allison, A., 1996. *Permitted and Prohibited Desires*, Boulder, Col., Westview Press.

Anderson, D. and Mosbacher, M., 1997. *The British Woman Today – A Qualitative Survey of Images in Women's Magazines*, London, Social Affairs Unit.

Araki, N., 1997. *Tokyo Lucky Hole*, Köln, Taschen.

——, 1998. *Tokyo – Marketplace of Emotions*, Zürich, Edition Stemmle.

Archer, R. and Simmonds, D., 1986. *A Star is Torn*, London, Virago.

Assiter, A. and Avedon, C., eds, 1993. *Bad Girls and Dirty Pictures*, London, Pluto.

Atkins, T., ed., 1976. *Sexuality in the Movies*, New York, Da Capo Press.

Baker, N., 1994. *The Fermata*, London, Picador.

Barthel, D., 1992. 'When men put on appearances: advertising and the social construction of masculinity', in Craig, ed., pp. 137–53.

Barthes, R., 1973. *Mythologies*, London, Paladin.

——, 1982. 'The metaphor of the eye', in Bataille, pp. 119–27.

Bataille, G., 1982. *The Story of the Eye*, London, Penguin.

——, 1994. *The Absence of Myth*, London, Verso.

Becker, E., Citron, M., Lesage, J., Rich, B.R., 1995, 'Lesbians and film', in Creekmur and Doty, eds, 1995, pp. 25–43.

Berger, M., Wallis, B. and Watson, S., eds, 1995. *Constructing Masculinity*, London, Routledge.

Betterton, R., ed., 1987. *Looking On*, London, Pandora.

Biskind, P., 1998. *Easy Riders, Raging Bulls*, London, Bloomsbury.

Blake, N., 1995. 'Tom Of Finland: an appreciation', in Creekmur and Doty, eds, pp. 343–53.

Bland, L., 1995. *Banishing the Beast*, London, Penguin.

Bockris, V., 1998. *Patti Smith*, London, Fourth Estate.

Boston, R., 1990. *The Essential Fleet Street*, London, Blandford.

Bradley, L., 2000. 'Sculley hits the glass ceiling: postmodernism, postfeminism, post-humanism and the X-files', in Helford, ed., pp. 61–90.

Brehm, M., 1996. 'Sex pictures', in Sherman, C., pp. 100–25.

Breton, A., 1987. *Mad Love*, Lincoln and London, University of Nebraska Press.

Bright, D., ed., 1998. *The Passionate Camera: Photography and Bodies of Desire*, London, Routledge.

Bright, S., 1997. *Sexual State of the Union*, New York, Simon & Schuster.

Bristow, J., 1997. *Sexuality*, London, Routledge.

British Medical Association Board of Science and Education, 2000. *Eating Disorders, Body Image and the Media*, London, British Medical Association.

Broadcasting Standards Commission, 1999. *Sex and Sensibility*, London, BSC.

Broude, N. and Garrard, M.D., eds, 1994. *The Power of Feminist Art*, London, Thames & Hudson.

Buckley, D., 1999. *Strange Fascination: David Bowie, the Definitive Story*, London, Virgin.

Burchill, J., 1986. *Girls on Film*, London, Virgin Books.

——, 1989. *Ambition*, London, Corgi.

Burston, P. and Richardson, C., eds, 1995. *A Queer Romance: Lesbians, Gay Men and Popular Culture*, London, Routledge.

Burstyn, V., ed., 1985. *Women Against Censorship*, Vancourver, Douglas McIntyre.

Butler, J., 1990. *Gender Trouble: Feminism and the Subversion of Identity*, London, Routledge.

Califia, P., 1994. *Public Sex*, Pittsburgh, Penn., Cleiss Press.

Capsuto, S., 2000. *Alternate Channels: The Uncensored Story of Gay and Lesbian Images on Radio and Television*, New York, Ballantine Books.

Carey, J., 1992. *The Intellectuals and the Masses*, London, Faber & Faber.

Carol, A., 1986. *Nudes, Prudes and Attitudes*, Cheltenham, New Clarion Press.

Chicago, J., Lucie-Smith, E., 1999. *Women and Art*, London, Weidenfeld & Nicolson.

Cleto, F., ed., 1999. *Camp: Queer Aesthetics and the Performing Subject – A Reader*, Edinburgh, Edinburgh University Press.

Cohan, S. and Hark, I.R., eds, 1993. *Screening the Male: Exploring Masculinities in Hollywood Cinema*, London, Routledge.

Colacello, B., 1990. *Holy Terror: Andy Warhol Close Up*, New York, HarperCollins.

Cooper, E., 1996. *The Sexual Perspective: Homosexuality and Art in the Last 100 Years in the West*, London, Routledge.

Copp, D., Wendell, S., eds, 1983. *Pornography and Censorship*, Buffalo, NY, Prometheus.

Cottingham, L., 1993, 'What's so bad about 'em?', in Institute of Contemporary Arts (ICA), *Bad Girls*, pp. 54–61.

Coward, R., 1999. *Sacred Cows: Is Feminism Relevant to the New Millenium?*, London, HarperCollins.

Craig, S., ed., 1992. *Men, Masculinity and the Media*, Newbury Park, Sage.

Creed, B., *et al.*, 1995. 'Lesbian bodies', in Grosz, E. and Probyn, E., eds, 1995, pp. 86–103.

——, 1998. 'The crash debate: anal wounds, metallic kisses', *Screen*, vol. 39, no. 2, pp. 175–92.

Creekmur, C.K. and Doty, A., eds, 1995. *Out In Culture*, London, Cassell.

Danto, A.C., 1990. 'Photography and performance: Cindy Sherman's stills', in Sherman, pp. 5–14.

——, 1994. *Playing with the Edge*, London, Thames & Hudson.

Davidson, D.K., 1996. *Selling Sin: The Marketing of Socially Unacceptable Practices*, Westport, Conn., Quorum Books.

Delacoste, F. and Alexander, P., eds, 1988. *Sex Work: Writings by Women in the Sex Industry*, London, Virago.

Dines, G., 1995, '"I buy it for the articles": *Playboy* magazine and the Sexualisation of Consumerism', in Dines, and Humez, eds, 1995, pp. 254–62.

Dines, G. and Humez, J., eds, 1995. *Gender, Race and Class in Media*, London, Sage.

Dittmar, L., 1998. 'The straight goods: lesbian chic and identity capital on a not-so-queer planet', in Bright, ed., pp. 319–39.

Donnerstein, E. and Malamuth, N., eds, 1984. *Pornography and Sexual Aggression*, London, Academic Press.

Donald, S., ed., 1996. *The Joy of Sexism*, London, John Broon Publishing.

Duggan, L. and Hunter, N. 1995. *Sex Wars: Sexual Dissent and Political Discourse*, London, Routledge.

Dyer, R., 1990. *Now You See It: Studies on Lesbian and Gay Film*, London, Routledge.

——, 1992. *Only Entertainment*, London, Routledge.

——, 1995. *The Matter of Images: Essays on Representation*, London, Routledge.

Edwards, T., 1996. *Men in the Mirror*, London, Cassell.

Ellis, B.E., 1990. *American Psycho*, London, Picador.

——, 1999. *Glamorama*, London, Picador.

Ellis, J., 1992. 'On pornography', in *The Sexual Subject*, pp. 146–70.

Ellis, K., 1986. *Caught Looking*, Toronto, Buffalo Books.

Ellmann, R., 1987. *Oscar Wilde*, London, Penguin Books.

Evans, D., 1993. *Sexual Citizenship*, London, Routledge.

Ewing, W.A., 1994. *The Body*, London, Thames and Hudson.

Faludi, S., 1991. *Backlash*, London, Verso.

——, 1999. *Stiffed*, New York, W. Morrow and Co.

Farson, D., 1999. *Gilbert & George: A Portrait*, London, HarperCollins.

Faust, B., 1980. *Women, Sex and Pornography*, Harmondsworth, Penguin.

Fleming, C. 1998. *High Concept*, London, Abacus.

Forestag, M., ed., 1988. *Perpetual Motif: The Art of Man Ray*, New York, Abbeville Press.

Foster, H., 1995. *Compulsive Beauty*, Cambridge, Mass., MIT Press.

Foucault, M., 1990. *The History of Sexuality, vol. 1*, London, Penguin.

——, 1992. *The Uses of Pleasure*, London, Penguin.

Frank, L. and Smith, P., eds, 1993. *Madonnarama: Essays on Sex and Popular Culture*, Pittsburgh, Cleiss Press.

Friedler, G., 2000. *Naked London*, London, Norton.

Gabler, N., 1994. *Walter Winchell: Gossip, Power and the Culture of Celebrity*, London, Picador.

Gamson, J., 1998. *Freaks Talk Back*, Chicago, University of Chicago Press.

Gibson, P.C. and Gibson, R., eds, 1993. *Dirty Looks: Women, Pornography, Power*, London, British Film Institute.

Giddens, A., 1993. *The Transformation of Intimacy*, Cambridge, Polity Press.

Gill, J., 1995. *Queer Noises*, London, Cassell.

Goffman, E., 1976. *Gender Advertisements*, London, Macmillan.

Golden, T., ed., 1994. *Black Male: Representations of Masculinity in Contemporary American Art*, New York, Whitney Museum of Modern Art.

Goldin, N. and Costa, G., 1998. *Ten Years After*, Berlin, Scalo.

Goldschmidt, P.W., 1999. 'Pornography in Russia', in Barker, ed., *Pornography and Democratisation*, Boulder, Col., Westview Press, pp. 318–36.

Grant, L., 1993. *Sexing the Millennium*, London, Harper Collins.

Greer, G., 1981. *The Obstacle Race*, London, Picador.

Griffin, S., 1988. *Pornography and Silence*, London, Women's Press.

Gross, L. 1991. 'Out of the mainstream: sexual minorities and the mass media', in Wolf and Keilwasser, eds, pp. 61–9.

Grosz, E. and Probyn, E., eds, 1995. *Sexy Bodies: The Strange Carnalities of Feminism*, London, Routledge.

Gruen, J., 1991. *Keith Haring: The Authorised Biography*, London, Thames & Hudson.

Gubar, S., 1989. 'Representing pornography', in Gubar and Hoff, eds, pp. 47–67.

Gubar, S. and Hoff, J., eds, 1989. *For Adult Users Only*, Bloomington, Indiana University Press.

Habermas, J., 1989. *The Structural Transformation of the Public Sphere*, Cambridge, Polity Press.

Hanke, R., 1992. 'Redesigning men: hegemonic masculinity in transition', in Craig, ed., pp. 185–98.

Hanson, E., 1999. *Out Takes: Essays on Queer Theory and Film*, London, Duke University Press.

Hargrave, A.M., 1992. *Sex and Sexuality in Broadcasting*, London, Broadcasting Standards Council.

Haring, K., 1996. *Journals*, London, Fourth Estate.

Hartley, J., 1996. *Popular Reality*, London, Arnold.

——, 1998. 'When your child grows up too fast: juvenation and the boundaries of the social in the news media', *Continuum*, vol. 12, 1998.

Haste, H., 1993. *The Sexual Metaphor*, Hemel Hempstead, Harvester Wheatsheaf.

Hebditch, A. and Anning, N., 1988. *Porn Gold*, London, Faber & Faber.

Helford, E.R., ed., 2000. *Fantasy Girls: Gender in the New Universe of Science Fiction and Fantasy Television*, Boulder, Col., Rowman & Littlefield.

Hibberd, M., Kilborn, R., McNair, B., Marriott, S. and Schlesinger, P., 2000. *Consenting Adults?*, London, Broadcasting Standards Commission, 2000.

Hickman, T., 1999. *The Sexual Century: How Private Passion Became a Public Obsession*, London, Carlton.

Hiromix Tashigawa. 1997. *Japanese Beauty*, Tokyo, Editions.

Hirsch, F., 1976. 'Midnight cowboy', in Atkins, ed., pp. 200–7.

Holmberg, C.B., 1998. *Sexualities and Popular Culture*, London, Sage.

Hooks, M., 1993. *Tina Modotti: Photographer and Revolutionary*, London, Pandora.

Horne, P. and Lewis, R., eds, 1996. *Outlooks: Lesbian and Gay Sexualities and Visual Cultures*, London, Routledge.

Hoskyns, B., 1998. *Glam! Bowie, Bolan and the Glitter Rock Revolution*, London, Faber & Faber.

Hughes, R., 1995. *Culture of Complaint*, London, Harvill Press.

Hunt, L., 1993. *The Invention of Pornography*, New York, Zone Books.

——, 1998. *British Low Culture*, London, Routledge.

Huntley, R., 1998. 'Slippery when wet: the shifting boundaries of the pornographic (a class analysis)', *Continuum*, vol. 12, pp. 69–81.

Institute of Contemporary Arts (ICA), 1993. *Bad Girls*, London, ICA.

Isaak, J.A., 1996. *Feminism and Contemporary Art*, London, Routledge.

Itzin, C. ed., 1992. *Pornography: Women, Violence, and Civil Liberties*, Oxford, Oxford University Press.

Jackson, S. and Scott, S., 1996, 'Sexual skirmishes and feminist factions', in Jackson and Scott, eds, pp. 1–31.

—— eds, 1996. *Feminism and Sexuality: A Reader*, Edinburgh, Edinburgh University Press.

Jeffords, S., 1993, 'Can masculinity be terminated?', in Cohan and Hark, eds, pp. 245–62.

Jensen, R., 1996. 'The Culture Wars, 1965–1995: a historian's map', *Journal of Social History*, vol. 29, no. 3, pp. 17–37.

Katz, I., 1998. 'Aesthetics of "intimacy"', in Bright, ed., pp. 204–15.

Kendrick, W., 1987. *The Secret Museum*, New York, Viking.

Kieran, M., ed., 1996. *Media Ethics*, London, Routledge.

Kitzinger, J. 1999. *The Representation of Teenage Sexuality in the Media*, Edinburgh, Health Education Board for Scotland.

Koons, J., 1992. *Jeff Koons*, Cologne, Benedikt Taschen.

——, 1994. *The Jeff Koons Handbook*, London, Taschen.

Krauss, R., ed., 1985. *L'Amour Fou*, New York, River Press.

Krzywinska, T., 1999. 'Cicciolina and the dynamics of transgression and abjection in explicit sex films', in Aaron, ed., pp. 188–209.

Lane, C. 2000. *Feminist Hollywood: From Born in Flames to Point Break*, Wayne State University Press.

La Valley, A., 1995. 'The great escape', in Creekmur and Doty, eds, pp. 60–70.

Lawrence, D.H., 1936. *Pornography and So On*, London, Faber & Faber.

Lloyd, F., ed., 1993. *Deconstructing Madonna*, London, Batsford.

Lucie-Smith, E., 1991. *Sexuality in Western Art*, London, Thames & Hudson.

Lumby, C., 1997. *Bad Girls: The Media, Sex and Feminism in the 90s*, Sydney, Allen & Unwin.

McElroy, W., 1995. *A Woman's Right to Pornography*, New York, St. Martin's Press.

MacInnes, J., 1998. *The End of Masculinity*, Buckingham, Open University Press.

McKenzie, W., 1998. 'Bad girls do it in public', *Continuum*, vol. 12, pp. 83–90.

MacKinnon, C., 1992. 'Pornography, civil rights and speech', in Itzin, C., ed., pp. 456–511.

——, 1994. *Only Words*, London, HarperCollins.

McNair, B., 1996. *Mediated Sex*, London, Arnold.

——, 1998. 'Journalism, politics and public relations: an ethical appraisal', in Kieran, ed., pp. 49–65.

——, 2000. *Journalism and Democracy*, London, Routledge.

McNair, B., Boyle, R., Haynes, R., Schlesinger, P., Dobash, R. and Dobash, R., 1998. *Men Viewing Violence*, London, Broadcasting Standards Commission.

Mapplethorpe, R., 1983. *Lady: Lisa Lyon,* Boston, Bullfinch Press.

——, 1985. *Certain People: A Book of Portraits*, Pasadena, Twelvetrees, 1985.

——, 1995. *Altars*, New York, Random House.

Mercer, K., 1992. 'Just looking for trouble: Robert Mapplethorpe and fantasies of race', in Segal and McIntosh, eds, pp. 92–110.

Merritt, N., 2000. *Digital Diaries*, London, Taschen.

Metzstein, M., 1993. '*Sex*: signed, sealed and delivered', in Lloyd, ed., pp. 91–8.

Miller, D., Kitzinger, J. and Williams, K., 1999. *The Circuit of Communication*, London, Sage.

Morrisroe, P., 1995. *Mapplethorpe*, London, Secker & Warburg.

Mort, F., 1996. *Cultures of Consumption*, London, Routledge.

232

Mulvey, L., 1975. 'Visual pleasure and narrative cinema', *Screen*, vol. 16, no. 3, pp. 6–18.

Mulvey. L. and Wollen, P., 1987, 'The discourse of the body', in Betterton, ed., pp. 211–16.

Muthesius, A. and Neret, G., eds, 1998. *Erotic Art*, London, Taschen.

Myers, K., 1987. 'Fashion 'n' passion', in Betterton, ed., pp. 58–65.

Naughton, J., 1999. *A Brief History of the Future: The Origins of the Internet*, London, Weidenfeld & Nicolson, 1999.

Nead, L., 1992. *The Female Nude: Art, Sexuality and Obscenity*, London, Routledge.

Neale, S., 1993. 'Masculinity as spectacle', in Cohan and Hark, eds, pp. 9–19.

Neret, G. 1998. *Erotic Art*, Köln, Taschen.

Nixon, S., 1996. *Hard Looks*, London, University College of London Press.

O'Pray, M., ed., 1989. *Andy Warhol: Film Factory*, London, British Film Institute.

Oakley, A., 1972. *Sex, Gender and Society*, London, Temple Smith.

——, (1974). *Housewife*, London, Penguin.

Ono, K., 2000. 'To be a vampire on "Buffy the Vampire Slayer": race and other socially marginalising positions on horror TV', in Helford, ed., pp. 163–86.

Paglia, C., 1990. *Sexual Personae*, London, Penguin.

——, 1992. *Sex, Art and American Culture*, London, Penguin.

——, 1995. 'Rape and the modern sex war', in Stan, ed., pp. 21–5.

Penrose, R. 1989. *Man Ray*, London, Thames & Hudson.

Phillips, G., 1976. 'The boys on the bandwagon: homosexuality in the movies', in Atkins, ed., pp. 157–71.

Polizotti, M., 1995. *Revolution in the Mind*, London, Secker & Warburg.

Probst, K., 1999. *Pornografic*, Twin Palms.

Pultz, J., 1995. *Photography and the Body*, London, Weidenfeld & Nicolson.

Reckitt, H. and Phelan, P., 2001. *Art and Feminism*, London, Phaidon.

Reid, M., 1998. 'Postnegritude reappropriation and the black male nude', in Bright, ed., pp. 216–28.

Robson, D., 1995. *The Art of the Nude*, New York, Shooting Star Press.

Rose, J., 1992. *Marie Stopes and the Sexual Revolution*, London, Faber & Faber.

Rowbotham, S., 1977. *Hidden from History*, London, Pluto Press.

Salaman, N., ed., 1994. *What She Wants: Women Artists Look At Men*, London, Verso.

Saunders, T. 1996. *Sex in Advertising*, London, Batsford.

Schneider, R., 1997. *The Explicit Body in Performance*, London, Routledge.

Schwichtenberg, C., ed., 1993. *The Madonna Connection*, New York, Westview Press.

Screen, 1992. *The Sexual Subject: A Screen Reader in Sexuality*, London, Routledge.

Segal, L., 1994. *Straight Sex: the Politics of Pleasure*, London, Virago.

Segal, L. and McIntosh, M., eds 1992. *Sex Exposed: Sexuality and the Pornography Debate*, London, Tavistock.

Sherman, C., 1990. *Untitled Film Stills*, London, Jonathan Cape.

——, 1996. *Cindy Sherman*, Madrid, Museo Nacional Centro de Arte.

Showalter, E., 1992. *Sexual Anarchy: Gender and Culture at the Fin de Siècle*, London, Virago.

Simon, W., 1996. *Postmodern Sexualities*, London, Routledge.

Simpson, M., 1994. *Male Impersonators,* London, Cassell.

——, 1996. *It's a Queer World*, London, Vintage.

Smalls, J., 1998. 'Public face, private thoughts', in Bright, ed., pp. 78–102.

Smith, A., 1993. 'What is pornography?', *Feminist Review*, no. 43, spring pp. 71–87.

Smyth, C., 1993. 'Bad Girls', in Tucker, M., ed., pp. 6–12.

——, 1994, 'What she wants and what she gets', in Salaman, ed., 1994, pp. 51–61.

——, 1996. *Damn Fine Art*, London, Cassell.

Snitow, A., 1985. 'Retrenchment versus transformation: the politics of the antipornography movement', in Burstyn, ed., pp. 107–20.

Sontag, S., 1982. 'The pornographic imagination', in Bataille, pp. 83–118.

Stan, A.M., ed., 1995. *Debating Sexual Correctness*, New York, Delta.

Steele, V., 1996. *Fetish: Fashion, Sex and Power*, Oxford, Oxford University Press.

Stein, J. and Plimpton, G., eds, 1992. *Edie: An American Biography*, London, Pimlico.

Sullivan, A., 1995. *Virtually Normal*, London, Picador.

Tang, I., 1999. *Pornography: The Secret History of Civilisation*, London, Channel 4 Books.

Tannahill, R., 1992. *Sex in History*, Scarborough House.

Tanner, M., 1994. 'Mother laughed: the Bad Girls' avant-garde', in Tucker, ed., pp. 47–80.

Tasker, Y., 1993, 'Dumb movies for dumb people', in Cohan and Hark, eds, pp. 230–44.

——, 1994. *Spectacular Bodies: Gender, Genre and the Action Cinema*, London, Routledge.

——, 1998. *Working Girls: Gender and Sexuality in Popular Cinema*, London, Routledge.

Taylor, T., 1996. *The Prehistory of Sex*, London, Fourth Estate.

Thompson, B., 1994. *Soft Core*, London, Cassell.

Thompson, H. 1988. *Generation of Swine*, London, Picador.

Tickner, L., 1987, 'The body politic: female sexuality and women artists since 1970', in Betterton, ed., pp. 235–53.

Tisdale, S., *Talk Dirty to Me*, London, Secker & Warburg, 1994.

Tolson, A. 1977. *The Crisis of Masculinity*, London, Tavistock.

Travis, A., 2000. *Bound and Gagged*, London, Profile Books.

Tucker, M., ed., 1994. *Bad Girls*, Cambridge, Mass., MIT Press.

——, 1994. 'The attack of the Giant Ninja Mutant Barbies', in Tucker, ed., pp. 14–46.

Vicinus, M., 1996, 'Turn-of-the-century male impersonator', in Miller and Adams, eds, pp. 187–213.

Warhol, A., 1989: *The Andy Warhol Diaries*, New York, Warner Books.

Watney, S., 1987. *Policing Desire: Pornography, AIDS and the Media*, London, Comedia.

Waugh, T., 1996. *Hard to Imagine*, New York, Columbia University Press.

——, 2000. *The Fruit Machine: Twenty Years of Writing on Queer Cinema*, London, Duke University Press.

Williams, L., 1990. *Hard Core*, London, Pandora.

——, 1994. 'What do I see, what do I want?', in Salaman, N., ed., pp. 3–12.

Williamson, J. 1978. *Decoding Advertisements: Ideology and Meaning in Advertisements*, London, Marion Boyars.

Willis, S., 1997. *High Contrast: Race and Gender in Contemporary Hollywood Film*, Durham, Duke University Press.

Winship, J., 1987, '"A girl needs to get street-wise": magazines for the 1980s', in Betterton, ed., pp. 127–41.

Wolf, M.A. and Kielwasser, A.P., eds, 1991. *Gay People, Sex and the Media*, New York, Harrington Park Press.

Wurtz, E., 1998. *Bitch*, London, Quartet.

Young, L., 1996. *Fear of the Dark*, London, Routledge.

INDEX

Aaron, M. 39, 122
Abstract Expressionism 181
academia 63–4
ACT UP 30
Adams, K. 98
Add N To (X) 78
Adjustor 176
Adult Lives 101, 105–6
Adult Video News 37
advertising: and homosexuality,
    129–40; and masculinity, 117–18; and
    pornography, 78–81, 89; and women,
    23, 115–21
Advertising Standards Authority 78, 117
Advocate, The 201
aestheticism 180
Ai No Corrida 40, 58
AIDS *see* HIV/AIDS
Ajamu 186
Aliens 122
Ali McBeal 128
All Saints 196
All That Jazz 70
Allison, A. 212
Altars 186, 225
Ambition 165, 122
American Family Coalition 186
American Psycho 127, 170, 222
Amis, M. 63, 68, 82, 84, 215
And the Band Played On 29
Anderson, D. 119
Anderson, G. 128
Anderson, P.T. 31, 40, 73–4, 85, 156
Aniston, J. 128, 139
Anning, N. 63
Appleyard, B. 7, 52, 61, 64, 149, 213
Aquinas, T. 28, 210
Araki, N. 170–1, 176, 223–4

Archer, R. 195
Aretino, P. 169
Aretino's Sonnets 38
Armani, G. 158
art: and pornography, 64–5, 165, 177–8,
    182–4, 190, 199–203; and striptease,
    90–1
Art and Feminism 226
As Good As It Gets 220
Assiter, A. 223
At Home with the Braithwaites 128, 140
Audit Bureau of Circulation in Britain 37
Austen, J. 191–2
Avedon, C. 15, 43

backlash 16–17, 21, 25, 31, 76, 160,
    206–7
Backlash 16, 149–50
Bad Girls 25, 128, 140, 194–5
Bangkok Bound 101
Bailey, F. 42, 85
Baker, N. 215
Barney, M. 226
Barrett Browning, E. 191
Barrymore, B. 141, 220
Barrymore, D. 120
Barthes, R. 99
Basic Instinct 70, 121–2, 124, 134, 142,
    152–4, 219
Bataille, G. 69–70, 169, 172–4
BBC (British Broadcasting Corporation)
    9–10, 18, 83, 86, 95, 104–5, 114, 141,
    145, 160, 210
BBC2 83–5, 101
Beardon, R. 197
Beatty, W. 149, 202
Becker, E. 142
Bedtime Stories 227

Behind the Green Door 39, 62
Bekert, K. 28
Bellmer, H. 171
Benglis, L. 198
Bennett, C. 210
Bergman, A. 89
Berkowitz, S. 10
Bernhard, S. 139, 141, 201
Bernhardt, S. 224
Betty Gets It 200
Bible John 55
Big Brother 10–11, 89, 102–4, 108, 141
Bigelow, K. 126, 218
Billy Elliot 156
Bird, A. 127
Birdcage 139, 145, 147
Biskind, P. 71, 137–8
Bjork 225
Black Male 112, 186, 220, 226
Black, R. 44, 56, 82, 84,
Blair, T. 26, 91
Bland, L. 15, 22, 28
Blow Job 65, 181
Blue Steel 126
Bockris, V. 196
Bostonians 21, 210
Bowie, A. 135
Bowie, D 135–6, 180, 219–20
Bogarde, D. 133
Bogart, H. 157
Boogie Nights in Suburbia 83
Boogie Nights 12, 40, 73–5, 90
Boston, R. 213
Bound 143, 220
Bourgeois, L. 197
Bow, C. 9
Boy George 142
Boys Don't Cry 126–7, 146, 219
Boys in the Band 134
Boyzone 142
Bradley, L. 128
Brando, M. 22, 181
Breaking the Waves 175
Breillat, C. 40, 58, 175, 212
Breton, A. 171, 180, 193
Bridget Jones's Diary 121
Bright, D. 25, 144, 210
Bright, S. 42, 53, 82, 144
British Board of Film Classification 58, 107, 211, 213, 216
British Low Culture 214
British Medical Association 119–20, 158–9, 218

British Sex 85
Broadcasting Act, 1990 214
Broadcasting Standards Commission 58, 59, 103, 107, 122, 140, 217
Brookside 179, 141
Broomfield, N. 100–1
Bronski Beat 136–7, 188
Brontë Sisters 191
Brooke, E. 21
Brookes, L. 117
Brooks, R. 224
Broude, N. 193, 198, 227
Brown, H.G. 23
Brown, N. 26
Buckley, D. 219
Buffy the Vampire Slayer 128
Bunuel, L. 175
Burchill, J. 128, 166–7, 194, 222
Burroughs, W. 187
Burton, J. 74–5
Bush, G.W. 27
Butler, J. 208
Butter, N. 213

Cage, N. 75
Cale, J. 224
Cameron, J. 122
Campbell, N. 9
Campion, J. 127
Capsuto, S. 129, 132, 141, 147, 220
Caravaggio 195
Carlton TV 85
Carpenter, E. 21
Carpenter, K. 201
Castaways 104
Cattaneo, P. 90
Caught Looking 47
Cave, N. 168, 222
Celebration 175
Censored 82, 83
Centre Folds 198
Chambre Closes 200
Changing Rooms 10, 141
Channel 4 31, 42, 82–5, 95, 99–103, 140–1, 179, 216, 223
Channel 5 58, 83, 95–6, 107
Chapman brothers 165, 222
Charlie's Angels 124, 196
Cheang Shu Lea 71
Cheaper Sex 209
Chegwin, K. 107
Chicago, J. 137–8, 192, 197, 199, 227
Chicken Knickers 199

Christensen, H. 76
Christian Action Network 147
Christian Coalition 160
Christopher, P. 82, 200, 203
Cicciolina, La 64, 177–8, 202
cinema: and homosexuality, 10–11, 133–40, 142–8; and masculinity, 149–57; and pornography, 70–6; and striptease, 89–90, 100; and transgression, 174–7; and women, 23, 121–8
Citron, M. 142
Cleland, J. 38, 169
Clift, M. 131
Cline, P. 195
Clinton, B. 27, 91, 93
Clinton, H. 9
Clinton–Lewinsky scandal 7, 91
Clockwork Orange, A 135
Close, G. 152
Cock and Cunt Play 197
Cocteau, J. 180
Come to Daddy 76
Coming 189
Coming to Power 24
Communications Decency Act, 1996 57
Company 25, 83, 84, 118, 216
Compromising Positions 58
confessional talk shows 88, 97–8
Confessions of a Window Cleaner 62
Connery, S. 152, 158
Conservative Party (UK) 9
Constance 71
Contagious Diseases Acts 15
Cooper, A. 136
Cooper, E. 180, 224, 225
Cooper, G. 151
Cosmo girl/woman 23, 115, 118
Cosmopolitan 23, 118
Cottingham, L. 25
Coward, N. 137
Coward, R. 25, 156
Cox, R. 186, 225
Coyote Ugly 124
Crash 166, 176
Crawford, C. 144
Creed, B. 143, 176
Cremaster 226
Crevel, R. 180
Crichton, M. 153
Criminal Law Amendment Act, 1885 15, 28
Cronenberg, D. 166, 176
Cruise, T. 9, 31, 56, 157

Cruising 134, 135, 143, 145
Crystal, B. 141
cultural capitalism 6, 9–11, 192, 206
Culture Club 136
Cumming, A. 90
Cunt Cheerleaders 197
Cunt Scum 189
Cure, The 136, 168
Current Opinion 21
Curtis, S. 133

Da Vinci, L. 180
Dahl, J. 122
Dahl, S. 116–17, 120
Daily Mail 82
Daily Record 142
Daldry, S. 156
Dalí, S. 171
D'Amato, A. 165
Dancer in the Dark 175
Danto, A. 183
Darwin, C. 20
Darling, C. 181
Daughters of Bilitis 134
Davidson, K.D. 96, 216
Dawsons Creek 141
De Caunes, A. 85
Dead Babies 63
Dean, J. 22, 131
Dearden, B. 133
Debating Sexual Correctness 54, 213
Decoding Advertisements 81
Deconstructing Madonna 215
Deep Inside Annie Sprinkle 44
Deep Throat 39, 62–3
DeGeneres, E. 141
Delacroix 168
Demme, J. 138
democratisation of desire 11–13, 182
Desperately Seeking Susan 218
Destiny's Child 190
Devil In Miss Jones, The 62
Diamond Dogs 136
Diaz, C. 139
Did You Do It? 66
Die Hard 152
Dietrich, M. 135
Diggler, D. 73, 74
Digital Diaries 202–3
Dillon, M. 138, 145
Dinner Party 197
Dirty Ejaculation 65
Dirty Harry 151

Dirty Looks 64
Dirty Pictures 186, 224, 226
Disclosure 121, 153–4
Dittmar, L. 144
Do The Right Thing 11
docu-soaps 88, 99–100
Dogma 174–5
Doing Rude Things 83
Donovan, M. 140
Douglas, K. 152
Douglas, M. 124, 143, 152, 154
Dover, B. 84
Dr Jeckyll and Mr Hyde 16
Drudge Report 91
Duggan, L. 210
Duran Duran 65–7
Dworkin, A. 25–6, 41, 167, 210, 212
Dyer, R. 11, 44, 113, 132, 146, 206, 213
Dyke TV 141

East Is East 226
EastEnders 141, 179
Easton Ellis, B. 170–1
Eastwood, C. 151
Easy Rider 122
Egoyan, A. 176
Eight and a half Women 121
8mm 12, 75–6
Eisenman, N. 200
Eisenstein, S. 131, 180
Eliot, G. 191–2
Ellen 140–1
Ellroy, J. 62
Emin, T. 165–6, 199
Eminem 168
Emmanuelle 62
Empire of the Censors 83
End of Alice 52
Enfield, H. 113–14, 118, 160
Engels, F. 210
Epstein, B. 219
Erin Brockovitch 124
Eromanga 170
Eurotica 57, 214
Erotic Diaries 58
Erotic Review 44
Erotica 66, 68–9, 227
Erotica: A Journey into Female Sexuality 82
Erotique Voilee 172
Eurotrash 57, 82, 85–6, 89, 213
Evans, D. 5, 24
Everett, R. 139–40, 147

Evil Angel Video 39
Evita 227
Ewing, W. 211
Exaltation 65
Exorcist 134
Exotica 176

Face 49, 76, 78, 129, 157–8
Factory 181–2
Fairbanks, D. 9
Fake Love 223
Falling Down 154
Faludi, S. 16, 25, 76, 149–50, 152, 209–10
Fanny Hill 38
Fantasy Club 99–100, 217
Fantasy Football 159
Farson, D. 189–90
Fashion 198
Fat Slags 160
Fatal Attraction 16, 121, 152
Faust, B. 23
Fear of the Dark 226
Felicia's Journey 176
Femme Mystique 23
Femme Productions 44
Fenton, B. 213
Ferman, J. 58, 107
Fermata, The 215
Fetish 100–1
FHM 48, 90, 159, 221, 160
Fight Club 156–7, 159
FilmFour 58, 83
Film Stills 198
fin de siècle 9, 15–16, 32
Fincher, D. 156
Fleming, C. 138
Flynt, L. 62, 71, 74, 76, 216
Fonda, H. 151
Ford, A. 105–6
Ford, J. 151
Forman, M. 71–2
Fosse, B. 70
Foucault, M. 2–3, 21, 27
Fourier, C. 223
Fox, C. 128
Frankfurt School 64
Frankie Goes To Hollywood 66, 136
Frear, S. 156
Freedland, J. 31, 61, 117, 211
French Connection 134
French, M. 209

Fresno State College Feminist Art
  Programme 197
Freud, S. 171–2
Friday, N. 66
Friedan, B 23
Friedkin, W. 134, 219
Friedler, G. 12, 96, 103
Friends 128
Fruit Machine, The 135
Full Monty, The 90, 99, 156

Gable, C. 150
Gabriel, P. 171
Garland, J. 195
Garrard, M.D. 193, 198, 227
Gately, S. 142
Gaultier, J.P. 85, 158
Gay Exchange 137
Gay Liberation Front 29
Gay Life 140
Gaytime TV 141
Gearon, T. 165–6
gender-bending 183, 201
Genesis 171
Gentileschi, A. 192–5
George the Cunt and Gilbert the Shit 189
Gibson, M. 116, 152, 156
Gibson, P.C. 64
Gibson, R. 64
Giddens, A. 5, 33
Gilbert & George 165–6, 177, 189–90
Giles, N. 168–9, 177, 223
Gill, A.A. 149
Gill, J. 137, 142
Gimme Gimme Gimme 145
Girls on Film 67, 128
girrl power 196
Gladiator 50, 156
glam 135–6, 180
Glamorama 170
Go West 135, 137
Goffman, E. 81, 115, 157
Golden, T. 226
Goldman, A. 219
Goldschmidt, P. 52, 213
Goldstein, Al 62
Good Machine 223
Gorbachev, M. 52
GQ 48, 90
Grace, D. 200
Grade, M. 82
Graham, H. 73
Grand, S. 21

Grant, C. 131, 150
Grant, L. 121
Grayson, L. 132
Greenaway, P. 121
Greer, G. 191–2, 226
Grey Advertising 117
Greyson, J. 135
Gross, L. 129, 200
Guardian 31, 61, 82, 84, 86, 117, 129,
  210–11, 216, 221
Guccione, B. 62
Guerrilla Girls 198
Guernica 174
Guy Show, The 159
Gysin, B. 187

Habermas, J. 81, 98
Hackman, G. 139
Hall, R. 28, 224
Hamilton, W. 75
Hanks, T. 138
Hanson, E. 220
Happiness 155
Hardcore (Channel 4, 2001) 84–5
Hardcore (Schrader, 1979) 63, 71, 73, 75,
  84, 216
Hardcore from the Heart 202
Hardcore, M. 44, 56, 82, 84–5, 207
Harel, P. 175, 176
Haring, K. 13, 187–9, 226
Harrelson, W. 71
Harris, L.A. 225
Harris, W. 186
Harrison, M. 170
Harron, M. 127, 170
Hartley, J. 93, 108
harvey, p.j. 196
Haste, H. 32
Haynes, T. 30, 136, 146, 180, 196, 210
Health Education Board of Scotland 118
Hebditch, A. 63
Heffner, H. 62, 210, 216
Hegel, G. 210
Helford, E.R. 218
Henry, B. 147–8
Heresies 24
Herzegovina, E. 117
Hiassen, C. 90
Hickman, T. 9, 21
Hidden from History 210
High Contrast 226
High Fidelity 156
Higher Education Statistics Agency 209

Hilditch, T. 48
History of Art 192
Hitchcock, A. 133
Hitchens, P. 53, 64
HIV/AIDS 6, 15–17, 27, 29–30, 41, 64,
  68, 138–9, 141, 146, 152, 183–4,
  187–8
Hoberman, J. 143
Hole 196
Holland Day, F. 225
Holliday, B. 195
Holmes, A.M. 52
Holy Smoke 127
Homegrown Video company 39
hooks, b. 112
Hornby, N. 156
Horne, P. 177, 181
Horses 182, 196, 224, 226
Hoskins, B. 176
Houellebecq, M. 175
How to Read a Dirty Movie 82
Hudson, R. 131, 138
Hughes, R. 225
Human League 136
Hunt, L. 50, 64, 214–15
Hunter, N. 210
Huntley, J. 213
Hustler 71–2
Hynde, C. 190

I Shot Andy Warhol 127, 219
Ibiza Uncovered 217
Ice Storm 149
I-D 49, 76, 157
Idiots, The 166, 175
If I Was your Girlfriend 201
IKU (2000) 71
In Bed with Madonna 139
In the Company of Men 154–5
In & Out 138–9, 145
Independent Television Commission
  (ITC) 59, 83
Inman, J. 132, 137
Interclimax 39
Interior Scroll 197
internet: and pornography, 10, 14, 39,
  47–9, 57–9, 83, 88, 91; and striptease,
  101–3
Internet Watch Foundation 58
Iron John 31
Isaak, J. A. 199
It Ain't Half Hot Mum 132
ITV (Independent Television) 95, 105

Jackson, S. 55
James, C. 214
James, H. 21
James, N. 210
James, O. 8
Januszczak, W. 171, 202
Japan 136
Jarman, D. 137
Jenny Jones 97, 104
Jerry Springer Show 97, 104
John, E. 136
Joplin, J. 196
journalism: and pornography, 52, 212–13;
  and sex scandals, 93–5
Joy of Sexism 160, 161
Judith Beheading Holofernes 195
Juliet 172
Justify My Love 65
Justine 175

Kahlo, F. 193–4
Kaufman, P. 170
Kaye, T. 78
Keating, F. 72
Kendrick, W. 213, 215
Kennedy, J.F. 91
Kensit, P. 221
Kermode, M. 76
Kidman, N. 121
Kidron, B. 101
Kiki of Montparnasse 172
Kilroy 97
Kimball, R. 7
Kindergarten Cop 152
Kinsey report 133
Kitzinger, J. 218
Kline, K. 138–9, 145, 147
Koons, J. 64–7, 69, 75, 87–8, 108, 177–8,
  183–5, 202
Kubrick, S. 133, 152
Kumashiro, T. 215
Kupferman, J. 61
Kruger, B. 198
Krzywinska, T. 42, 212

La Bute, N. 154–5
La Prière 172
La Valley, A. 205
Labour Party (UK) 26
Lady: Lisa Lyon 183
Lake, R. 97–8
l'amour fou 171
Lane, C. 124–6, 127

lang, kd 135, 144
Last Action Hero 152
Last Days of the Board 216
Lawrence, D.H. 61
Lawson, M. 47, 212
Le Violon d' Ingres 172
L'Ecole des Filles 38
L7 196
Lee, A. 149
Lee, S. 10–11
Lennon, J. 219
Leone, S. 151
Lesage, J. 142
Levinson, B. 153
Lewinsky, M. 7, 13, 91, 93
Lewis, R. 177, 181
Lezzie Smut 44
Liberal Party (UK) 26
Liebowitz, A. 19
Lies 173
Life and Times of Rosie the Riveter 22
Like a Prayer 65
Liman, D. 155
Little Red Corvette 201
Lives of John Lennon 219
Loach, K. 156
Loaded 48, 90, 159–60
Local Government Act, 1988 26
Lolita 52, 179
London Fields 63
London Weekend Television 140
Lonesome Cowboys 181
Love, C. 71–2, 196
Lowe, C. 131, 137
Lucas, G. 138
Lucas, S. 199
Lucie-Smith, E. 192, 197, 227
Lunas, B. 173
Lunch in Fur 193–4
Lyle, A. H. 186, 225
Lyne, A. 16, 152, 179

McElroy, W. 15
Macgregor, C. 91
Mackinnon, C. 47, 54, 167, 212
McNair, B. 8
Ma Gouvernante 193
Mad About Boys 119
Made in Heaven 64–5, 75, 164, 177–8
Madonna 13, 25, 65–70, 72, 75–6, 87–8,
     107, 116, 139–40, 143–4, 184–5, 193,
     201–3, 215, 218–20, 227–8
Madonna Connection 215

Madonnarama 215
Magnolia 31, 156
Major, J. 91
Malcolm X 11
Man In A Polyester Suit 185
Man Ray 172, 174, 182, 185, 223
Man Who Fell to Earth 147
Man Who Sold the World 135
Mandela, N. 216
Mandelson, P. 26
Manson, M. 136
Mapplethorpe, R. 13, 29, 134–5, 166,
     180–8, 190, 196, 224–6
Marie Claire 25, 118
Marlowe, C. 180
Marquis of Queensberry 181
Married Love 21
Martin, D. 158
Marx, E. 20
Marx, K. 20, 210
Matrix 143
Mattachine Society 134
Maupin, A. 29
Maxim 159–60
Mayfair 49
Medhurst, A. 129, 145
mediated prostitution 41
Mediated Sex 54, 82
Meisel, S. 65–6, 116
Men Behaving Badly 160
Men's Health 160
Mercury, F. 136
Merlet, A. 192
Merritt, N. 202–3
Metzstein, M. 67
Michael, G. 136
Michelangelo 180
Midler, B. 138
Midnight Cowboy 134, 139, 219
Mill, J. S. 20
Miller, D. 208
Milligan, S. 78
Minelli, L. 137
Minogue, K. 83
Minneapolis Ordinance 15
Minotaur Hunt 227
Mirren, H. 128
Mitchell, J. 196
Modotti, T. 193–4
Money 63
Monroe, M. 22, 181
Moore, D. 12, 89–90, 99, 108,
     153–4

Moore, J. 73
Moore, M. 183
Morgan, R. 47
Morrisey, P. 181
Morrisroe, P. 180
Mosbacher, M. 119
Mugabe, R. 30
Mulvey, L. 23, 126, 193, 210
Murdoch, R. 85
Music 227
My Bed 199
My Best Friend's Wedding 139, 147
My Hustler 181
Myers, K. 173, 175
Myers, M. 227

Nabokov, V. 52
Nagashima, Y. 202
Naked 12, 95
Naked London 96, 103, 108
Naked Los Angeles 96, 103
Naked New York 96, 103
Naked Shit Pictures 189
National Endowment for the Arts (NEA) 165, 182, 186, 224
NBC 102
Nead, L. 21, 169, 173–4, 219
Near Dark 126
New Queer Cinema 146, 220
New Statesman 210
New York Dolls 136
New York Times 61
News of the World 119, 166
newspapers: and homosexuality, 140, 147; and pornography, 82
Newton, H. 64, 200, 215
Next Best Thing, The 139, 140
Nicholson, J. 220
Nixon, S. 157
Nochlin, L. 205
Noe, G. 175
Noire et Blanche 172
Norton, E. 159
Norton, G. 141

Oakley, A. 24, 208
Object of My Affection, The 139
Observer 68
Obstacle Race 191
Olivares, R. 199
Olivier, L. 133
On Our Backs 24, 44
Ono, K. 128

Ono, Y. 197
Open your Heart 65
Oppenheim, M. 193–5
Opposite of Sex, The 140
Oranges Are Not The Only Fruit 140, 219
Oshima, N. 40
Out 90
Out on Tuesday 140
Outrage 30, 131

Pacino A. 134
Paglia, C. 42–3, 63, 167, 184, 191, 221–2, 224, 226–7
Paine, T. 51
Panorama 18, 25, 86, 104
Parker, A. 227
Parris, M. 26
Pemberton, A. 211
Penthouse 37, 48–9, 76
People vs Larry Flynt, The 71–3, 215
Perfect Moment 182, 186, 224
Perretti, J. 132
Pet Shop Boys 131, 137, 142
Petrie, R. 158
Phelan, P. 227
Philadelphia 138
Philips, M. 7, 58–9, 208
Piano, The 127
Picasso, P. 174, 178, 183
Picture of Dorian Grey, The 180
Pierce, K. 126–7, 146
Pierson, F. 186, 224
Pimps, Hookers, Hustlers, and their Johns 101
Pink Prison 71
Piss Christ 165, 186
Pitt, B. 122, 156
Playbirds Continental 59
Playboy 22, 48, 62, 158, 216
Pleasantville 22
Plimpton, G. 224
Point Break 126
Poison 146
pop music: and feminism, 196; and homosexuality, 131, 135–7, 142; and pornography, 64–9
Porn Wars 86
pornographication 12–13, 81–2
Pornography: A Secret History of Civilisation 42, 85, 86
porno-roman 215
pornosphere 12, 38, 42, 44, 47, 49, 56–7, 59, 61, 64, 75, 81, 87, 95, 205, 207

Portillo, M. 9, 27, 147
Power of Feminist Art, The 226
Prefab Sprout 168
Prehistory of Sex 208
Presley, E. 22, 138, 181
Prime Suspect 128
Prince 29, 62, 201, 209
Probst, K. 74–5
Probyn, E. 200
Prodigy 168
psychoanalysis 171
public sphere 81, 88–108, 217
Pulp 136
Pultz, J. 184, 211
Pussy Power 71

Queen 136
Queer As Folk 137, 141
queer.com 5
Queer Noise 137
Quek, G. 83
Question Time 142
Quills 170

Ramsey, L. 127
Rankin 177
Rape of Sardanapolus 168
Raw Nudes 177
Raven, C. 54, 86, 213
Ray of Light 68
Reagan, R. 7, 151
Rebel Rebel 136
Reckitt, H. 227
Red Shoe Diaries 83
Red Light Zone 82, 100, 223
Red River 151
Redford, R. 149
Reed, L. 224
Reeves, C. 210
Relax 66
REM 136
Rendez-vous 214
Rent 137
Representation of Teenage Sexuality in the Media 218
Reynolds, B. 73, 90
Rheims, B. 200, 203
Ricci, C. 140
Rich, B.R. 142
Rich, R. 146
Richardson 78
Richardson, M. 21, 72
Riefenstahl, L. 185–6

Rinetti, S. 84
Rio 67
Riot Grrrls 196
Ritchie, G. 140
Roberts, J. 124, 139, 140
'Rock 'n' Roll Nigger' 196
Roeg, N. 147–8
Romance 40, 58, 165–6, 175, 212
roman-porno 170
Roos, D. 140
Rope 133
Roseanne 141
Ross, D. 201
Ross, G. 22
Ross, J. 66
Rowbotham, S. 20, 210
Roxy Music 136
Royal Television Society 82
Royalle, C. 44
Russo, V. 147

Sade, Marquis de 171, 172, 188
Samois Group 24
Scarlett's Story: Part 1 91
Schiffer, C. 117
Schlesinger, J. 134, 139, 219
Schneeman, C. 197, 199
Schneider, R. 196, 197, 201, 203, 225–6
Schrader, P. 63, 71, 75
Schumacher, J. 75, 154
Schwarzenegger, A. 152, 156
scientia sexualis 21, 43
Scott, G.C. 63, 71
Scott, R. 50, 122, 126, 156
Scott, S. 55
Scottish Television 98
Scottish Women 98
Searchers 151
Secret Museum, The 63, 215
Secret Garden 66
Section 28 26, 31, 142, 147, 207
Sedgwick, E. 181, 224
Segal, L. 24, 26, 210
Seidelman, S. 128, 218
Serrano, A. 165, 186
Seul Contre Tous 175
Sex 25, 66–70, 72–5, 96, 139, 202
Sex: the Annabel Chong Story 83
Sex Bomb 85
Sex in the City 128, 218
Sex, Gender and Society 208
Sex in History 208
Sex and Sensibility 107, 217

Sex and Shopping 83, 86
Sex and the Single Girl 23
Sex Work 100
Sexual Century 9, 21, 85
Sexual Personae 167
Sexual Pictures 189
Sexy Bodies 200
She-Devil 218
Sherman, C. 198–200
She's Gotta Have It 11
Shilts, R. 29
Shopping 137
Showalter, E. 15–17, 21
Showgirls 70, 89–90, 124, 218
Sid the Sexist 160
Sign o' the Times 209
Silence of the Lambs, The 138
Simmonds, P. 195
Simple Minds 136
Simpson, A. 44
Simpson, D. 137–8, 144, 158
Simpson, M. 88, 129, 157–8, 220
Sin 137
Sinatra, F. 158
Sky One 85
Slade 136
Sleep with Me 219
Smack My Bitch Up 168
Smith, B. 195
Smith, C. 26
Smith, F. 226
Smith, J. 144
Smith, P. 182–3, 196
Smith, W.A. 58, 214
Smiths, The 136
Snitow, A. 24
Snoop Doggy Dogg 186
Soap 142
Soderberg, S. 122, 124
Solonz, T. 155
Somerville, J. 137, 188
Songs for Drella 225
Sontag, S. 19–20, 120, 184–5, 209
Soutar, B. 31, 142
Spartacus 133, 152
Sperm Eaters 189
Spice Girls 196
Spielberg, S. 138
Spiteri, S. 76
Springfield, D. 137
Sprinkle, A. 44, 82, 202
Staller, L. (Cicciolina) 64
Stallone, S. 90, 151, 156

Stan, M.A. 210
Star is Torn, A 195
Starr, R. 217
Starr Committee 7, 93
Starship Troopers 124
Steele, V. 55
Stein, J. 224
Stevenson, R.L. 16
Stewart, J. 133, 151
Stiffed 149
Stipe, M. 13, 136, 210
Strange Days 126
Straw, J. 58, 214
Streisand, B. 138, 201
Striptease 89–90, 100
Stone, O. 154
Stone, S. 122, 142–3
Stonewall 27, 29, 132–5, 145, 179, 181
Stopes, M. 21
Story of the Eye, The 172
Stuff 159
style magazines: and masculinity, 157–61; and pornography, 76–8; and striptease, 90; and women, 119
Suede 136
Sullivan, A. 19, 20, 29, 145, 208
Sumari, H. 178
Summers, A. 59
Summer of Sam 10–11
Sun 142
Sun-Woo, J. 173
Sunset Boulevard 220
surrealism 171–4, 180, 193–4
Survivor 89, 102
Susie Bright: Sex Pest 82
Swank, H. 146
Sweet 136
Sweet Hereafter 176
Swingers 155
SX TV 214

Tales of the City 29, 141
Tanaka, N. 215
Tannahill, R. 27–8, 208, 210
Tanner, M. 194, 197
Tarantino, Q. 219
Taschen 65
Tashigawa, H. 202
Tasker, Y. 121
Tatchell, P. 30
Taylor, E. 181
Taylor, T. 27, 208

television: and homosexuality, 10, 132,
140–1, 145; and masculinity, 159–60;
and pornography, 82–6; and striptease,
95–108, 216; and women, 127–8
Tennant, N. 131, 137
That Gay Show 141
Thatcher, M. 26
Thelma and Louise 122, 126
Theroux, L. 84, 100
Thompson, B. 63
Thompson, H.S.T. 208–9
Thompson, R.F. 188
Thurman, U. 9
Tickner, L. 118, 203
Time 50
Titanic 120
Titian 168
TIVO 220
To Die For 121
Toilet of Venus 21
Tokyo Lucky Hole 170
Tolson, A. 149
Tom of Finland 180, 224
Tom Jones 107
Top Gun 138, 219
Tricia 97
Tucker, M. 194–5, 198
Tupac Shakur 186
Two-Lane Blacktop 122

U2 137
UK Cam Girl 102
UK Dolls 102

Valentino, R. 150
Vanity Fair 12, 140, 90, 144
Vechten, C.V. 225
Velazquez 21, 168
Velvet Goldmine 136, 146, 180
Velvet Underground 78, 173, 223
Venus in Furs 78
Venus of Willendorf 168
Verhoeven, P. 70, 89, 124, 142–3,
219
Versace, G. 158
Vice – the Sex Industry 101, 105–6
Vice – the Sex Trade 95
Vicinus, M. 224–5
Victim 133
Video Appeals Committee 57, 211,
213
Village People 135–7
Vinterberg, T. 175

Viz 160
Vogue 65, 139, 216
Voight, J. 134
Von Trier, L. 71, 76, 174–5

Wachowski brothers 143
Wahlberg, M. 73
Wakamutsu, K. 215
Walker, C. 186
Wall Street 154
Warhol, A. 103, 177, 180–3, 187, 189,
224, 227
Wars of the Roses, The 154
Watney, S. 207
Waugh, T. 135, 219, 225
Wayne, J. 151
Weaver, S. 121
Weight of Water, The 218
Weird Weekends 84, 100
West, F. 55, 176
Weston, E. 193
Westwood, V. 76
Weldon, F. 57, 211, 213
W.H. Smith 47
What Women Want 116
Whatever 175
Where Life Begins 66
Where the Streets Have No Name
137
White, E. 135, 183–5
Whitehouse, M. 59
Whitford, F. 221–2
Wild One 22
Wilde, O. 9, 13, 16–17, 19, 28, 180–1,
131, 209
Wilde 17, 209
Will & Grace 141
Williams, L. 40, 63, 70, 211–12
Williams, R. 139, 147
Williamson, J. 81
Willis, J. 107
Willis, S. 121–2, 226, 160
Winchell, W. 93
Winship, J. 56, 118
Winslet, K. 120
Winterson, J. 140
Without You I'm Nothing 201
Witkin, J.P. 173
Wolfe, T. 7
Wollen, P. 193
Woman 114, 118
Women Against Censorship 24
Women and Art 226

Women's Institute 12, 96, 108
women's magazines 114–15, 118–20
Wonder Boys 154
Wood, J. 186
Woolf, N. 76
Woolstonecraft, M. 191
Word 85
Working Girls 121
www.jennicam.com 102

X-Files 128
Xena the Warrior Princess 128, 218–19

'YMCA' 135
Yorkshire Ripper, The 55
Young, L. 226
Your Friends and Neighbours 155–6

Zellweger, R. 121
Ziggy Stardust 135–6, 180